D1201652

MONEY IN A THEORY OF FINANCE

Money in a Theory of Finance

By

John G. Gurley *and* Edward S. Shaw

with a Mathematical Appendix by

Alain C. Enthoven

THE BROOKINGS INSTITUTION

WASHINGTON, D. C.

Published January 1960

Second printing August 1962
Third printing February 1964
Fourth printing February 1966
Fifth printing March 1968
Sixth printing January 1970
Seventh printing October 1971
Eighth printing August 1976

ISBN O-8157 3322-4
Library of Congress Catalog Card Number 60-7985

Printed in the United States of America

THE BROOKINGS INSTITUTION is an independent organization engaged in research and education in the social sciences. Its principal purposes are to aid in the development of sound public policies and to provide advanced training for students in the social sciences.

The Institution was founded December 8, 1927, as a consolidation of three antecedent organizations: the Institute for Government Research, 1916; the Institute of Economics, 1922; and the Robert Brookings Graduate School of Economics and Government, 1924.

The general administration of the Institution is the responsibility of a self-perpetuating Board of Trustees. In addition to this general responsibility the By-Laws provide that, "It is the function of the Trustees to make possible the conduct of scientific research and publication, under the most favorable conditions, and to safeguard the independence of the research staff in the pursuit of their studies and in the publication of the results of such studies. It is not a part of their function to determine, control, or influence the conduct of particular investigations or the conclusions reached." The immediate direction of the policies, program, and staff of the Institution is vested in the President, who is assisted by an advisory council, chosen from the professional staff of the Institution.

In publishing a study the Institution presents it as a competent treatment of a subject worthy of public consideration. The interpretations and conclusions in such publications are those of the author or authors and do not necessarily reflect the views of other members of the Brookings staff or of the administrative officers of the Institution.

Foreword

THIS VOLUME discusses the role of financial markets and institutions in a growing economy. The authors develop for the first time a theory of finance of which monetary theory is a part. Their treatment is technical and is addressed more to the professional economist than to the general reader. The purpose is to make a pioneering contribution that will place money in the broader context of financial assets. Like all pioneering ventures in economic research, it is expected to induce controversy, refinements, and further theoretical contributions.

The study began as an investigation of trends in commercial banking in the United States. At once it became apparent that a body of theory was needed that would explain at least hypothetically the relations of commercial banking to other nonbanking financial institutions. The development of such a theory to explain the financial developments of this century became a first objective. When the first draft of the study was completed, it was felt that the theoretical chapters should be further elaborated in a separate book, and that the historical and interpretative chapters should be published later. This, then, is the first volume of a broader study, to be followed by another dealing with the empirical evidence.

During the course of their work, the authors have published for review and criticism several preliminary papers offering early formulations of their theory. These include: "Financial Aspects of Economic Development," *American*

Economic Review, September 1955; "Financial Intermediaries and the Saving-Investment Process," *The Journal of Finance,* May 1956; and "The Growth of Debt and Money in the United States, 1800-1950: A Suggested Interpretation," *The Review of Economics and Statistics,* August 1957.

To the authors who have undertaken this difficult assignment and have shown exceptional skill and perseverance in producing this theoretical volume, the Institution is deeply indebted. To Alain C. Enthoven of the RAND Corporation, who has prepared a Mathematical Appendix, we are also indebted. The Advisory Committee, consisting of Lester V. Chandler, Evsey D. Domar, George Garvy, Raymond W. Goldsmith, and Walter S. Salant, and others have made many helpful criticisms and suggestions with respect to both the earlier and the present manuscript. The Institution is especially grateful for their assistance. Some members of the Committee have reservations about portions of the study, but all are agreed that it should be published.

To the Ford Foundation, whose grant for general support helped to finance this study, and to the Merrill Foundation for Advancement of Financial Knowledge, Inc., whose special grant helped to finance this research, the Institution expresses its deep appreciation.

The views expressed by the authors are their own and are not to be regarded as necessarily those of the Trustees, Officers, or other staff members of the Brookings Institution; nor should they be regarded as reflecting the views of the Ford Foundation or the Merrill Foundation for Advancement of Financial Knowledge, Inc.

ROBERT D. CALKINS
President

November 1959

Authors' Preface

A distinguished member of our Advisory Committee detected traces of iconoclasm in the method and conclusions of this volume. It is true that we have found icons in our way and regarded them with some distaste. But we have been concerned far less with challenging familiar doctrine about money and finance than with the positive goal of designing a way of thinking about financial phenomena in general that comprises a theory of money in particular.

Though the text is formal, and at times even austere, it is for the most part unadorned by mathematical pyrotechnics. That is reserved for the Appendix, written by Alain C. Enthoven, RAND Corporation. Dr. Enthoven develops the model of Chapter III, adding elements of realism and applying tests of stability. We are greatly indebted to him not only for the Appendix but also for his advice and assistance on successive versions of the text. He, in turn, acknowledges valuable advice from Richard R. Nelson and Robert M. Solow.

We have also been aided by the considerate comments and criticisms of the members of our Advisory Committee. Walter S. Salant, as a member of this Committee and of the senior staff of The Brookings Institution, has labored far beyond the call of duty to cleanse our manuscript of its errors and to enrich it with his own insights. Josef Attiyeh and Sidney G.

Winter, Jr., research fellows at The Brookings Institution in 1958-1959, generously contributed their mathematical skill at crucial points. For his extraordinary patience with our false starts and for his encouragement when we seemed to be making progress, we are deeply grateful to Robert D. Calkins, President of The Brookings Institution.

Mrs. Yvette Gurley narrowly escapes implication as an author of this volume. She has been critic, counsel, research staff, and audience through the duration of our project, and in these capacities she has improved the volume in numerous ways.

The main body of this study is unique in one respect: there are almost no footnotes and no bibliography. This does not mean that our work has broken with the past—the many references in the Appendix testify that it has not. We are writing here for professional economists, and we take it for granted that they will recognize, without benefit of reference, our dependence on intellectual forebears. They will appreciate how freely this study has drawn against the monetary theorist's line of credit with such writers as Lord Keynes, Joan Robinson, J. R. Hicks, James Tobin, and Don Patinkin. Special acknowledgment is due Patinkin, since his work has exposed most clearly some of the problems, relating mainly to determinacy of the price level and neutrality of money, that lie near the core of our project.

Empirical observations are rare in the present work, and the few policy prescriptions appear solely for the purpose of clarifying analysis. The successive models are constructed to neo-classical specifications, so that it would call for reckless temerity to deduce from these models a set of guides for policy in the real world. A second volume, now in preparation, will apply our way of thinking about money and finance to American experience. Fortified by empirical and institutional materials, it will venture into the embattled territory of policy.

The authors represent different generations of graduate study at Stanford University. Their common experience includes tutelage by the two men to whom this book is dedicated with respect and affection, Professors Elmer D. Fagan and Bernard F. Haley. The dedication entangles Professors Fagan and Haley in our work as accessory after as well as before the fact, but with exoneration for the consequences.

JOHN G. GURLEY
EDWARD S. SHAW

Contents

CHAPTER I

Introduction

THIS IS A THEORETICAL STUDY of finance. It is a study of how debt, financial assets, financial institutions, and financial policies shape, and are in turn shaped by, general levels of prices and output. Although we direct particular emphasis to one financial asset, money, to one financial institution, the monetary system, and to one facet of financial policy, monetary control, we draw into the analysis a wide range of financial assets and institutions. We attempt to develop a theory of finance that encompasses the theory of money, and a theory of financial institutions that includes banking theory.

Two closely related considerations attracted us to this study. First, major improvements and extensions in time series of financial data had been made or were in prospect, including Raymond W. Goldsmith's studies of saving and financial intermediaries, Milton Friedman's work on money at the National Bureau of Economic Research, and Federal Reserve projects on flow-of-funds and banking statistics.[1] Such rich veins of empirical material are rarely ac-

[1] See Raymond W. Goldsmith, *A Study of Saving in the United States* (1955) and *Financial Intermediaries in the American Economy Since 1900* (1958); "A Flow-of-Funds System of National Accounts Annual Estimates, 1939-54," *Federal Reserve Bulletin* (October 1955), "Summary Flow-of-Funds

cessible to economists, and the temptation to examine them for any new interpretations they might suggest regarding financial development in the United States was too strong for us to resist.

Second, we were aware of the inadequacy of the analytical tools at hand for exploiting the financial data we found so tempting. It bothered us that we could stare so intently at the Federal Reserve's elaborate tabulations of flow-of-funds, for example, or at Goldsmith's elegant details of growth in debt, financial assets, and financial intermediaries—all the time appreciating and admiring the empirical work—without much idea of what they might mean for anyone who would want to draw on experience for understanding processes of growth and cyclical change.

Economists have been largely preoccupied with markets for current output, real wealth, and labor services. They have put relatively little effort into working out conditions of supply and demand on financial markets except in connection with money, government debt, and the foreign exchanges. Their disposition has been to eliminate other financial assets and other debt, and most financial institutions as well, by consolidating the balance sheets of creditor and debtor, on the grounds that we owe domestic debt to ourselves or that the real effects of financial asset accumulation by lenders are neutralized by the real effects of debt accumulation by borrowers.

One result is that books on money and banking and on

Accounts 1950-55," *ibid.* (April 1957) and "A Quarterly Presentation of Flow of Funds, Saving, and Investment," *ibid.* (August 1959); Federal Reserve System, *All-Bank Statistics United States 1896-1955* (1959); and the many studies published by the National Bureau of Economic Research under its Financial Research Program. Several projects in money and banking are being prepared at the National Bureau by Milton Friedman and Anna Schwartz, Phillip Cagan, and Richard T. Selden.

monetary theory have paid insufficient attention to finance in the broad sense, as their titles so clearly indicate. They have made little attempt to deal in any systematic way with financial assets, financial institutions, and financial policy generally. At the same time, the "analysis" one finds in books on finance has tended to evolve methods and traditions of its own and to become a descriptive-historical discipline apart from the main stream of economics. It has been long on description, short on generalization, and the generalizations it has established cannot be linked easily with those of economics proper to work out the interplay among markets for current output, labor services, and financial assets.

Markets for Financial Assets

The logical way for an economist to study finance is to study it as a market problem. He should be able to state the factors that determine the demand for any financial asset and the factors that determine the supply of that asset. And there should be a statement defining market equilibrium. That is to say, there should be a demand function, a supply function, and a market-clearing equation to select the effective points of demand and supply from the first two equations. Each set of demand, supply, and market-equilibrium equations defines a market that is susceptible to analysis in its own right—to partial analysis. The full collection of these markets for financial assets is the domain of finance.

There are far too many of these markets in a developed society for analysis of each. Even for partial analysis they must be grouped, with the basis for classification varying according to the problem. In this book we are interested, for one thing, in the interrelationships between methods of financing expenditures for current output of goods and services and levels of real output and prices. Individual nonfinancial spending units (consumers, business firms, and government bodies) purchase current output for the most part from their own current incomes: most expenditures are internally financed. Part of the expenditures, however, is externally financed by new security issues, which we call "primary securities," consisting of bonds, equities, mortgages, consumer debt, and so on. Ultimate borrowers may sell primary securities directly to ultimate lenders, in which case, of course, the latter acquire the primary securities.

Alternatively, primary securities may be sold to financial institutions. Then the institutions acquire primary securities and issue claims against themselves in the form of demand deposits, savings deposits, and similar debts. These claims we call "indirect securities." In this case, ultimate lenders acquire these indirect securities instead of the primary securities themselves. So we classify financial markets into a market for primary securities and a market for indirect securities. The latter divides further into a market for money (means of payment) and a market for nonmonetary indirect securities (time deposits, savings deposits, savings and loan shares, and so on).

The economic system comprises these financial markets and a collection of real markets. The latter include markets for goods, both current output and the capital stock or real wealth, and for labor services broadly defined.

These sweeping market classifications, in both the financial and real sectors, do not preclude refinement of classification as the analysis proceeds. Thus the market for consumer goods may be set apart from the market for investment goods, the market for bonds from the market for corporate stock, and the market for savings and loan shares from that for shares in open-end investment companies.

The economist's way to study finance, to repeat, is to study it as a market problem. He may study it in terms of partial analysis, locking up in *ceteris paribus* the "feed-in" of influences from any or all of the other markets in the economic system to the one market that concerns him, and resisting the temptation to follow through the "feed-back" of influences from "his" market to the others. Or he may study simultaneously all financial and real markets in the context of general equilibrium analysis, working with a static or a growth model in which solutions for equilibrium on all markets are obtained simultaneously, with full accounting for the give and take of feed-in and feed-back.

This book employs general equilibrium analysis throughout, though it is necessary and convenient at times to use partial analysis of the money market and other financial markets. It is important for the monetary economist to have a broad view of the economy, to see how the money market fits into other markets of the economy, and to see the interplay that takes place among all markets. Without this broad view, one can stray quite wide of the mark in assessing the role of money in the economic system. This book also analyzes the role of money, within a general equilibrium framework, in a state of stationary equilibrium and in a growth setting.

The Chapters Ahead

The analysis begins with a rudimentary economy that contains a minimum of financial markets and financial institutions and progresses step by step to increasingly complex financial structures. The purpose at each step is to see how financial and real markets interact to produce equilibrium levels of real output and prices, the emphasis all along being on the supply of and demand for money. For the reader's convenience, the financial profile of the chapters is given below.

Financial Profile of Chapters

Chapter	Financial Markets	Financial Institutions
II.	Market for money only, with emphasis on the demand for money.	Governmental monetary system composed of Policy Bureau and Banking Bureau.
III.	Markets for money and for one type of primary security.	Same as above.
IV.	Market for primary securities, with emphasis on growth in quantity and diversity of primary securities.	Same as above.
V.	Markets for money and for differentiated primary securities.	Same as above.
VI.	Markets for money, differentiated primary securities, and nonmonetary indirect assets.	Governmental monetary system and nonmonetary financial intermediaries (private and governmental).
VII.	Same as above, with emphasis on supply function of money.	Central bank, member commercial banks, nonmonetary financial intermediaries.

Chapter II starts with an economy that has only one financial market, that for money, and only one financial institution, a governmental monetary system. This monetary system is operated by the government sector and is composed of a Policy Bureau and a Banking Bureau. The former stipulates monetary policy by issuing instructions to the latter concerning the stock of money. The Banking Bureau purchases current output (or makes transfer payments) and creates money. The money issued by the government sector is accumulated by consumers and business firms. Simple as this model is, it will clarify concepts, show the relationships among the three markets for money, current output, and labor services, and introduce the demand function for money. The supply function of money is made as simple as possible: the stock of money is just what the Policy Bureau says it shall be. This device on the supply side of the money market has been employed to avoid, at this early stage, taking account of those determinants of the money stock that reflect profit considerations of a private banking system and the network of controls imposed by a central bank over its members. This approach makes it easier to concentrate on the demand side of the money market.

Chapter III introduces a second financial market, that for homogeneous bonds (perpetuities) issued by business firms and acquired by consumers and the Banking Bureau. There are now four markets in the economy—for labor services, current output, money, and primary securities (business bonds). The latter market has its price, the rate of interest on bonds. The government sector, with its Policy and Banking Bureaus, does no transacting on markets for labor services and current output but only on the two financial markets. The function of the Banking Bureau, on orders from the Policy Bureau, is to purchase or sell primary securities and in the process create or destroy money balances. Consumers acquire money or primary securities or both, while business firms issue primary debt and accumulate money balances. The governmental monetary system is still the only financial institution.

The new financial market that is introduced in Chapter

III—that for primary securities—is examined closely in Chapter IV. The purpose here is twofold: to analyze the factors that determine the growth of primary securities, which at a given bond rate is equal to the growth of spending units' financial assets, and to consider change in the quality, as distinct from the quantity, of primary securities. Primary security growth and the accumulation of financial assets are discussed within the framework of the model of Chapter III. The last part of Chapter IV then takes up the factors that affect differentiation of primary securities, and the techniques used for getting these securities distributed from borrowers to lenders.

Having introduced the many different types of primary securities in Chapter IV, we turn next, in Chapter V, to the way these differentiated securities and their interest rates affect the demand for money. The growth process involves continuous qualitative change in primary security issues, and this evolving pattern of differentiation presents lenders with the problem of reorganizing portfolios to assure maximum prospective yield. The demand for money, as one portfolio component, is sensitive to the mutations in quality of the other components.

Chapter VI brings into the analysis a third financial market and a second financial institution. The new financial market is that for nonmonetary indirect assets, such as savings deposits and savings and loan shares. The new financial institution is the group of nonmonetary financial intermediaries which purchase primary securities and issue nonmonetary indirect assets. The governmental monetary system is retained, though it is now allowed to issue time deposits as well as money. In these pages, we analyze the factors determining the demand for and supply of nonmonetary indirect assets, the way in which the activities of nonmonetary intermediaries (both private and governmental) affect the demand for money, the differences and similarities between these intermediaries and the monetary system, and the impact of nonmonetary intermediaries on the efficiency of monetary control.

At long last, in Chapter VII, the governmental monetary system is replaced with a system that conforms closely to the American type: there is a central bank that imposes direct controls, in the form of rationed reserves, a deposit rate on reserve balances and perhaps a reserve requirement, on its member commercial banks. In previous chapters, the Banking Bureau issued the stock of money that it was instructed to issue by the Policy Bureau. Now the instructions are replaced by a more or less intricate control mechanism operated by a central bank over commercial banks that are privately organized to make profits. Consequently, the maximum stock of money permitted by the controls may be different from the amount of money that commercial banks wish to produce under the profit motive. The supply side of the money market, as a result, becomes a good deal more complicated. In discussing supply, we consider, first, creation of money by commercial banks not under control by a monetary authority; then we consider principles and techniques of monetary control, and, finally, the effects of monetary control on the viability of the banking system.

Methods and Lacunae

Mathematical economists and econometricians—who we hope will be attracted to some of the problems we tackle—may regret that we have not built financial variables into a complete, dynamic model of growth. They will find, however, a mathematical treatment in the Appendix, written by Dr. Alain C. Enthoven, of much of the material contained in Chapters II, III, and IV. The method we have chosen is the presentation of rigorous analysis unencumbered with mathematics.

We have adopted in this book the framework of neo-classical economics, with its assumptions of full employment, price flexibility, absence of money illusion and distribution effects, and so on. We have done this not because we believe that this is the way the world actually is, but rather because in such a framework money is likely to matter the least—perhaps not at all—so far as real effects are concerned. We have played the game according to the ground rules of neo-classical economics in order to show that even here money is not a veil, that it may have an important role to play in determining the level and composition of output. The role of money, however, becomes increasingly important as one moves further and further away from neo-classicism.

There are many behavior equations implicit in this book. We do not pretend that they are realistic in the sense that they accurately describe how consumers and business firms behave on all markets of the economy. They do, however, suggest quite clearly, we believe, the role of finance in markets for goods and labor under varying conditions. These behavior equations could be altered fairly drastically without affecting our main conclusions about finance.

We are uncomfortably aware of large problem areas neglected in this volume. The analysis touches very lightly on the role of finance in short cycles. It does not advance in the least the theory of risk and uncertainty, which is especially relevant to finance in the short run. It skims over international aspects of finance, and has little to say in the traditional area of corporation finance. Furthermore, there are few statistics in this volume. They must come later in order of publication even though they came first in our own experience. We spent many months studying the financial history of the United States in the light of views we present here about markets for money, primary securities, and nonmonetary indirect financial assets. The results encouraged us to develop and present the theory first and return to the data later.

CHAPTER II

Rudimentary Finance

THIS CHAPTER DEALS WITH finance in the context of a rudimentary economy. Our model of such an economy has no close historical counterpart, and some of its institutional arrangements are not realistic. But it is a convenient device for presenting some concepts and principles of finance that will be useful in more realistic settings.

We begin by describing this rudimentary economy in terms of its social accounts: its balance sheets, its income accounts, and its flow-of-funds accounts. Then we turn to its markets, specifying conditions of supply and demand that prevail both in stationary equilibrium and during growth. There are only three markets: one for labor services, another for current output, and the third for money. The first two are real markets, and the third is a financial market. Two very important financial markets are missing—for primary securities (such as corporate and government bonds, equities, and mortgages) and for nonmonetary indirect financial assets (such as savings deposits and savings and loan shares).

The rudimentary economy has money, a monetary system for creating money and for administering the payments mechanism, and a monetary authority. Under one set of specifications, policy of the monetary authority regarding the stock of money is trivial because it can affect only price levels on the markets for current output and labor services. Under a different set of specifications, however, monetary management does have a bearing on real levels of output and income.

The rudimentary economy's capacity for growth is limited by its financial system. With no financial asset other than money, there are restraints on saving, on capital accumulation, and on efficient allocation of saving to investment that depress the rate of growth in output and income. Some of the restraints on real growth that are evident in this model are reminiscent of the financial handicaps faced by the American economy about the time of the Revolution and by some underdeveloped countries today. In the final section of the chapter, some of the simpler expedients for easing these financial handicaps are discussed.

Sectors, Markets, and Social Accounts

Any economic system is an aggregate of spending units including consumer households, business firms, and governmental bodies. In this section, we describe how these decision-making units operate in the rudimentary economy, the nature of their assets and liabilities, their incomes and expenditures, and their lending and borrowing.

SECTORS AND MARKETS

Spending units are grouped into three sectors: consumer, business, and government. There is no foreign sector in the model; it is an economy with no international transactions.

Nor is there a financial sector comprising institutions, such as commercial banks and insurance companies, that incur debt of their own in order to acquire the debt of others. All trading is confined to the three sectors.

What are the characteristics of these sectors? The consumer sector makes consumption expenditures, buying goods and services from business firms. It obtains income by selling personal productive services to the other sectors. It does not accumulate tangible wealth, such as land or capital equipment (including houses). Money is its only asset and it does not go into debt.

The business sector consists of unincorporated firms. We make the arbitrary and unrealistic assumption that these firms are economic ultimates, not owned by natural persons. This sector holds tangible wealth, and it combines these real assets with productive services bought from the consumer sector to produce output. Part of this output is sold to the consumer sector, part to government as "government goods." The remainder of output, private investment goods, is sold within the business sector to augment its own stock of wealth. Business firms do not borrow by issuing new securities, and they retain all of gross profits including depreciation allowances. They hold money balances as their only financial asset.

The government sector has the paramount functions of issuing money, providing a clearing and payments mechanism for transfer of money, and defining monetary policy. The money is a fiat issue with no backing whatever. It may be currency or deposits subject to check by the consumer and business sectors. It is money in the literal sense of means of payment. To keep our model extremely simple, we suppose that the stock of money either remains constant or increases. It cannot decrease because we do not permit the government to collect taxes or to issue nonmonetary debt. When the government determines that an increase in the stock of money is advisable, it either makes purchases of goods and pays for them by creating money or disposes of new money through transfer payments.

Money is government debt in this model, issued to cover or finance the amount of government expenditures determined by monetary policy. The government is monetary system and monetary authority. As a foretaste of more complex monetary systems to come, we imagine that the system of the present model is composed of a Policy Bureau (an embryonic central bank) and a Banking Bureau (a forebear of commercial banks). The former stipulates monetary policy by issuing instructions to the latter regarding the stock of money. The Banking Bureau carries out the instructions, creating money for purchase of goods and services or for transfer payments.

There are three markets in this economy—for labor services, for current output (consumption goods, government goods, private investment goods), and for money. Since there is no market for nonmonetary securities such as stocks or bonds, there is no "financial circulation" as distinct from the "income circulation," and in the economy's array of prices there are no rates of interest. Only goods currently produced are traded, existing tangibles being barred from the markets.

SECTORAL AND SOCIAL BALANCE SHEETS

The rudimentary economy may be examined first in terms of its sectoral balance sheets. Such balance sheets, drawn up as of the close of a fiscal period, appear in Table 1. Tangible assets—capital equipment, buildings, inventories—appear only on the business balance sheet. Net worth for each sector is the difference between its assets and liabilities. Money appears as the debt of government and the financial asset of the consumer and business sectors. It is a heritage of government spending financed sometime in the past by borrowing through the issue of a form of debt that is generally acceptable as the means of payment.[1]

The three balance sheets may be combined into one for all three sectors. They may also be consolidated. The com-

TABLE 1

Sectoral Balance Sheets

Business Sector			
Assets		*Liabilities*	
Money	50	None	
Tangible	900	*Net Worth*	
		Accumulated savings	950

Government Sector			
Assets		*Liabilities*	
None		Money	100
		Net Worth	
		Accumulated savings	—100

Consumer Sector			
Assets		*Liabilities*	
Money	50	None	
		Net Worth	
		Accumulated savings	50

bined balance sheet in Table 2 simply sums up the assets, liabilities, and net worth of the three sectors. The consolidated balance sheet, also in Table 2, highlights the fact that only tangible assets and the equity or net worth in those assets have survived the consolidation. Money as the financial asset of private sectors is netted out against money as the

[1] The meaning of borrowing and lending in this context is explained below on pp. 23-25.

debt of government, so it disappears. Consolidation rips away the money veil. This suggests the simple truth that not only money but all other financial phenomena, too, are the consequence of autonomy and specialization among spending units in earning and spending income in an interdependent society. Spending units are federated in a capitalist economy, rather than consolidated, and finance in various forms serves in many ways as a substitute for economic centralization. Economic specialization—in earning income and in disposing of it—is the basis for debt, financial assets, and financial institutions.

TABLE 2

Social Balance Sheets

COMBINED BALANCE SHEET				CONSOLIDATED BALANCE SHEET			
Assets		*Liabilities*		*Assets*		*Liabilities*	
Money	100	Money	100	Tangible	900	None	
Tangible	900						
		Net Worth				*Net Worth*	
		Accumulated savings	900			Accumulated savings	900

The information in Tables 1 and 2 provides no way of knowing whether a money stock of 100 exceeds private demand for money balances, equals, or falls short of it. And one cannot guess at this point what the results of an excess stock or demand would be for the growth of wealth and for the accumulation of savings in net worth. The monetary authority has supplied money by spending and borrowing, and it is up to the private sectors to work out a solution for excess demand for or excess stock of money balances through subsequent transactions in labor services, current output, and money. We shall turn to this presently, but for now we continue with description rather than an analytical explanation of the model.

NATIONAL INCOME AND PRODUCT ACCOUNTS

Balance sheets catalogue tangible and financial assets, debt, and equity at the end of fiscal periods. National income and product accounts, on the other hand, record the economy's expenditures for output and its incomes from selling this output during some fiscal period.

The incomes actually earned in the sale of gross national product are always equal to the expenditures actually made in purchasing this product: gross national income is always equal to gross national expenditure (product). This basic identity is shown in Table 3, which is an abbreviated set of national income and product accounts for our rudimentary economy.

On the right side, consumption goods and services are produced by business firms and purchased by the consumer sector. Business firms make gross purchases of investment goods produced within the business sector itself. The government purchases goods and services from both private sectors. The sum (100) of these expenditures gives rise to an equivalent amount of income. On the left side of the chart, there is income for the consumer sector, in the form of salaries and wages. The income of the business sector is its gross retained earnings, or gross saving, including depreciation allowances. There are no taxes and so no income for government.

Part of the spending is for investment in capital goods. These expenditures, less depreciation allowances, would be represented by a rise in tangible assets on the social balance sheets. There would also be an equivalent increase in net worth on these balance sheets. This is the net saving of the economy, reflected in the national income and product accounts by the excess of gross national income over the sum of personal consumption, government expenditure, and depreciation allowances. The income that the economy has left over after purchasing consumer goods and government goods and after allowing for depreciation is its net saving,

TABLE 3

National Income and Product Accounts [a]

INCOME		PRODUCT	
Income of the consumer sector	80	Personal consumption expenditures	75
Gross saving of the business sector	20	Gross private investment expenditures	15
Tax receipts of the government sector	0	Government purchases of goods and services	10
Gross National Income	100	Gross National Product or Expenditure	100

[a] Government may make transfer payments to either private sector. They would appear twice in the income column of national income and product accounts—once as an addition to the income of the receiving sector and once as a negative item charged against government income.

and this is always equal to its net purchases of private investment goods. Thus the rise in tangible assets on the social balance sheets would necessarily be equal to the increase of savings in net worth.

National income and product accounts *by themselves* have nothing to report about changes in financial assets and debt on the sectoral and combined balance sheets. Only if we can identify the sectors making the various expenditures and can determine the means by which these expenditures are financed—only then can we determine changes in financial data. The national income and product accounts describe completely the changes in items on the nation's consolidated balance sheet, and that is all. And this balance sheet has no entries for debt and financial assets.

The one statement about finance that can be extracted directly from the income and product accounts—and hence from the consolidated balance sheet—is this: gross national income is always and necessarily sufficient to finance, to buy and pay for, gross national output. The economy as a whole, if it has no external trading, never needs to borrow funds because its income and expenditure are always in balance. And if it never borrows it never lends. This information is not very exciting for the student of finance. Concentrating on such an aggregative level of activity, with financial claims and counterclaims canceled out, conceals the fact that some parts of the economy do borrow and others lend. If we want to discuss these borrowing and lending activities, we must study the economy as a federation, not a consolidation of its sectors.

Preoccupation with national income and product accounts, which largely ignore financial transactions, may have led too many economists to consolidate financial accounts out of economics, relegating financial analysis to its own lonely and sometimes not very fruitful course of development. Because part or all of finance is commonly aggregated or netted out of economic analysis, economists may inadvertently have given too little weight to the bearing of finance on economic activity.

FLOW-OF-FUNDS ACCOUNTS

In principle it is not difficult to expand national income and product accounts into accounts that show the expenditure and income of each sector and also the lending and borrowing transactions among sectors. These accounts—money-flows or flow-of-funds accounts—itemize changes in all parts of the sectoral and combined balance sheets. They record not only the changes in tangible assets and net worth on balance sheets but also the changes in financial assets and debt.

A first step in developing flow-of-funds accounts is to identify sectoral budgets, each recording the sector's receipts and expenditures on income and product account. If a sector has an excess of expenditure over income, it has a deficit budget on income and product account. If a sector has more income than expenditure, it has a surplus budget. And if a sector's income and expenditure are equal, it has a balanced budget. We may now examine the budgets of the three sectors on the basis of entries in Table 4.

Our consumer sector reports a budget surplus of 5. This is the excess of consumer income (80) over consumer expenditure (75). It is also the excess of consumer saving (5) over consumer investment in tangible wealth, which we assume is nil. Our business sector also reports a budget surplus of 5. This is the excess of business receipts (100) over business expenditures (95), both on income and product or "nonfinancial" account. It is also the excess of business saving (20) over business investment in tangible wealth (15). The government sector has incurred a budget deficit of 10, because it has spent 10 on income and product account while its income has been nil. The three sectors aggregatively have a balanced budget, with receipts equal to expenditures on income and product account, income (80 for consumers and 20 for business) equal to national product (75 in consumption, 15 in investment, and 10 in government goods), and saving equal to investment.

The sum of sectoral surpluses is identical with the sum of sectoral deficits: surpluses of 5 for each of the private sectors match the government deficit of 10. When all sectors are

TABLE 4

Flow-of-Funds Accounts[a]

Transactions Category	Consumer Sector		Business Sector		Government Sector		National	
	Sources	Uses	Sources	Uses	Sources	Uses	Sources	Uses
Nonfinancial								
Consumer income	80			80			80	80
Consumer expenditure		75	75				75	75
Government expenditure			10			10	10	10
Investment expenditure			15	15			15	15
Total	80	75	100	95	0	10	180	180
Financial								
Money		5		5	10		10	10
Grand total	80	80	100	100	10	10	190	190
Memoranda								
Income	80		20				100	
Saving	5		20			—10	15	
Investment				15				15
Surplus	5		5				10	
Deficit						10		10

[a] "Sources" are sources of funds, and "uses" are uses of funds.

accounted for, this identity is inescapable. Since receipts and expenditures on income and product account are the same for all sectors taken together, any sectoral surpluses are necessarily balanced by deficits in other sectors. Since saving and investment, measured *ex-post,* are the same for all sectors taken together, a budget surplus representing the excess of saving over investment for some sectors must be balanced by budget deficits representing the excess of investment over saving for other sectors.

The combination of sectoral budgets in Table 4, with a government deficit and surpluses in both private sectors, is only one of several possible combinations in the rudimentary economy. Still more combinations could emerge if we were to change the specifications of the economy, say to permit tax collections by government or investment expenditure by consumers. The combination we have chosen is purely illustrative and might be replaced by any other that would be in keeping with the model and that would satisfy the rules of social accounting—that sectoral budget surpluses or deficits represent the difference between receipts and expenditures on income and product account or between saving and investment, while the community's budget is eternally in balance, measured *ex-post*.

We consider now the financial aspects of these income-expenditure patterns or budget combinations. The government sector in the model finances its expenditures—its deficit—by issuing new money. Budget surpluses in the consumer and business sectors imply that these sectors acquire money equal to their surpluses. Each surplus sector acquires money and nothing else with its excess income, or its excess of saving over investment, simply because there are no other financial assets to acquire and because trading in tangible assets has been barred. If there were a budget deficit in either the consumer or business sector, it could be financed only by reducing previously accumulated money balances. Neither of the private sectors is permitted to issue its own debts or equity securities, and neither can run off new money from its own printing press. A sector neither accumulates nor dishoards money when it has a balanced budget.

Issues of new money by the government to finance its deficit are necessarily equal to acquisitions of money by the private sectors, where the surpluses are. The government borrows by issuing a non-interest-bearing security in the form of money, and the private sectors lend by accepting this security in their money balances. Because government incurs a deficit, its net financial assets (financial assets minus debt) must decline; because the private sectors realize surpluses, their net financial assets must rise; because money is the only form of debt and financial asset in our model, the financial solution of unbalanced budgets consists simply of an increase in the stock of money issued by government and accumulated in private balances.

What the government borrows, by issue of money, is command over current output. What private sectors lend, by accepting additions to money balances, is also command over current output. The government is able to spend more than it earns on income and product account because the private sectors spend less and release their savings in exchange for the financial asset, money. Income is distributed among sectors according to one pattern, spending according to a different pattern, and this difference in distributions is possible only because there is at least one form of debt and financial asset.

In this rudimentary economy, there is a very simple structure of debt and financial assets. Money is the only debt that can be issued to obtain external financing for deficits or excesses of investment over saving. The same money is the only financial asset that any sector can acquire as it transfers its excess of saving over investment to deficit spenders. Increases in debt are equal to deficits, and increases in the stock of money are equal to increases in debt.

In the actual world, of course, relationships among deficits, debt, and money—or among surpluses, financial assets, and money—are far more complex. Later on both private and government debt in various forms will be taken into account. We shall allow for divergence between debt and deficits, between total borrowing and monetary expansion, between lending and growth in savers' money balances.

NOMINAL AND REAL MAGNITUDES: STOCKS AND FLOWS

Most of the flow and stock magnitudes that have been discussed so far may be measured either in nominal or in real terms. The nominal amount of something means the dollar amount of it uncorrected for changes in the prices of current output; it is the dollar amount in current—that is, prevailing—prices. The real amount of something, on the other hand, is the nominal amount divided by an index of the price level of current output or by some other appropriate price index. Thus nominal gross national expenditures, for example, are these expenditures in current prices, while real gross national expenditures are higher or lower depending on whether current prices are lower or higher than those that prevailed in the base period. If prices have risen, real expenditures are less than nominal expenditures; if prices have fallen, the opposite is true.

In the following pages, the "demand for money" means a demand for a stock of money; as of any moment of time, spending units have a certain demand (in nominal or real terms) for a given stock of money (in nominal or real terms). The "incremental demand for money" means an increase in spending units' demand for money during a period of time. The "supply of money" means an increase in the nominal stock of money. The real demand for money and the real stock of money are the nominal demand for money and nominal stock of money divided by an index of the price level of current output.

Patterns of Economic Behavior

The social accounts of the rudimentary economy are a record of purchases and sales, borrowing and lending, debt and financial-asset position. They describe how spending units have behaved on the economy's markets. They do not explain motives of behavior—why spending units behave as they do. This is the matter to be considered now.

Business firms are suppliers on the market for current output (goods). Their real output in any short period depends in part on the stock of capital goods that has been accumulated from real net investment in the past. But it depends, too, on the amount of labor services provided by consumers and on the technical conditions affecting efficiency of production. We assume that real output can be increased in proportion with capital and labor if, with given techniques of production, the two factors increase in the same proportion. And we suppose that real output increases less than proportionally with the amount of either factor alone.

Consumers supply labor to firms in a constant amount unaffected by the money wage rate or the real wage rate per unit of time: there is a given supply of labor. The labor is fully employed, and its real wage rate is equal to its marginal product.

Total product over and above aggregate real wages covers depreciation of existing capital goods and, in addition, provides a real rent to the firms as owners of existing capital. The rental rate, equal to the marginal product of capital, is a percentage—a natural rate of interest. In marginal terms, the net rental rate is the change in firms' net earnings as a percentage of the change in their capital stock.

Net national product, then, is divided between real wages for consumers and real rents for firms, with the rate of return to each sector equal to the marginal product of the factor that the sector supplies.

Firms apply depreciation allowances automatically to capital replacement. Net rental earnings may be applied to either of two uses. They may be invested to increase the real stock of capital, or they may be allocated to accumulation of real money balances. It will be recalled that, in this economy, firms do not pay dividends to consumers. We suppose that each firm has in mind a division of its total assets between real capital and real money balances that equalizes the real rental rate on capital with the real marginal advantage of holding cash. Each firm desires a "balanced portfolio."

The preferred allocation of business net rental earnings (equal to net income or net saving of business) in any period between capital goods and money depends on a number of factors. Demand for net investment is stimulated by a relatively high marginal real rental rate. Given this rental rate, it tends to be discouraged by a relatively large stock of existing capital goods, because of risk considerations affecting firms as their scale of operations expands. Given the rental rate and the stock of existing capital, demand for net investment is stronger as firms' existing real money balances are large in relation to those desired. And, of course, demand for new investment and also for money is more intense when business earnings are relatively high.

The real incremental demand for money by firms is limited by the excess of their net rental earnings (saving) over their net investment. Firms wish to devote a relatively large share of earnings to real money balances as the existing stock of capital is large, as the marginal rental rate is low, and as money balances already on hand are deficient in comparison with those desired.

At the beginning of any fiscal period, firms may desire to balance their budgets for the period ahead or they may prefer budgets unbalanced on either the surplus or deficit side. In the first case, they propose to divert all earnings to real investment, standing pat on existing money balances. In the second case, involving a surplus budget, they wish to divert part of net earnings to real investment, part to money. If a deficit is desired, firms plan to dishoard money and to increase capital goods by more than net saving alone would finance. Real incremental demand for money by firms is nil in the first case, positive in the second, and negative in the third. In each case, business incremental demand for money reflects the desire of firms to achieve an appropriate allocation of total assets between capital goods and means of payment.

Consumer households in the rudimentary economy supply labor in exchange for wages. They spend their real wage income on consumption, or they save it. Consumer saving may be used for no other purpose than to increase consumer real money balances, since consumers do not invest in tangible assets and since money is the only financial asset in the rudimentary economy. Consumers may desire to dissave and so to spend on consumption at the expense of a decrease in real money balances.

The stock of money balances that consumers desire tends to rise with consumer real income, though not necessarily in fixed proportion. Consumers demand additional money in any period because their initial stock is less than their desired stock. They spend all of income on consumption when they have on hand the money balances they want. They wish to dishoard when the money on hand is excessive. It may be that consumers do not attempt in any one period to correct the entire difference between the money balances held and those desired.

What we have had to say about consumer demand for money defines completely consumer demand for goods as well. Consumption is related positively to consumer income and to consumers' real money balances on hand. It is related negatively to desired money balances; the "real-balance effect" of money on consumption depends on the difference between real money held and real money wanted. In contrast, demand for increments of money is related positively to consumer income and to desired money balances, negatively to money balances on hand.

We have defined patterns of behavior for firms and consumers. The remaining sector, government, has less freedom of action. It receives no income. If it demands goods and services, it must pay for them by issue of money; that is, if it demands goods and services, it must supply money for the balances of consumers and firms. The existing nominal stock of money is accumulated from government deficits in the past, and the existing real stock of money is the nominal stock deflated by the price level for goods and services. Government may sit idle or it may dissave, and its dissaving is financed by expansion in the nominal money stock.

When government spends in the income stream, its spending adds to private incomes and to private money balances. So far as its spending displaces private spending, there is no net effect on private incomes, but private money balances gain. In the main, we will suppose that government spends for goods and services, but we shall give brief attention to government spending through transfer payments to the private sectors. Why the government chooses to spend or not to spend, to issue money or not to issue it, we shall consider later at some length. For the moment, we may be content with saying that the government's decision is a matter of monetary policy.

In this economy firms and consumers are motivated by anticipated real advantages and they plan in real terms. It is real income, real rates of return, and real values of assets that bear on decision making. Given real values of these variables, firms and consumers are completely indifferent to nominal values; they make the same decision at all levels of prices and wages in terms of the pricing unit. In the usual phraseology, firms and consumers are free of money illusion. Moreover, the private sectors take it for granted, though with a degree of uncertainty, that any present level of prices for goods and labor will be maintained indefinitely. That is, we assume static price expectations. This is a special case of unitary elasticity of price expectations.[2]

In this economy, furthermore, markets for goods and labor are competitive. All prices for goods and labor are perfectly flexible. Any excess of real amount demanded over real supply on the market for goods precipitates an immediate rise in levels of prices and money wage rates. Any excess supply results at once in falling prices and money wage rates. On this and other grounds, our rudimentary economy is a far cry from Keynesian models. It is, rather, in the neo-classical tradition.

The Market for Money

In the preceding section, we have run quickly over the conditions of supply and demand on the markets for labor services, current output (goods), and money. Money is our

[2] In general, price expectations are of unitary elasticity when a change in current prices changes expected prices in the same direction and in the same proportion. Hence, if expected prices are equal to current prices, a change in current prices is expected to be permanent. See J. R. Hicks, *Value and Capital* (1948), p. 205.

primary concern in the rudimentary economy. The nominal stock of money outstanding at any moment is equal to the historic accumulation of government deficits. The real stock of money outstanding at any moment—the purchasing-power aggregate of money balances—is the nominal stock deflated by an index of prices for current output. The supply of money on our money market is the current issue of nominal money. This supply is one source of change in the real stock of money. The other source of change is inflation in prices of goods and services, which reduces the real stock of money, or deflation in prices of goods and services, which increases it.

The real incremental demand for money balances can be satisfied by government issue of nominal money or by a fall in prices of current output. Private sectors demand money balances for their purchasing power; their demand is for real balances, not nominal balances, and it can be satisfied equally well by new issues or by price deflation.

Why do private sectors desire real money balances? Why do they stand ready to save in order to bring the balances they have in line with the balances they desire? Obviously there is no Keynesian speculative liquidity-preference in this economy, simply because there are no securities other than money and no market rate of interest on such securities; money is not desired as a way of avoiding the risk of decline in market prices of bonds. What, then, are the motives that induce consumers to accumulate cash at the expense of consumption and induce firms to accumulate money at the expense of investment?

In thinking about motivation for holding money balances, we find it convenient to resort to the fiction of an *implicit* deposit rate on money. This implicit rate is to be distinguished from the *explicit* rate sometimes paid by monetary systems on checking accounts or time deposits. We suppose that consumers in our model demand increments in real balances to the limit at which the marginal implicit deposit rate is equal to the marginal utility sacrificed in foregoing consumption to accumulate money. Firms press their demand for money to the limit at which the marginal implicit deposit rate is equal to the marginal real rental rate on capital goods.

Prices of goods and labor are flexible in the rudimentary economy. While private spending units regard present price levels as the best measure of future price levels, they do not hold this expectation with complete confidence. As they see it, there is some chance that price levels will decline. Unless this chance is counterbalanced by probability of price inflation, the private sector has the prospect that deflation in prices of current output and labor services will return a real capital gain to money balances. This possible gain is one component of the implicit deposit rate.

Demand for money in the rudimentary economy depends also on the fact that no spending unit expects with certainty to maintain a balanced budget continuously and forever. Each spending unit expects, with more or less certainty, to fluctuate day by day between a budget surplus and a deficit. That is to say, it expects "budget rotation." Each spending unit anticipates budget deficits, which can be financed only by dishoarding money. Unless money balances are accumulated for possible dishoarding sometime, various costs and losses involved in matching expenditure precisely with income at all times can be expected. These costs and losses that money-holding averts are the second element of implicit deposit rate. They are costs and losses entailed in getting along without money, in continuously synchronizing money receipts and money payments.

For business firms, though not for consumers, money represents a disposition of saving that is an alternative to another asset, capital goods. We assume that real investment is subject to increasing marginal risk, that anticipations with respect to the marginal rental rate on capital goods are not held with complete confidence. In view of this risk, firms in the rudimentary economy diversify their assets by allocating saving partly to capital goods and partly to money for portfolio balance. Anticipated losses on real investment that are avoided by holding money are another element of money's implicit deposit rate.

Money is desired, then, because its implicit marginal return is equal to or above marginal returns to consumption and investment. Its marginal return depends on anticipated deflation of prices, on advantages of budget rotation, and on risks of real investment. The economy does not apportion its real stock of money between three distinguishable varieties of money balance, one for each of the three factors underlying deposit rate. Money is one asset, not three, and its desired amount equates the marginal return on money with the marginal return on alternative dispositions of income.

We have said that real incremental demand for money is stimulated by growth in real income of consumers, by growth in real income and in real capital goods of firms, as well as by a decline in the marginal rental rate on capital goods. This demand for money is stimulated, too, by the reduction in real money balances below their desired level that may result from inflation of prices. Whether growth in real balances desired by the private sectors is more or less rapid than growth in income and tangible assets depends on relative changes in the marginal utility of consumption, marginal rental rate on capital, and the implicit deposit rate.

Demand for money confronts the stock of money on the market for money. The market attains an equilibrium when money demand is equal to money stock. This market, to be sure, is not an institutional market place. It is instead a logical construct of specifications regarding demand and supply and their equilibrium. In the present model, given our assumption of continuous full employment on the market for labor, equilibrium on the market for money is reached inevitably when there is equilibrium on the market for goods. That must be so, since incremental demand for money is defined as the desired allocation of income to hoarding, as alternative to consumption and investment, and incremental stock of money is identical with the government's demand for goods.

Stationary Equilibrium

We assume that each of our markets and the three markets together abhor disequilibrium that their structure of responses to excess demands or excess supplies propels them to equilibrium. We consider now the profile of equilibrium, partially for each market and generally for the economy as a whole, when the economy is in the doldrums of a stationary state. We are particularly concerned with the monetary aspects of stationary equilibrium.

Stationary equilibrium is simply the absence of real growth. In such a state, each sector keeps its budget balanced; business gross income exactly provides for capital replacement; consumer income goes entirely to consumption; and there is no government demand for current output.

On the market for current output, in this milieu, the net national product is equal to real wage income of the consumer sector. The consumer sector spends its entire income on current output so that, with business and government putting in no bids, the market for net output is precisely cleared. On the market for money, no additions to real balances are desired by business because the real stock of wealth, the marginal rental rate on capital, and business gross income are constant and because existing real money balances yield an implicit deposit rate equal to the marginal rental rate on tangible assets. No additions to real balances are desired by consumers because consumer income is constant and because existing real balances bear the desired relationship to income. Since no additions to real balances are desired by the private sectors and no nominal issues of money are being made, at the existing price level, the market for money is precisely cleared. The monetary specification for stationary equilibrium is that the actual and desired real stocks of money balances are equal to each other.

This appropriate real stock of money may comprise any positive nominal stock, from the minutely small to the indefinitely large. Spending units want real balances, and any desired real stock of money can be contrived from numerous combinations of nominal money and price level. In stationary equilibrium, our rudimentary economy is a quantity-theory world. The nominal stock of money is an adventitious datum cast into the structure of the model, and spending units adapt it to their desired real stock of money by bidding prices of goods and labor to the appropriate level.

To demonstrate the structure of the economy, one may perform imaginary experiments with its nominal stock of money and its price level. Suppose that an initial stationary equilibrium is disturbed by a feat of magic that suddenly doubles all money wage rates and all prices. The effect is to reduce real money balances to one half of those desired. Business demand for investment goods declines because firms set about to restore their optimal balance of tangible assets and money. Consumer demand for goods declines as consumers set about to save in order to restore their desired cash position relative to income. There is excess supply on markets for goods and labor, an excess of *ex-ante* saving over *ex-ante* investment, because of the effect of higher prices in reducing real money balances—because of the real-balance effect of inflation in decreasing private demand for goods and labor. With prices and wages perfectly flexible, the economy drives its price and wage levels back to their original equilibrium positions. The arbitrary act of inflation impoverishes the community's creditors, the holders of money, and they respond to impoverishment by economizing on demand for goods and labor until original levels of prices and wages are restored. Of course, the inflation enriches government, the issuer of money, by reducing the real value of its debt, but we assume that government demand for goods and services is not affected by the real value of the debt.

There is a second experiment that would give us results comparable to the first. Let real money balances be halved, not by a doubling of prices and wages, but by destruction of nominal money. Once again the real-balance effects in the private sectors lead to excess supply of goods and labor, excess of *ex-ante* saving over *ex-ante* investment, excess real demand for money. Initial equilibrium is restored, not at the original price and wage levels but at levels reduced by one half to match the contraction in nominal money.

The economy's private sectors demand real money balances. They can fabricate the desired real volume of money balances from any amount of nominal money by adjustment of price and money wage levels. Price and wage levels are flexible, and the appropriate changes in them are not obstructed by perverse and unstable expectations about the course they are taking, their ultimate limit, and the reason for their movement.

Real Growth with Price Deflation

Growth is easier to visualize in the rudimentary economy than absence of growth. Suppose now that the labor supply is growing at some constant rate and that there is parallel growth in the stock of capital, with no change in technology. Marginal products of labor and capital do not change, but total wages and total rents are increasing. Suppose, too, that each sector is maintaining a balanced budget. Government spending and money-issue are nil. Among the economy's variables, only the nominal stock of money stands still.

Demand for increments of real money must be positive in this growth process. In our economy the desired real stock of money is positively affected by growth in the stock of capital goods and in business and consumer incomes. Unless the actual real stock of money keeps pace with the desired stock, growth generates excess demand for money. And excess demand for money is equivalent, of course, to excess supply on markets for goods and labor. Unless incremental demand for money is satisfied, there develops a general glut of physical resources and output during the growth process.

For the moment, our premise is that government does not satisfy real incremental demand for money by new nominal issues. Hence the endemic excess demand for money is satisfied by continuous deflation in prices of goods and labor. The economy fits the real money stock to its desired level by continuous mark-down of prices and money wage rates. There is an unseen hand on the market for money as well as on the markets for current output and labor services.

In the process of balanced growth that we have been talking about, one can suppose that the real stock of money grows in constant proportion with labor, capital, and output. If growth merely multiplies firms and consumers, leaving per-capita wealth and income the same, demand for money increases just because of growth in population. Then money's income velocity is fairly assumed to remain constant. If, on the other hand, growth increases per-capita income, income velocity of money may vary in a different way. It will fall if money is a "luxury good" with a relatively high income elasticity of demand. If so, growth requires a more rapid deflation of prices than when it is accompanied by stable velocity.

Government policy of keeping nominal money constant has no effect on economic development in our model. Price deflation is wholly competent to take over the job of satisfying real incremental demand for money. Deflation is a necessary and constructive part of this growth process, dissipating excess demand for money and maintaining full employment for the accumulating stock of productive resources. All prices are perfectly flexible, and the continuous decline in general price indexes does not in any way distort price relationships between goods and labor, consumption goods and investment goods. Monetary policy is neutral, that is to say, with regard to employment of resources and to relative prices of output and resources.

Real Growth with Price Stability

The growth process increases spending units' desired real stock of money and, when equilibrium is maintained, requires continuous expansion in the real size of the monetary system—in the actual real stock of money. We have shown that real incremental demand for money during growth can be satisfied, in the rudimentary economy, by deflation of prices and money wage rates. But it can be satisfied too by growth in nominal money at stable levels of prices and money wage rates.

If price and wage levels are to be stable during growth, the private sectors of the rudimentary economy must maintain surplus budgets and government must run a continuous deficit. The private sectors must save, lend, and accumulate nominal money while government must dissave, borrow, and issue money. With the qualification that government spending is somehow kept from affecting the pattern of output and relative prices, private real demand for money can be satisfied equally well by growth in the real value of government debt as the result of a falling price level or by new debt issues at a stable price level.

Monetary Policy

The Banking Bureau in the rudimentary economy is the money factory. When the nominal stock of money is to increase, it is this Bureau that purchases goods and services from the private sectors and settles for its purchases by putting new money to the credit of sellers. There are two other participants in the market for money. The private sectors hold the money stock as their only financial asset and employ it as their means of payment. The third participant is the Policy Bureau whose function is to state the rule of growth in nominal money—to stipulate monetary policy.

Who determines the nominal stock of money? The finger might seem to point to the Banking Bureau, the rudimentary economy's equivalent of commercial banks. It creates nominal money, and private sectors will accept any amount of its product at par in exchange for goods and services at their market prices. The Bureau appears to "take the initiative" in producing nominal money, and no one refuses its product.

The apparent answer is wrong. The role of the Banking Bureau is passive. It is a money spigot to be turned on or off according to the decisions of private spending units and the Policy Bureau. At each step in the community's growth, the monetary system is confronted with the private sectors' real incremental demand for money balances. This demand can be satisfied, as we know, by any among innumerable combinations of change in price level and in the nominal stock of money. Once the Policy Bureau specifies the price level that it prefers, the appropriate nominal stock of money is settled. This appropriate stock, then, is determined by private real demand for money and by the price-level decision of the Policy Bureau. The Banking Bureau has no choice other than to create the appropriate nominal stock of money. The private sectors "determine" the real stock of money; the private sectors and the Policy Bureau "determine" the appropriate nominal stock; and the Banking Bureau makes this appropriate stock available.

ALTERNATIVES OF POLICY

We have already considered two alternatives of policy. First, the monetary authority may decide on a constant nominal stock of money and rely upon price deflation to satisfy real demand for money. Second, the Policy Bureau may decide on a constant level of prices and wages and resort to money-issue in order to satisfy real demand for money. Does either alternative have a net advantage over the other?

On the terms of our rudimentary economy, there is no

government demand for goods under the policy alternative of price deflation. Under the alternative of price stability, goods are bought by the Banking Bureau. Unless government were to allocate goods in precisely the same way as private spending units would have allocated them, the alternative policies would have different real effects on the economy's growth. A choice of policy would necessarily take into account the relative contributions of private spending and government spending to the community's welfare.

Assume, however, that any government purchases of goods and services would not disturb the pattern of demand for current output. Then is there a rational basis for choice in our economy between the two ways of satisfying real demand for money—price deflation and money-issue? Apparently not. When the desired real stock of money rises above the existing real stock, price deflation and money-issue are equally efficient in creating real money to close the gap. Monetary policy in this context is trivial, and the monetary system's only important function is to maintain an efficient payments mechanism.

Government in our economy may let price deflation maintain monetary equilibrium. If it decides upon stable prices, it might so arrange its spending or transfer payments that government financing still would not affect the pattern and rate of real growth. As a third alternative of policy, government may use money management to intervene in the growth process. Given a target of stable levels for prices and money wage rates, government could satisfy private demand for money by new issues, in effect borrowing voluntary private saving to finance its own deficit-spending on current output. This current output could be allocated to an investment program or to other social goals that would modify the course of real development. Moreover, by issuing money for transfer payments that would not be distributed in the same way as private incomes from production, government could impose distributive effects on the community that would also modify the course of real development.

Monetary policy might call for wage-price inflation rather than for deflation or stability. Any rise in money wage rates and in prices reduces the real value of money balances outstanding and opens a gap between actual and desired real balances. It involves a loss in real wealth for private sectors as creditors of government and a corresponding gain in real wealth to government as debtor. If the private sectors undertake to restore real money balances by saving a larger share of income and by devoting a smaller share of saving to real investment, government can absorb this saving by money-issue and apply it to social projects. A policy of price stability in the rudimentary economy induces voluntary private saving when growth in capital and income stimulate demand for money, and government can absorb this saving by money-issue. A policy of price inflation induces a still higher rate of voluntary saving, on our assumption of static price expectations, and diverts still more of the net national product to government use. Inflation induces the higher rate of saving because spending units demand money not only in response to growth of capital and income but also in order to recoup real balances lost through inflation.

MONETARY POLICY AND ECONOMIC FRICTION

Any act of monetary policy has two aspects in the rudimentary economy. One is the issue of nominal money by government which goes into the balances of firms and consumers. This aspect of monetary management we have called trivial, or neutral, in the sense that, after allowance for related changes in price and wage levels, it does not affect rates of growth in capital, employment, and output. The second aspect of monetary management is the purchase of goods and services or the transfer payments which money-issue finances—the "use" of funds that is associated with money-issue as the "source." We have imagined that government could, if it wished, avoid disturbing markets for goods and labor by its use of funds. Then monetary policy is neutral in both aspects.

We have also pointed out that government could, if it wished, deliberately disturb markets for goods and labor, applying proceeds of money-issue to developmental or other projects. It could impose distributive effects on relative demands for consumption and investment, or for different kinds of investment, that would have non-neutral effects on the rate and pattern of real growth. Money-issue must be spent on something, and the spending program can give the monetary authority a real grip on economic activity.

Quite apart from such distributive effects, money management ceases to be trivial if we change any of three assumptions regarding the rudimentary economy. Suppose, first, that prices and money wage rates are rigid rather than flexible. Then there can be no deflation of prices and money wage rates as an efficient alternative to money-issue in satisfying real incremental demand for money. As real capital and income grow, growth in real demand for money can be satisfied only by growth in nominal money. If real incremental demand for money is not satisfied, the excess demand results in chronic underemployment of labor and capital and retardation of growth. Price flexibility is the unseen hand that may maintain monetary equilibrium with a given nominal stock of money. Price rigidity shackles the unseen hand.

If there is downward price rigidity, the money-issue aspect of monetary policy is vital to real growth with full employment. If there is upward price rigidity, because of price controls or for other reasons, money-issue becomes a more powerful instrument for diverting real output to government spending programs. Then money can be imposed on consumers and firms, at a stable price level, and this compulsory private saving can be used to finance government investment or dissaving.

Rigidity of prices puts the burden of satisfying real demand for money upon nominal money-issue. Administered inflation or deflation of price and wage levels may be regarded as a special case of rigidity, since it removes prices and wages from the influence of excess demand or supply on the money market. In our economy, a decree raising prices and wages would reduce real balances below those desired, create excess real demand for money, and require a faster rate of growth in nominal money, through new issues, to avert excess supply on markets for goods and labor.

We may introduce a second friction into our model by assuming that price expectations are not of unitary elasticity. With some misgivings, spending units hitherto have taken it for granted that any equilibrium price level is the permanent price level; they have had static price expectations, a special case of unitary elasticity of price expectations. If spending units lose this simple faith, price deflation again may be disqualified as an efficient alternative to money-issue in satisfying the real incremental demand for money that results from growth in real capital and income.

Suppose price expectations are of greater than unitary elasticity. Then a change in current prices will change expected future prices in the same direction but in greater proportion. Hence, as the real demand for money rises during output growth, given nominal money, the process of price deflation serves only to increase this demand even more and to bring about further price deflation. The failure of the monetary system to supply nominal money, then, may result in underemployment or, in the extreme case, in collapse of money prices. Conversely, a rise in current prices sets up expectations of proportionally greater increases in future prices and so reduces real demand for money. Hyperinflation is the culmination of the process. In general, when price movements widen the gap between actual and desired real balances, policy concerning money-issue ceases to be trivial; price deflation is not a perfect substitute for money-issue.

The conclusion that monetary policy is not trivial also holds when price expectations are of less than unitary elasticity. Then a change in current prices changes expected future prices in the same direction (if elasticity is greater than zero) but in smaller proportion. Under these circumstances, price deflation during output growth reduces the real incremental demand for money below what it would be under conditions of unitary elasticity of price expectations. Conversely, price inflation increases real incremental demand for money above what it otherwise would be. Consequently, the policy choice between changes in nominal money and changes in prices becomes an important one.

A third friction can be put into the model in the form of money illusion: spending units define their goals and make their plans in nominal rather than in real terms. The effect is that the choice between change in nominal money and change in price level, as alternative responses to incremental demand for money, ceases to be trivial, and monetary policy is not neutral in its real effects. Price deflation cannot satisfy incremental demand for money because it is more nominal balances, not more real balances, that spending units desire. And price inflation cannot remove excess supply of money, because excess balances are measured nominally. Under these circumstances, money management is a delicate and important process of creating just the right amount of nominal balances. It is the community's sole expedient for maintaining monetary equilibrium as the growth process continuously changes demand for money.

We conclude that monetary policy *can* be trivial in the rudimentary economy. It is trivial if there are no distributive effects from government spending, if prices are flexible, if price expectations are of unitary elasticity, and if money illusion is absent. When monetary policy is trivial money-issue plays a neutral role in real growth, and the nominal growth rate of the monetary system is irrelevant to the public welfare.

Financial Restraints on Real Growth

It is difficult to attain a satisfactory rate of growth in real output. Such a growth rate may not be achieved for a number of reasons, some social, some psychological, some political, and some economic. What is significant here is that the rudimentary economy places severe financial restraints on growth of real output. An immature financial system is in itself an obstacle to economic progress. In this section we consider ways in which limitations on lending and borrowing hamper real growth in the rudimentary economy.

The output that an economy is capable of producing depends on the input of labor services and on the size of the capital stock, given the state of the productive arts. Labor services aside, net output capacity expands as the capital stock increases—as there are saving and investment. However, net output capacity depends only partly on the level of investment. It depends also on the efficient allocation of investment among alternative capital projects.

The design and performance of a financial system may stimulate saving and investment in efficient uses or it may retard saving and divert it to inefficient uses. The financial system in our rudimentary economy does not pass with a high score on these counts. Especially in a regime of private enterprise, it is not congenial to a rapid growth of real output.

RESTRAINT ON THE LEVEL OF INVESTMENT

If capital is to accumulate in the rudimentary economy, there must be domestic saving to finance it, since no borrowing is permitted from abroad. The domestic saving must come from the private sector, since government has no income. Within the private sector, there is consumer saving only for accumulation of real money balances and, even then, only as consumer demand for real balances is satisfied by issue of nominal money rather than by price deflation. Such consumer saving, along with any business saving also directed to increases in real money balances, necessarily flows to the government sector for its disposition. Only business saving not allocated to real money balances is available for private investment. If government were to incur its deficits on transfer payments to business, rather than on spending for goods and services, all saving could flow to private capital formation. If the model were relaxed a bit, so that firms might dishoard their money balances to satisfy consumer demand for money, there would be a direct route for the flow of consumer saving to business. However, economies in money balances of business could hardly be very significant before the implicit deposit rate on these balances would rise enough relative to the rental rate on capital goods to inhibit further transfers.

The financial system of the rudimentary economy offers to private spending units just one kind of financial asset, money, as an enticement to saving. It provides business with no financial instrument of its own to issue as an inducement to saving by consumers, and government is not allowed to issue nonmonetary debt. The financial system makes no attempt to stimulate private saving either by offering different kinds of financial assets or by allowing an explicit rate of interest on financial assets. As a result, we must suppose, the propensity to save and the rate of growth in capital will be relatively low, given the distribution of income between consumers and firms.

RESTRAINT ON FLOW OF SAVING TO INVESTMENT

The financial system of the rudimentary economy provides two channels for the flow of saving to investment in capital goods. Each firm directs its own saving to its own investment projects to the extent that its saving exceeds its incremental demand for money. And all saving, both by consumers and firms, that is allocated to accumulation of real money balances flows to government. If incremental demand for money is satisfied by price deflation, saving flows to investment in tangible assets only through the first channel. If prices and money wage rates fall by less than is required to satisfy incremental demand for money, governmental issues of nominal money draw saving through the second channel for such allocations as government policy specifies. Government has various options in its deficit-spending: it may invest the flow of private saving in social capital; it may finance private investment through transfer payments; or it may spend in ways that do not increase the stock of capital goods.

This financial regime evidently puts heavy responsibility on the government sector for investment planning. First, the rate of private saving depends on monetary policy regarding the price level. Second, allocation of private saving for accumulation of money is more or less efficient according to the government's selection of investment projects.

Private enterprise in allocation of saving to investment is minimized in the rudimentary economy. Consumers may direct their saving only to the government sector. And each firm has access, except through government transfer payments, only to its saving. If government were to permit incremental demand for money to be satisfied only by price deflation, the economy would have no specialization in saving and investment. There would be no markets where firms could compete for private saving, where investment opportunities could be ranked according to their marginal efficiencies, and where price in the form of the bond rate of interest could disqualify the less efficient projects. There would be no private mechanism for merging the saved income of numerous spending units to finance investment on the large scale. Private security issues and markets for disposing of them to savers are indispensable to private enterprise in accumulation and allocation of capital.

SAVING, INVESTMENT, AND MONEY

The financial system of the rudimentary economy is inefficient since it provides neither the array of financial assets that would stimulate saving nor the array of financial markets that would allocate saving competitively to investment. But it is clearly better than no financial system at all, because it does provide one financial asset—money.

The existence of money as a financial asset gives each spending unit the opportunity to spend more or less than its income. It opens the way to borrowing and lending. Since the spending unit with income to spend is not necessarily the spending unit with the most rewarding opportunities to spend, lending by savers and borrowing by investors permits a more efficient allocation of spending to output in our economy than presumably would be feasible in a still more primitive society. Any financial asset permits the reallocation of income among spenders and allows some potential spenders to pit their spending options against others. The trouble with the rudimentary economy is that it provides only one financial asset and does not fully exploit financial incentives to saving and financial media for efficient dispersion of saving among investment opportunities.

Innovations in Finance

A financial system restrains growth if it ties the distribution of spending too rigidly to the distribution of income and if it does not make institutional provision for selective matching of surplus budgets in some sectors with deficit budgets in others. Spending units can be expected to look for ways around such restraints. Indeed, in any economy, the financial structure is continually reshaped by the efforts of spending units to break out of the confines of existing financial arrangements.

In the remainder of this chapter, we consider briefly some of the simpler financial devices that have been used in relatively underdeveloped economies to expedite the flow of saving between spending units. Any one of them might be grafted to our rudimentary economy to raise its rate of real growth.

ELEMENTARY FINANCIAL EXPEDIENTS

The early economic history of the United States offers interesting illustrations of ways to ease financial restraint on real development. The formation of partnerships was a common device for mobilizing saving in the American colonies before the emergence of corporate organization and of private markets in corporate securities. The merging of business budgets by partnership arrangements widened the range of investment opportunities for any given dollar of saving. The pooling of consumer saving in mutual societies also lowered barriers to the flow of funds into relatively urgent uses.

Another popular technique for raising funds in colonial times was the lottery, which has a long tradition the world over as a substitute for private security issues. If the value of prizes is set well below the value of lottery tickets sold, the game obviously can be played to the advantage of its operator. And the operator may spend his winnings on investment. The colonial governments used lotteries not only to gain funds for themselves but also to extend grants to private individuals and business firms. The colonies—and the states, too, later on—also permitted individuals to conduct lotteries to finance designated investments. The lottery ticket may not be a perfect substitute for a bond or stock certificate, but in many countries it has been one of the first steps along the road of financial development.

Government has tapped private saving by money-issue, by lottery, by taxation, by sale of goods produced under government auspices, by direct appropriation of private output, and by sale of monopoly charters or religious privileges. It has applied saving from such sources to its own investment projects or it has released command over saved resources to private enterprise through numerous techniques of transfer payment. In our own colonies, these transfer techniques included bounties to encourage investment in preferred categories, premiums for output of exceptional quality, and subsidies for desired enterprise that was slow to gain momentum.

All governments, in societies both primitive and advanced,

have exploited private real demand for money, in the manner of government in our model. They have invented devices, too numerous for listing here, to stimulate real demand for money at given levels of output and income in the community. Money was early made receivable for taxes in this country and elsewhere, and usually receivable as legal tender for payment of debts, with penalties provided for creditors who preferred other means of settlement. In physical appearance, in denomination, in provisions for convertibility, and in other ways, efforts were made to increase real demand for money. Primitive price controls and rationing cannot be omitted from this list of devices for increasing the real yield to government of its money-issue.

Financial devices that we have yet to discuss are principally of two types. One involves tangible assets, and we turn to it below. The second involves various kinds of elemental primary securities, both private and governmental. These primary issues have come to be the main reliance, in private enterprise economies, for soliciting saving and for taking efficient advantage of a division of labor between spending units that save and other spending units that invest. Primary issues enter our model in the next chapter.

FINANCE BY EXISTING TANGIBLE ASSETS

In our rudimentary economy, there is no trading in existing assets. But financial restraint has often been relieved, especially in underdeveloped countries, through transfers of land and other tangibles.

Tangible assets may serve the same purpose as money balances do in the rudimentary economy: to transfer surplus budgets of some spending units to the finance of deficit-spending by other units. Any existing asset that a sector is willing to acquire as an alternative to spending on current output releases resources for other uses, including new investment. A community's natural endowment in land is perhaps the least ambiguous illustration of the existing asset that costs the community as a whole little or nothing in terms of current productive effort and that can be traded to savers as a means of diverting their claims on current output into capital formation. But any other existing asset—*objets d'art,* for example, or estates of an erstwhile ruling class—can be used in the same way.

Public lands served admirably in the United States, both in colonial times and later, to secure funds for development purposes. The most famous instances were the land grants to canal and railroad companies by federal and state governments. Most land granted to railroad companies was intended for sale to raise funds for railroad construction. To the extent that the companies sold the land, their need to obtain external funds by other means, including security sales, was reduced. That this was no small matter is suggested by the fact that the land grants to railroads amounted to almost 10 per cent of the entire area of continental United States. Land transactions replaced security transactions at a time when security markets were underdeveloped and a "land-office business" was possible. Many savers certainly preferred to accumulate land instead of securities in those years, and the saving they released clearly was allocable to new investment.

Summary

Our model of the rudimentary economy contains three sectors and three markets. The three sectors comprise nonfinancial spending units, grouped into consumers, business firms, and government. The three markets are those for labor services, current output, and money. Money is the only financial asset in the economy, and it is issued by the governmental monetary system, the only financial institution. This monetary system is composed of a Policy Bureau and a Banking Bureau, the former an embryonic central bank that instructs the latter concerning its purchases of current output (and transfer payments) and its issues of money, which are acquired by consumers and firms.

Private spending units demand real money balances because money has an implicit marginal deposit rate that exceeds the marginal returns to consumption and investment. The marginal deposit rate of money rises as spending units anticipate price declines, as their anticipated deficit budgets grow, and as there is increasing marginal risk of real investment. The real demand for money balances is stimulated by these factors, the last two of which are related to growth in real income and in real capital, and by a decline in the marginal rental rate on capital goods. The appropriate nominal stock of money is determined by private demand for real money and the price-level decision of the Policy Bureau. The private sectors determine the real stock of money; the private sectors and the Policy Bureau determine the appropriate nominal stock; and the Banking Bureau makes this appropriate stock available.

Firms and consumers are motivated by anticipated real advantages and plan in real terms: they are free of money illusion. The current price level is expected, with some uncertainty, to be permanent. Markets for current output and labor services are competitive; prices are flexible. It is a neoclassical world.

In this setting, there is only one price level associated with any given nominal stock of money: the price level is determinate. If government purchases of goods and services do not disturb the pattern of demand for output, there is no rational basis for choice, in this neo-classical world, between the two ways of satisfying excess real demand for money—by price deflation and by issues of money. Monetary policy in this context is neutral in the sense that it cannot affect the real variables of the economy, such as rental rate, output, and wealth. Changes in nominal money simply change price and money wage rate levels and that is all.

Monetary policy is not neutral, however, if government purchases of goods and services (and, hence, issues of nominal money) alter the economy's relative demands for consumption and investment, or for different types of investment. Monetary policy also ceases to be neutral if prices and money wage rates are not perfectly flexible, if price expectations are not of unitary elasticity, or if there is money illusion. In any of these cases, the choice between money-issue and price changes is not trivial; the choice does matter for the real variables of the economy.

The financial system of the rudimentary economy is not congenial to rapid growth of real output because it fails to provide the array of financial assets that would stimulate saving and the array of financial markets that would allocate saving competitively to investment. Simple financial techniques have been used by underdeveloped countries to offset these deficiencies. These techniques include the formation of partnerships and mutual societies, the use of lotteries, transfer payments by government to private sectors, devices for increasing demand for money, and transfers of land and other existing tangibles.

CHAPTER III

Money and Primary Securities

THE LEVEL OF ECONOMIC ACTIVITY and the rate of its expansion are depressed by primitive financial arrangements that limit each spending unit's expenditure essentially to its income. If spending for output is distributed according to income—if only savers can purchase investment goods—economic specialization is inhibited and economic resources may not be drawn to their most efficient uses. Of course, economic specialization and the highly developed finance that goes with it do imply various social costs, but the presumption is that social gains outweigh them.

In the rudimentary economy of Chapter II, financial arrangements were not congenial to private real investment. They restrained private economic development in a strait jacket. But where there are attractive private investment opportunities and where nonfinancial barriers to exploitation of these opportunities have been removed, investors can be counted upon to escape from the strait jacket by the means previously discussed. Eventually markets are developed for private primary securities to relax even more effectively the restriction of budget-balancing on private expenditures.

In the model we introduce now, there are private securities and a market for trading in them, so that some spending units may invest more than they save and others may lend saved income and accumulate interest-bearing securities as well as money. This economy generates two kinds of debt and financial asset, a homogeneous bond and money. It has two financial markets, one for bonds and one for money, where bids and offers are cleared at an equilibrium bond rate of interest and price level.

The plan of this chapter calls, first, for a brief description of this second model. Next, we shall lay out the conditions of supply and demand on the economy's four markets—for labor services, current output (goods), primary securities (bonds), and money. The third step will be to analyze separately the market for money, especially the demand for money as one component in financial portfolios. The remainder of the chapter is concerned with general-equilibrium analysis and the role of money in determining the price level, rate of interest, and level and composition of output.

Sectors, Markets, and Finance

In this section we describe our second economy in terms of its sectors, its markets, and its financial structure.

SECTORS, BUDGETS, AND MARKETS

There continue to be the three sectors of consumers, nonfinancial business firms, and government. In equilibrium, consumer spending units have either balanced or surplus budgets, while firms have either balanced or deficit budgets. Government receives no income and does not spend on income and product account; it is the monetary system, with dealings confined to the markets for bonds and money. There still is no foreign sector.

The business sector owns all real capital and combines it with labor services from the consumer sector to produce the national output. Depreciation of capital goods is covered automatically by replacement, and the remaining net national product is divided between wages and interest paid to consumers and rental income to firms. Business firms are ultimates, with no equity securities outstanding. They do issue homogeneous bonds, assumed to be perfectly safe, to supplement their saving for accumulation of both real capital and money balances. There are no dividends so that business net income and net saving are the same.

The security that firms sell is homogeneous and gilt-edged, and it is a perpetuity paying $1 annually. The terms of sale can be expressed either as a market rate of interest or as a security price, an absolute number of dollars representing the present worth of future payments on the security at market rate of interest. There will be occasion to measure bonds in three ways: in number, in nominal present worth, in real present worth.

The consumer sector sells labor services to firms in exchange for wage income. This sector holds business securities yielding interest income. Interest due on business securities held by the monetary system is diverted to consumers, but it is not construed as a reward for holding either money or bonds. So all interest payments by business accrue to consumers. The consumer sector allocates its income between consumption expenditures and saving, and the saving is allocated to accumulation of money and bonds. Consumers own no tangible wealth.

Government again has its Policy and Banking Bureaus, the former responsible for policy and the latter for money-issue and administration of the payments mechanism. But this time the Banking Bureau does not buy goods and services or make transfer payments. Instead its money-issue is in payment for purchases of business bonds through open-market operations. Government's budget is balanced at zero on income and product account. It follows that there is also an *ex-post* balanced budget aggregatively for the private sectors. Any budget surplus in the consumer sector is equal to a budget deficit in the business sector. And the financial assets in which consumer spending units "invest" their budget surpluses must be equal to business debt less business money balances. With budget surpluses of one private sector equal to deficits of the other, lending by one is equal to borrowing by the other. Government purchases of business bonds supply nominal money for private portfolios of financial assets.

The three sectors of spending units carry out their transactions on the four markets—for labor services, goods, bonds, and money. The two private sectors transact on all markets, while government is confined to markets for bonds and money. The congeries of markets determines real national income, the distribution of income between firms and consumers, the allocation of income to consumption and investment, all relative prices including bond rate of interest, and absolute levels of prices for goods and labor. It determines, too, real stocks of bonds and money; that is, nominal stocks deflated by the absolute level of prices for goods.

PRIMARY AND INDIRECT SECURITIES

The gilt-edged bonds of firms in this model are a form of primary security. Primary securities, in the broadest sense, include all liabilities and outstanding equities of nonfinancial spending units, that is of spending units whose principal function is to produce and purchase current output, and not to buy one type of security by issuing another. Primary securities are contrasted with indirect securities, which are defined as issues of financial institutions. In this economy, the only financial institution is the governmental monetary system, and money is the only form of indirect security. The financial profile of the model is this: business issues the only form of primary security and accumulates money; government purchases primary securities and issues money as the only form of indirect debt; and consumers acquire either primary securities or money or both.

DIRECT AND INDIRECT FINANCE

These financial transactions are mainly complements of income and product transactions. In most postures of this economy, income and spending on income and product account are not similarly distributed between sectors of spending units. Consumers save, voluntarily or not, releasing command over current output in exchange for financial assets, bonds and money. Firms incur debt, equal in value at issue price to increases in consumer financial assets, as their way of absorbing consumer saving. Consumers save, lend their savings, and add to their financial-asset portfolios; firms invest in excess of their own savings, borrow consumer savings, and add to business debt. Issues of primary securities and acquisitions of financial assets reflect intersectoral division of labor between saving and investment, between receiving and spending income.

There are purely financial transactions not directly concerned with the transmission of saving from one sector to investment in another. Business may incur primary debt not only to finance its deficits, and so to supply financial assets for consumers, but also to build up its own money balances. Consumers may adjust their portfolios by switching between money and bonds.

The Banking Bureau may buy the nominal primary

securities issued in any period, and prior issues as well, paying with money newly created. In this case, consumers, as the surplus sector, add money and not primary securities to their portfolios. On the other hand, the Banking Bureau may buy no bonds, or even reduce its portfolio, so that all intersectoral financing of output for the period is settled by a direct flow of primary securities from firms to consumers. The Banking Bureau, on instructions from the Policy Bureau, has the option of intermediating part of the financial flow, rather than all or none, taking up a portion of primary issues so that consumers receive an increment of financial assets that is partly bonds and partly money. Intermediation by the monetary system permits indirect finance by consumer saving of business investment. Direct finance pours primary securities into consumer portfolios, while indirect finance substitutes money for primary securities in these portfolios.

Patterns of Economic Behavior

We are concerned now with determinants of demand and supply in the four markets and with amounts of labor services, current output, primary securities, and money demanded and supplied in market equilibrium. In a more formal presentation, this section would be an array of demand functions, supply functions, and market-clearing equations—one each for every market.

OUTPUT AND REAL INCOME

As in the rudimentary economy, the supply of labor is given independently of the wage rate. Real capital is the accumulation of net investment on the basis of private net saving in the past, and it is automatically maintained out of depreciation charges against current gross product. Real income or output is the product jointly of labor services and capital goods. We carry over from the rudimentary economy the rules applying to determination of output and to its distribution between real wages and real rent. Business firms' gross rental income from capital is divided among depreciation, interest on outstanding business debt, and their net income or saving. Markets for labor and output are assumed to be competitive, their prices flexible.

THE BUSINESS SECTOR

Funds flow to firms from two sources, net income and borrowing. These sources finance uses of funds on the current output market for net investment, on the money market for increments in money balances, and on the bond market for debt redemption. The goal of business management is to reach an optimal or balanced asset-debt position, with potentialities of net profit, considering risk, superior to any alternative combination of capital goods, real money balances, and real debt. When the optimal position has been attained, there is equality after allowances for risk among the marginal rental rate on capital, the marginal implicit deposit rate on money balances, and the market rate of interest on business bonds.[1]

The same variables affect business decisions to invest, to acquire money, and to adjust debt by borrowing or redemption. Business demands on all markets are flow-demands for increments in stocks of capital, money, and bonds. The target

[1] The rental rate on capital is equal to the sum of firms' net profits and interest payments as a percentage of their capital stock.

of firms is a balanced assortment of assets and debt. Our model does not specify how rapidly firms set about closing any gap between existing and desired stocks. Presumably there is always such a gap during growth, and the gap is closed for the aggregate of firms only in stationary equilibrium. During growth there may be equilibria of stocks, not with the levels that are the ultimate targets of accumulation, but instead with levels along a planned path or trajectory of accumulation.

A rise in the marginal rental rate increases the rate of net investment, increases the disposition of firms to borrow, and reduces real incremental demand for money. It encourages borrowing and dishoarding of money to finance capital accumulation. A rise in the bond rate of interest decreases desired net investment, borrowing, and incremental demand for money. Reductions in the marginal rental rate and the bond rate of interest have opposite effects on business choice among capital, money, and bonds.

Business firms are guided in their decisions not only by relative prices but also by their real income net of depreciation and of the interest on outstanding debt. A rise in net income stimulates their demand for net investment and real money balances, and encourages borrowing. Opposite results follow a decline in net income.

Business decisions are assumed to take into account also the proportion of outstanding real debt to existing real stocks of capital goods. The burden of debt on business is a ratio of the real value, at face amount, of outstanding bonds to real capital, and it is taken as an index of the special risks that are run by external financing. Any rise in this burden has the "debt effect" of discouraging net investment and real incremental demand for money, and of encouraging debt redemption. As the debt burden is eased, firms are more disposed to borrow for the sake of adding to the stock of capital and to money balances.

Finally, business management makes no allocations of funds without considering existing real stocks of money balances. An increase in real balances reduces incremental demand for money, since it reduces any deficiency of existing balances relative to those desired. An increase in real balances diverts incremental demand away from money to alternative uses of funds in investment and debt redemption. Opposite effects follow from a decrease in real money held.

TABLE 5

Market Behavior of Business Firms

	Response (In real terms)		
Stimulus	Demand for Investment	Incremental Demand for Money	Supply of Bonds
Marginal real rental rate	+	—	+
Bond rate of interest	—	—	—
Real net income	+	+	+
Debt burden	—	—	—
Real money balances	+	—	—

To summarize, firms make no adjustments in capital goods, money, and primary debt without taking into account five factors: marginal real rental rate, bond rate of interest, real net income, debt burden, and real money balances. These are the factors that motivate business bids and offers in the markets for current output, bonds, and money. Table 5 is a guide to the relationships between the five factors and business transactions on three markets. The *plus* sign indicates that business response (in the columns) is in the same direction as the stimulus (in the rows); the *minus* sign indicates that business response is in the opposite direction.

THE CONSUMER SECTOR

The real income of consumers consists of real wages and all real interest on business debt. This flow of funds is allocated in three directions: to consumption, to real increments in money balances, and to real increments in bond portfolios. Consumers choose, that is to say, between expenditure for current consumption and saving; saving adds to consumer portfolios of financial assets; and these assets may be apportioned between bonds and money.

Consumers' real demands for goods, bonds, and money are motivated by a common set of variables: real consumer income, existing real stocks of bonds and money, and the rate of interest. An increase in real income of consumers raises their real demand for goods and their real incremental demands for money and bonds. An increase in the rate of interest raises their real incremental demand for bonds, lowers that for money, and puts some restraint on consumption.

Consumers have in mind some long-run plan of asset accumulation for money and bonds together. In any relatively short period, consumers wish to move only part way toward this ultimate estate from their existing one. Like firms, consumers have a desired trajectory of accumulation. An increase in present portfolios of real bonds brings the savings objective closer to realization and reduces present real incremental demand for bonds. Similarly an increase in present real money balances decreases real incremental demand now for such balances.

Consumers work toward short-run and long-run objectives for their total financial assets, and they work also for optimal portfolio "mix"—for the right combination of bonds and money. As a result, an increase in present real bond holdings shifts incremental demand from bonds to both consumption and money, and an increase in real money shifts incremental demand from money to both consumption and bonds. Consumers define their principle of behavior in this way, that the optimal uses of funds flowing to them achieve a balance among marginal utility of consumption, the rate of interest, and the marginal implicit deposit rate for real money.

Table 6 is drawn up in the same way as the preceding

TABLE 6

Market Behavior of Consumers

	Response (In real terms)		
Stimulus	Demand for Consumption	Incremental Demand for Money	Incremental Demand for Bonds
Bond rate of interest	−	−	+
Real consumer income	+	+	+
Real bond holdings	+	+	−
Real money balances	+	−	+

table on business market behavior. The signs indicate whether consumer response on markets for goods, bonds, and money is positively or negatively related to the stimuli of the rate of interest, real consumer income, real bond holdings, and real money balances.

THE GOVERNMENT SECTOR

The government sector is confined to open-market operations that simultaneously affect the markets for bonds and money. The Banking Bureau holds a portfolio of business bonds—of outstanding bonds not held by consumers—and it is indebted for the outstanding stock of money. The Bureau may buy or sell bonds, paying for them by issuing money or taking payment by retiring money. In the basic version of the model, the entire money stock is founded on domestic business bonds in the Banking Bureau's portfolio. In a modified version, to be introduced later, only part of the money stock is based on domestic business bonds, the remainder being issued against an external asset such as government or foreign bonds or gold.

Any government transaction pursuant to monetary policy is two-edged. Government issues money by buying bonds, and retires money by selling bonds. Its primary target is the money market, but there is a fallout of secondary effects on the bond market. Because bonds are homogeneous and the bond market competitive, there is no opportunity in the present model for application of "credit" policy side by side with monetary policy.

OTHER SPECIFICATIONS OF THE MODEL

Spending units in this economy, as in the rudimentary economy of Chapter II, are free of money illusion. Their decisions are motivated by real variables and are not distorted by compensating changes in nominal values that leave real stocks, real flows, or relative prices unchanged. Price expectations are static, in that current prices are expected to be permanent, though there is a penumbra of uncertainty about the future that induces cautious firms and consumers to protect themselves against possible adverse price movements. Static expectations are a special case of unitary elasticity of price expectations. Further, all markets are competitive and prices are flexible. Aggregative behavior is not sensitive to possible distribution effects that increase the wealth or income of one private sector at the expense of the other. Briefly, the stage is set according to neo-classical rules; it shifts only toward the end of this discussion to a context that is more familiar in modern economics.

We allege that the second model has an equilibrium solution, that it is capable of reaching some position of general equilibrium in which excess demands on all markets are nil, and that it tends to return to such a position after disturbance. The model's behavior patterns suggest that it is inherently stable.

The Market for Money

In previous pages we have reviewed conditions of supply and demand on all markets in the second model, even though our focus of interest is finance and, in particular, money. Partial analysis of money alone, or of money and bonds, can lead one astray in this model because real markets and financial markets are interacting. Actual stocks of money and bonds, in relation to desired stocks, affect demands for goods and labor, while the stock of capital, national output, and other real variables are determinants of both supply and demand on financial markets. One senses the full significance of finance only in the context of general-equilibrium analysis. Before we discuss general equilibrium, however, we take a moment to analyze supply and demand in the money market alone.

THE SUPPLY SIDE OF THE MARKET

The stock of money is government debt that bears no interest (no explicit deposit rate) and that is accepted generally as the community's means of payment. It may be measured in nominal terms as the dollar aggregate of money balances or in real terms as the purchasing-power aggregate. The nominal stock of money can be changed only by decision of the Policy Bureau and by market transactions of the Banking Bureau. The real stock of money can be changed both by new issues of nominal money and by inflation or deflation of an index of prices on the goods market.

The "supply" of money is not the stock of money but rather is new issues of money. In real terms, it is the real value of increments in the nominal stock of money. It confronts the real incremental demand for money. This demand can be satisfied either by new issues at a given price level or, given nominal money, by adjustment in the price level. The real incremental demand for money is a measure of the difference between desired and existing real money balances of consumers and firms. It is a measure of the private sectors' shortage of real money.

THE DEMAND SIDE OF THE MARKET

Consumers save in order to accumulate a portfolio of real money and real bonds. To adjust the real-money component of their portfolios, consumers may modify either their rate of consumption or their bond holdings. Firms have a mixed financial position, owning money and owing debt. Their bond liability always exceeds their money asset, and the difference is equal to their accumulated net investment less their net worth or accumulated savings.

What are the motivations for money-holding in this economy? Again we resort to the fiction of a marginal implicit deposit rate on money as a measure of motivation for money-holding. As in Chapter II, total desired money balances are not compartmentalized by motive into, say, transactions, precautionary, and speculative balances. Money is one asset, not three. It is classified only as desired balances and existing balances, the difference between the two being incremental demand for money.

Consumers want an inventory of financial assets. They want it so that future flows of money spending do not have to be entirely dependent on concurrent flows of money receipts. Synchronizing flows of funds is inconvenient and expensive, and the costs can be avoided by retaining a pool or inventory of funds in financial-asset form. Consumers may want an inventory of financial assets, too, for speculative account, on the possibility that deflation in prices of goods will yield real capital gains on portfolios of money and bonds. Even though the mean expectation favors price stability, the expectation is not certain and is not inconsistent with a financial hedge against deflation.

Consumers find it advantageous to diversify their financial inventory between money and bonds because the value of either asset in terms of the other may vary. If the inventory might be drawn upon in the near future, money could be the preferred component because the income from interest on bonds might fall short of turnover costs in buying and selling bonds and of short-period capital losses on bonds. Desired money balances are raised relative to balances on hand, so that incremental demand for money is generated, when a rise in consumer income and spending threatens to increase short-period drains on the inventory of financial assets. Some of the increase in income is devoted to saving, and part of the saving is directed to money balances because the diversified inventory of financial assets returns a higher yield than an inventory of bonds alone.

Both money and bonds are vehicles for speculation on the price level of current output: they appreciate equally when the price level falls. But money is also a vehicle for speculation on the price level of bonds—on the market rate of interest. While the mean expectation is that the interest rate will not change, the expectation is not certain. Because any interest rate may be succeeded by a higher one, consumers' desired money balances rise relative to existing balances with each increment in the financial-asset portfolio, given their income and the interest rate. The implicit deposit rate of money is credited with possible capital loss avoided by substitution of money for bonds.

Given consumer income and total financial-asset inventory, desired money balances vary inversely with the bond rate. As the bond rate slips to lower levels, bonds become more expensive and more vulnerable to market depreciation. Potential losses avoided on financial assets are greater per dollar of money substituted for bonds; the rise in the implicit deposit rate of money, accompanying the decline in bond yield, generates incremental demand for money as the cheaper and safer component of inventory. While consumers are induced to demand money incrementally, along with bonds, by each increase in total financial assets, they are induced to intensify demand for money relative to demand for bonds by each increase in their income and each fall in the interest rate. Inventory policy regarding financial assets calls for diversification.

Business firms are chronic deficit spenders. And they are chronic debtors, with real assets exceeding net worth. This excess measures their net debt, the difference between their gross debt outstanding and their money balances. Gross debt may exceed net debt because firms find it profitable to hold money as well as real capital, and to have a mixture of money and outstanding bonds. Considerations that underlie consumer preference for diversifying financial assets between bonds and money also underlie business preference for holding both money and capital goods at the expense of a larger amount of gross debt.

Business firms, for the same reason as consumers, increase their real incremental demand for money when their net income and spending rise and threaten to raise short-term demands on their liquidity. Firms also increase their incremental demand for money when the marginal rental rate on capital falls, and when their existing real balances are reduced relative to those desired.

Since individual firms face an uncertain future, they resist an increasing ratio of debt to capital goods. They are afraid of excessive risk from trading on their equity, of a growing debt burden. With these risks in mind, a rise in their debt burden will reduce their demands for assets, including money, and will reduce their supply of bonds. However, such risks may induce them to prepare for short-period bulges of investment over saving by seeking a higher ratio of money to debt than would otherwise be appropriate.

Uncertainty concerning the price level and the interest rate may induce firms to reduce their net debt position and to hold money balances. Whatever the outlook for deflation in the price level, a fall in the current yield on bonds will persuade firms to increase their incremental demand for money and their supply of bonds.

Aggregate incremental demand for money, in real terms, by consumers and firms together, rises with real national income, with the real capital stock, and with real bond holdings in financial-asset portfolios. On the other hand, such demand moves inversely to the marginal rental rate, the rate of interest, real money balances on hand, and primary debt outstanding.

"INSIDE" MONEY AND "OUTSIDE" MONEY

In the rudimentary economy of Chapter II, money was government debt, issued in payment for governmental purchases of goods and services or in transfer payments. It was a claim held by consumers and firms against government. From the standpoint of the private sectors, it was a net external or outside claim. Given the nominal amount of this outside money, its real value varied inversely with the price level, and each such change in its real value represented a wealth transfer between the private sectors and government. This wealth transfer affected private demands for money, goods, and labor but it was assumed not to affect government demand. Therefore, the wealth transfer, due to a change in the price level, had a net effect on aggregate demands for money, goods, and labor. The conclusion followed that only one price level was appropriate to general equilibrium in any particular real context; any other price level would produce imbalance on all markets. The price level, in other words, was determinate in the rudimentary economy.

In the second model, money is still government debt, but it is issued in payment for government purchases of private securities. It is a claim of consumers and firms against the world outside the private sectors, but it is counterbalanced by private debt to the world outside, that is, to government in this model. It is based on internal debt, so we refer to it as "inside" money.

Given the nominal amount of inside money, its real value varies inversely with the price level. The governmental monetary system neither loses nor gains in real terms by such variation in the real amount of its debt because there is an equal change in the real value of its claims against firms. And the two private sectors together do not lose real wealth to government as the price level rises nor gain real wealth as the price level falls. That is, a change in the price level does not result in a wealth transfer between the private economy and government when money is inside money. Instead it results merely in a wealth transfer between consumers and firms, the former gaining and the latter losing in our second model when the price level falls. This transfer is a distribution effect of price-level instability that we are pledged, by neo-classical rules of static analysis, either to treat as a short-run phenomenon or to neglect.

Since a change in the price level, when money is inside money, does not affect government's behavior and has no net effect on total wealth in the private economy, is the price level determinate in our second model? Is only one price level appropriate in any particular real context, or will any price level do?

The traditional answer would be that the price level is not determinate, and that any price level would be compatible with general equilibrium. On this view, the second model is a barter economy, moneyless and bound by Say's Law of Markets. Our own conclusion, to which we return in Chapter V, is that price changes do have net effects other than distribution effects which point to one and only one price level as "right" for general equilibrium in a given complex of real variables and nominal money.

The proof that our second model, with only inside money, is really a money economy and not simply a barter economy can be put in a homely, intuitive way. Although the private economy issues bonds, and so can adapt the nominal stock of bonds to any price level in order to maintain some one real stock of bonds, it has no control over nominal money. Hence it cannot adapt the nominal stock of money to any price level in order to maintain the desired real stock of money. Given nominal money, there is only one price level that provides to consumers the desired portfolio mix of real bonds and real money and to firms the desired proportion of real money to real debt. Change in the price level from an equilibrium position has no net effect, it is true, on aggregate private wealth, but it does have effects on the composition of this wealth that will tend to drive the price level back to its starting point. Price inflation and deflation have no net effect on aggregate wealth; the distribution effects between private debtors and creditors we are pledged to put aside; but there is still a portfolio-mix or diversification effect that makes the price level determinate.

To illustrate our point, imagine an initial equilibrium with a price level of 100, nominal and real bonds in consumer portfolios of $90, nominal and real money of $10. Total nominal and real bonds are $100, with $90 of them in consumer portfolios and $10 of them in the monetary system. In the private sectors, the bond-money ratio of 9-1 is appropriate to the interest rate on bonds in equilibrium. Now imagine that the price level doubles to 200 and that nominal bonds are also doubled (to $200) by business firms, to avoid distribution effects. Given the monetary system's nominal bonds of $10 and hence nominal money of $10, consumer portfolios of nominal bonds rise to $190. At the higher price level, real business debt is still $100 but consumers hold $95 in real bonds, and real money balances are only $5. The bond money ratio has risen, in real terms, from 9-1 at the price level of 100 to 19-1 at the price level of 200. The latter ratio is inappropriate to the initial bond rate, real income, and real wealth. At the new price level, then, there will be excess real demand for money, excess real supply of bonds and goods, so that the system is destined to grope its way back to the initial level of prices and initial stock of nominal bonds.

Stationary Equilibrium in the Second Model

We have examined the institutional structure of the second model and its behavior patterns. Now we are concerned with the model's appearance in stationary general equilibrium and especially with its financial aspects. Stationary equilibrium is marked by absence of growth. There is no net saving and investment, no borrowing and lending, no buying and selling of bonds by the monetary system. The interest rate, marginal rental rate, and other relative prices are appropriate to existing stocks and flows on all markets. At the prevailing price level, real values of bonds and money are in keeping with portfolio preferences of consumers and firms.

The second model is a quantity-theory world. Consider two alternative stationary equilibria. In one of them, nominal quantities of money and bonds and price levels for goods and labor are twice nominal quantities and price levels in the other. Real values of bonds owed and owned, and of money, are identical in the two equilibrium positions and bear the same relation to real income and the stock of capital. The alternative states of equilibrium report identical real flows, real stocks, and relative prices. Doubling of nominal money is neutral in its effects on the real profile of equilibrium, because differences in nominal money are associated with equi-proportional differences in prices and nominal bonds. Consumers and firms are unaffected in their real behavior by the nominal scale factor applied to the stock of money, the stock of bonds, and prices for goods and labor. A change in nominal money, therefore, has no effect on the real variables of the economy.

To illustrate, suppose that in the first position of equilibrium the price level is 100, nominal bonds are $100, with $90 of them in private portfolios and $10 of them in the monetary system, so that private sectors also hold nominal money of $10. In the second equilibrium position, the price level is 200, nominal bonds are $200, with $180 of them in private portfolios and $20 of them in the monetary system. In both positions of equilibria, the real value of bonds in private portfolios is $90, and real money balances are $10: the bond-money ratio remains at 9-1. Doubling of nominal money, with equi-proportional adjustments in nominal bonds and the price level, gives no incentive for any change in relative prices or in preferred real stocks and real flows.

Let us now trace out the movement from one position of equilibrium to another. Suppose that an initial equilibrium position is disturbed by an open-market operation in which the Banking Bureau buys bonds from consumer portfolios to increase the nominal stock of money. The immediate result is that, at the initial bond rate and price level (including money wage rates), consumers' portfolios are over-supplied with real money and under-supplied with real bonds. In response to their excess liquidity, consumers step up their demands for both consumption goods and bonds, so that goods prices and money wage rates rise and the rate of interest falls. Price inflation reduces the real value of business primary debt, the burden of debt, and firms' money balances; falling bond rate stimulates business deficit spending; and the outcome is that firms offer new issues of nominal bonds to finance both investment and larger nominal holdings of money. The new issues of nominal bonds are sold directly to consumers, and this causes the bond rate to rise back to its original level. The limit of this inflationary process, tracing from an initial injection of nominal money, is an equi-proportional rise in nominal money, nominal bonds, prices of goods, and money wage rates, with no effect on real stocks and flows and relative prices, including the rate of interest.

Consequently, the addition of private domestic primary securities to our model, with a market of their own, does not affect our conclusions of Chapter II about money's role. Any nominal amount of money is consistent with a given real profile of stationary equilibrium, because spending units can establish the real stock of money at the desired level by suitable adjustments in the price level and nominal primary debt. Money is neutral in so far as any real effects are concerned. When the inflationary process is over, and the rate of interest has returned to its initial level, the increase in capital goods associated with the temporary fall in bond rate of interest has been eliminated.

Real Growth in the Second Model

What is the role of money in a growth setting? This section is concerned with requirements for accumulation of money and primary debt in the second model when the model's capacity to produce and its output are undergoing balanced growth. Labor is growing at a constant rate, the stock of capital at the same rate, and technology is not changing. Marginal products of labor and capital are constant, so that aggregate real income follows the same growth line as the productive factors. We assume here, reserving further discussion of the matter for Chapter IV, that the growth rate of primary debt has been brought into line with the growth rate of real income.

REAL GROWTH WITH PRICE DEFLATION

As in the rudimentary economy, real growth in the second model stimulates real demand for money balances. There is a rising aggregate of income in both sectors of consumers and firms that makes money-holding more attractive, and the growth of capital and of financial assets also increases demand for money.

If general equilibrium is to be preserved in the growth

process, the real stocks of money and bonds must grow, and their growth must be in the relative proportions preferred by firms and consumers at a stable marginal rental rate and interest rate. The point we wish to make now is that the desired growth in debt and financial assets can be secured by deflation in prices of goods and in money wage rates without expansion in nominal money by purchases of business securities by the Banking Bureau. The community of consumers and firms is competent to adapt growth in real debt and real financial assets to growth in tangible wealth and output, maintaining balance desired by firms between gross and net debt and by consumers between bonds and money.

This process of financial growth by deflation of prices is more complex than the process involved in the rudimentary economy, but the end-product is the same. Since nominal money is assumed constant, nominal bonds must also be constant to preserve the stable ratio of real money to real bonds that is implied by conditions of balanced growth. However, since we allow for new issues of nominal bonds by business firms engaged in the growth process, the total of nominal bonds will remain constant only if an equivalent amount of outstanding bonds is retired. Any friction or lag in this adjustment of primary debt results in distribution effects between firms and consumers that will be dissipated by short-period interruptions in the growth process. Given the neoclassical ground rules of our model, however, adaptation of old debt to new price levels does not affect the trend line of growth.

To illustrate this process, suppose that general equilibrium at one moment in the course of growth is associated with real income of $100, real primary debt of $100, with $90 of it in consumer portfolios and $10 of it in the monetary system—so that private sectors also hold $10 of real money. The price level is 100. Later in the course of growth, let all real demands for money, primary securities, and primary debt be doubled, with nominal money given. In the new equilibrium, then, the price level is halved to 50, which doubles the real stocks of money and bonds, though the nominal amount of each is the same. Issues of nominal bonds during the transition have been offset by the retirements that are necessary to avoid distribution effects of price deflation.

REAL GROWTH AT A STABLE PRICE LEVEL

Given growth in the labor force, the stock of capital, and output, the second model generates growth in real demand for money by both consumers and firms, and monetary equilibrium is maintained by parallel growth in the real size of the monetary system. The monetary system may grow in real size without expansion of nominal money and exclusively by deflation in prices and money wage rates. It may grow in real size even with contraction of nominal money and correspondingly more severe price and wage deflation. There is an indefinitely large number of combinations of change in nominal money with change in price and wage levels that can yield the necessary growth in real money balances. One combination, of course, is expansion of nominal money parallel with expansion in real demand for money, with prices and money wage rates remaining constant.

Price stability in the rudimentary economy implied deficit spending by government and some diversion of real output from the private to the government sector. Price stability in the second model does not require a change in the distribution between sectors of income and spending, saving and investment. It requires only that the nominal money issued by government and the net issues of nominal bonds by business firms increase equi-proportionally with real income. The difference between deflation and price stability is simply a difference between increments of nominal money and nominal bonds—small increments of both for deflation, larger increments for price stability.

Monetary Policy in the Second Model

The unseen hand of neo-classical economics is a deft manipulator in the second model. Provided with some nominal amount of money by the Banking Bureau, it attunes both relative prices and the absolute price level to the community's full-employment capacity for real output and to relative demands for labor, goods, bonds, and money. Money does matter in this economy, even if it consists entirely of "inside" money based on the monetary system's portfolio of domestic business bonds. It matters in the sense that there must be some nominal money from which the unseen hand can fabricate, through determination of the price level, the real money that is demanded by firms and consumers as one component of financial position.

The unseen hand is so efficient, however, in adjusting the price level and nominal bonds that, once the monetary system has provided any positive nominal amount of money, the system has nothing important to do except to manage the payments mechanism efficiently. Monetary policy is trivial in the sense that it can affect only the price level and money wage rates. It cannot affect any real variable, not the real quantity of money and not any other real stocks or any real flows or any relative prices. If the Policy and Banking Bureaus are driven by sheer boredom to experiment with the quantity of money, the unseen hand follows the rules of quantity theory to neutralize the "mischief" of their monetary management. There is simply no rational objective of monetary policy.

The second model can get along without recurring monetary intermediation between savers and investors. All financing of firms' net investment by consumers' saving can be direct, none of it indirect, because price deflation and adjustments in nominal bonds can preserve portfolio balance. If portfolio balance at the stable rate of interest is threatened, say, by excessive accumulation of bonds and by shortage of money, there is no necessity for monetary intermediation because the private sectors are competent to retire superfluous nominal bonds and, by price deflation, to create additional real money balances. The economy has its own built-in substitute for intermediation by the Policy and Banking Bureaus.

Monetary Policy in a Modified Second Model

The second model is a money-economy. It has a money stock and a determinate price level. Money is one "good" in the model, and only one real value of money is appropriate for each state of general equilibrium. As the model stands, however, money is neutral in the sense that manipulation of nominal money has no real effects. Monetary policy has no bearing on real growth; any nominal stock of money is satisfactory for each state of general equilibrium, and the monetary authority need not waste its time looking for a uniquely "right" amount. However, any one of various modifications in the model can give a more impressive role to nominal money and to policy concerning nominal money. This section considers a few of these modifications. Still others are reserved for discussion in Chapter V.

A COMBINATION OF INSIDE AND OUTSIDE MONEY

Now we imagine that nominal money consists no longer of inside money alone, as in the basic version of our second model where it was created exclusively on the basis of domestic business bonds in the monetary system's portfolio, or of outside money alone, as in our rudimentary economy where it was a net claim of the private sectors against government. Instead, nominal money is now composed of a combination of inside and outside money, the latter created, say, on the basis of gold in the monetary system's portfolio. This change in specifications certainly makes the second model more realistic, but it does more than that. The important result is that monetary policy ceases to be trivial or neutral and that some nominal stock of money is uniquely right for each state of general equilibrium.

Suppose that stationary equilibrium prevails. Firms are in their desired financial position, with net debt bearing the appropriate relationship to tangible assets and gross debt properly adjusted to net debt. Consumers are also satisfied, with financial assets in the correct relationship to income and properly diversified between money and business bonds. In this stagnant context the Banking Bureau increases nominal money, inside variety, by an open-market buying operation. Are there *real* effects of this easy-money policy?

The answer is clearly "yes." The outside money, backed by gold, is not matched by domestic business bonds in the Banking Bureau's portfolio. Hence, if the open-market operation increases total nominal money by, say, 10 per cent, it adds to the Bureau's bond holdings by more than 10 per cent, assuming gold holdings are constant. This means that the open-market operation increases the proportion of money balances to business bonds held by consumers and of money balances to net debt for business firms, for the Banking Bureau has increased its share of total business bonds. At the initial price level, the open-market operation achieves a real transfer of bonds from private sectors to the monetary system, changing portfolio composition for private spending units. At a price level increased in proportion to nominal money, with nominal bonds of business adjusted in the same degree, the real composition of private portfolios would still be more heavily weighted with money than before the monetary system took action. The impact of the open-market operation on portfolio balance cannot be nullified by a proportional increase in the price level, money wage rate, and nominal bonds of business. The increase in money, relative to bonds, in private portfolios is acceptable to the private sector only at a lower rate of interest. And the ultimate equilibrium will also involve, as the result of monetary expansion, a larger real stock of capital, a higher level of real income, and a price level that is higher but proportionally less so than the increase in nominal money.

Money has ceased to be neutral, and monetary policy is trivial no longer in the second model. Open-market buying by the monetary system touches off growth in real wealth and income, at the expense of some inflation. Open-market selling by the monetary system depresses real wealth and income, with accompanying deflation. These are the conclusions for the case of stationary equilibrium.

They can be illustrated as follows. Assume an initial position of equilibrium with price level of 100, nominal and real money of $20, consisting of $10 of inside money based on business bonds held by the Banking Bureau and $10 of outside money based on gold. Total business debt is $100 of which $10 is held by the Banking Bureau and $90 by consumers. Equilibrium is now disturbed by an open-market buying operation in business bonds of $20, which doubles nominal money. Equilibrium cannot be restored in quantity-theory fashion by doubling nominal bonds and the price level, since then the initial portfolio mix of bonds-to-money for private spending units of \$90-\$20 is reduced, in real terms, to \$85-\$20. With nominal money, nominal bonds, and the price level doubled, the Banking Bureau has raised its real bond holdings from \$10 to \$15. In the private sector, real bonds have become less plentiful relative to real money so that one element in a new equilibrium will be a reduced rate of interest. This in turn raises the equilibrium real stock of capital and the real level of income.

Similar conclusions regarding the neutrality of money apply under conditions of growth. Imagine that balanced growth is occurring at some rate n in all real and nominal stocks and flows, with relative prices and the absolute price level stable. The stock of money has both inside and outside components, with each increasing at rate n. If the monetary system doubles the rate of expansion for total nominal money and both of its elements, the only effect is doubling of other nominal variables including the price level. But if the monetary system doubles the rate of expansion in nominal money solely by accelerating purchases of business bonds, there are real effects. Then the monetary system absorbs a larger share of real bond issues, leaving a smaller share for private investors. The adjustment in private portfolio-balance requires some decline in the rate of interest, some increase in the growth rate of capital and income, and an increase in the price level proportionally smaller than the rise in rate of monetary expansion. Conversely, if the monetary system takes up a smaller proportion of real bond issues, expanding outside money rather than inside money, the real effects begin with a rise in the bond rate and restraint on real growth.

Growth involves expansion in financial assets of which

our model provides two varieties—a homogeneous bond and money. It is the real value of financial assets which influences behavior of consumers and firms on all markets. Any combination of circumstances, such as a money stock with both inside and outside components, which makes it possible for the second model's monetary system to manipulate the proportion of real money to real bonds, empowers the monetary system in some degree to regulate the real value and real composition of private portfolios. Then the monetary system can play the role of financial intermediary, in real terms, and can vary its participation in the risks of growth. By intermediating a little more, it relieves private spending units of some risk in bond-holding. By intermediating a little less, it intensifies private risks. The result is some reduction in the bond rate in the first case, some increase in the bond rate in the second case. And the change in this one relative price affects the whole contour of real growth.

MONETARY POLICY AND THE NEO-CLASSICAL RULES

We have come to the conclusion, first, that our model is a money-economy in which nominal stocks of money and bonds and the price level have a job to do in maintaining equilibrium in the markets for goods and labor, in assuring equality between investment desired by firms, as deficit spenders, and saving desired by consumers for release to firms. Our second conclusion has been that monetary policy is trivial, and money neutral, in the second model as first formulated: that real demand for money can be satisfied equally well by price deflation or nominal monetary expansion; and that the private sectors can transfer real saving and maintain portfolio balance with or without intervention by the monetary system. The third conclusion is that monetary policy may be significant, and money non-neutral, if the money stock is not exclusively inside or outside money.

These conclusions are valid under the neo-classical specifications we have built into the second model—absence of money illusion, freedom from distribution effects of change in the price level and bond rate, stability of expectations regarding the price level and bond rate, perfect competition and flexibility of prices on markets for labor, goods, and (except for intervention by the monetary system) for bonds. The conclusions are valid for analysis of the model in terms of static equilibrium for the stationary state or in balanced growth. That is to say, they are valid under circumstances in which money is least likely to matter and is most likely to be merely a veil over the real aspects of economic behavior. These are the circumstances in which the private sectors are most efficient in manipulating real money and real bonds by adjustments in the price level and nominal bonds.

Money's role becomes more pivotal in real behavior if our model is lifted out of its context of neo-classical, static equilibrium analysis. Anything one does to reduce the efficiency of a change in the price level, relative to a change in nominal money, as a means of adapting the stock of money to its desired quantity, enhances the real significance of monetary policy. Any obstructions to adapting nominal primary debt to changes in the price level make it more important for the monetary system to operate continuously on the markets for bonds and money.

Price deflation cannot create real money, to satisfy incremental demand for it, if prices and money wage rates are inflexible. And price deflation cannot accommodate demand for money if, because of money illusion, it is nominal rather than real money that spending units want. Again, price deflation that excites expectations of further deflation and so intensifies demand for money is a poor substitute for expansion of nominal money.

In the second model, distribution effects of price-level instability result, in any short run, from the partitioning of the private sector into debtors and creditors. If real growth brings about endemic incremental demand for money, the persistent downward pressure on the price level tends constantly to transfer wealth from debtor firms to creditor consumers. The real effect of such a transfer is to depress saving and investment, retard growth in real capital, and inhibit growth in output. Distribution effects are avoided if the endemic incremental demand for money is satisfied at a stable price level by nominal monetary expansion.

Static neo-classical analysis averts distribution effects of movements in the price level by perfectly flexible refunding of nominal bonds. The number of bonds outstanding is corrected for movements in the price level and simultaneously with movements in the price level. As one leaves such a frictionless world, the more convinced one must be about the real costs of price-level instability in terms of short-period disturbances to the rate of saving and investment and to allocation of saving among investment opportunities. It is easy to visualize a world without distribution effects, but such a world is remote from our own. Continuous intermediation by the monetary system is a necessary crutch for the private sectors to lean upon in directing real saving to investment and in maintaining portfolio balance.

Summary

In the rudimentary economy, there were three markets: for labor services, current output, and money. The feature of our second economy is the addition of a fourth market, that for primary securities. These securities are gilt-edged, homogeneous perpetuities (bonds) of business firms. There continue to be three sectors: consumers, business firms, and government. However, government has no income and no spending on income and product account; it is the monetary system, composed as before of a Policy and a Banking Bureau. The two private sectors transact on all markets, while the government transacts only on the two financial markets. The Banking Bureau, on orders of the Policy Bureau, purchases or sells primary securities and creates or destroys money. The financial profile of the economy is that business firms issue the only form of primary security and acquire money, the only form of indirect security; government purchases primary securities and issues money; and consumers acquire either primary securities or money or both.

Business firms may sell their primary securities directly to consumers or they may sell them to the Banking Bureau. The first is direct finance, in which consumers acquire primary securities; the second is indirect finance, in which consumers and firms acquire money balances.

The real demand for money balances emanates from consumers and business firms. Both sectors increase their real demand for money when their real incomes rise. The real demand for money increases, too, when consumers acquire additional real holdings of financial assets (bonds and money) and when firms acquire real capital relative to real debt. A lower rate of interest on bonds stimulates private real demand for money, while a lower marginal real rental rate works in the same direction for firms. The nominal stock of money is once again determined by the Policy Bureau in the context of its policy aims and of private sectors' real demand for money. The Banking Bureau makes this stock available without hesitation or protest.

The nominal stock of money in the rudimentary economy was entirely "outside" money; that is, it was a net claim by the private sectors on an "outside" sector—the government. The nominal stock of money in our second economy is wholly of the "inside" variety; that is, it is based on private internal debt, and it is entirely counterbalanced by business primary debt. Hence, in contrast to the rudimentary economy, any change in the price level now results in wealth transfers only between the two private sectors, one gaining and the other losing by equal amounts. Neo-classical rules ignore the effect of such wealth transfers on aggregate demands for labor services, current output, and money. It would seem, therefore, that any price level is compatible with given aggregate real demands. Nevertheless, the price level is determinate in the second economy as it was in the first. This is because the private sectors desire a diversified financial position. Given the nominal stock of money, there is only one price level that achieves the desired mix between real primary securities and real money.

Within the neo-classical framework, monetary policy has neutral effects on the real variables of the economy when all money is of the inside variety—as it did when all money was of the outside variety in the rudimentary economy. A change in nominal money has no other effect than to change proportionally prices and money wage rates. In the same way as before, moreover, monetary policy ceases to be neutral if there is rigidity of prices, if price expectations are not of unitary elasticity, if there is money illusion, or if we admit distribution effects of wealth transfers.

Even within a strict neo-classical framework, however, monetary policy may not be neutral on real variables when there exists a combination of inside and outside money; that is, when the Banking Bureau holds both business bonds and "foreign" securities or gold behind its monetary liabilities. Then an increase in nominal money, owing to the Banking

Bureau's purchase of business bonds, increases the Bureau's holdings of real bonds proportionally more than its real monetary liabilities. This means that private sectors' real holdings of business bonds are reduced relative to their real holdings of money. Hence, the equilibrium interest rate is lower, and other real variables in the economy will adjust. A combination of inside and outside money, then, permits the monetary authority to get a grip on levels of real income and wealth.

CHAPTER IV

Financial Growth and Security Differentiation

THE PURPOSE OF THIS CHAPTER is to extend our analysis of financial growth in two directions. First, we shall analyze the factors that determine the growth of spending units' financial assets, using the model of the previous chapter as a basis for discussion; that model contained a number of very restrictive assumptions, and some of these will be relaxed.

Second, we shall consider the effects of change in the quality, as distinct from the quantity, of primary securities. The market for loanable funds is really a congeries of markets where funds trade against differentiated securities at a multitude of market rates of interest. This market supplies to asset-holders a far more extensive selection of financial assets than the simple diet of money and bonds in our second model. And the selection of financial assets evolves in the growth process. In this volume far less attention is given to differentiation of primary securities than the subject deserves. But it cannot be passed by because demand for money is not the same when the only alternative is gilt-edged perpetuities as when the alternatives are numerous.

Before getting into these subjects, it is necessary to elaborate an earlier comparison between primary and indirect securities.

Primary and Indirect Securities

Financial assets in the second model were composed of homogeneous bonds (perpetuities) of business firms and money issued by a governmental monetary system. The distinction between primary and indirect securities was clear-cut. When we allow, however, for a wide variety of securities from nonfinancial spending units, as we do in this chapter, and for a wide variety of securities from financial intermediaries, as we do later on, the distinction becomes less sharp. Nevertheless, we continue to make the distinction and it is the purpose of this section to explain why.

Primary securities include all debt and equity issues of nonfinancial spending units. The latter have been defined as those units whose principal function is to produce and purchase output, and not to buy one type of security by issue of another. Primary securities include corporate equities and bonds, accounts payable, short-term business debt to banks, consumer debt, mortgages, federal and state and local government debt, foreign securities, and all the varieties of each of these main types. Gold is not included since it is treated as a real asset. Unfunded credits to surplus accounts in the net worth of spending units are not included, either. These represent internal finance, an alternative to primary security issues.

Primary securities are one of two components in the financial-asset holdings of nonfinancial spending units. The other component is indirect securities, the debt issues of financial intermediaries including the monetary system. Indirect securities may also be divided, for some purposes, into those issued by the monetary system (monetary indirect debt) and those issued by other financial intermediaries (nonmonetary indirect debt). In addition, depending on the problem, monetary indirect debt may itself be divided into means of payment (currency and demand deposits) and others (time deposits).

Financial intermediaries are interposed between ultimate borrowers and lenders to acquire the primary securities of the borrowers and provide other securities for the portfolios of the lenders. Their revenues accrue mainly from interest on primary securities, and their costs are predominantly interest on indirect securities and expenses of administering securities. These characteristics are generally sufficient to set off financial intermediaries from nonfinancial spending units, and indirect from primary securities.

Still, our classification is ambiguous in some instances, though the volume of securities that are difficult to classify at any time is not likely to be significant. To illustrate some ambiguities, the issues of holding companies whose principal function is to control subsidiary spending units may or may not be counted as primary issues. It is possible to attribute both primary and indirect securities to some intermediaries. For example, bank deposits are indirect debt but bank stock issues may be regarded for some purposes as primary in that they reflect the "spending unit" aspect of bank operations. Any issues qualifying as money and made on the security of gold probably should be classified as indirect debt, even though gold is counted as a commodity rather than as a primary security. Moreover, it is necessary at times to create a special category for secondary intermediaries, such as sales finance companies, which may be largely interposed between ultimate borrowers and intermediaries proper.

Nevertheless, the distinction between primary and indirect securities seems to be a useful one for the problems analyzed in this book. It is a useful tool for analyzing the relationship between real growth and financial growth, for isolating the function of intermediation for special study, and for considering the relative roles of monetary and nonmonetary intermediaries in the growth process.

It should be noted that financial growth may refer to at least two different things. First, it may refer to the growth of primary securities, which is equal to the growth of the financial assets of nonfinancial spending units, after adjustment for capital gains or losses, whether these assets are in the form of primary or indirect securities. Second, it may refer to the growth of primary plus indirect securities. The absolute amount of this growth is the same as the first if all primary issues during a period are sold to nonfinancial spending units, so that no growth occurs in indirect securities. It is twice as large as the first if all primary issues are sold to financial intermediaries, so that growth of indirect securities equals growth of primary securities.

Growth of Primary Securities and Financial Assets

Financial assets in the second model consisted of money balances and primary securities, the latter being homogeneous bonds issued by business firms. These bonds were purchased either by the governmental monetary system, which paid for them with newly-created money, or by consumers, who thus acquired either bonds or money, or both. Business firms, too, accumulated money balances, while the government had no income or spending on income and product account.

In stationary equilibrium, at any level of real income, there was a certain demand by the private sectors for real financial assets, consumers demanding real money and bonds, and business firms real money. These real demands could be satisfied, in a neo-classical environment, with any positive amount of nominal financial assets held by private sectors. Thus, a given level of real income could be associated with any nominal portfolio level.

Real growth in the second model generated issues of primary debt and incremental demand for real financial assets. We intend now to look into this process somewhat more thoroughly than we did in the previous chapter. In much of the discussion to follow we assume that stable prices accompany real growth and that real growth is balanced, in the sense that all flows on every market and stocks of labor, capital goods, bonds, and money expand at a uniform percentage rate. It is also assumed at first, for convenience, that business firms do not accumulate money balances—that all financial assets are acquired by consumers, except those acquired by the monetary system. We shall first study primary security issues in this framework, then the accumulated stock of primary securities. After that we turn to financial growth when the real growth process commences with a zero (or very small) stock of primary securities. Finally, we discuss the contours of financial growth that are associated with various departures from the second model.

PRIMARY SECURITY ISSUES: IMMEDIATE DETERMINANTS

In any period along the growth path, the issues of primary securities by business firms are equal to the acquisitions of financial assets by consumers—both desired in equilibrium. Primary issues are equal to the firms' budget deficit; acquisitions of financial assets to consumers' budget surplus. This assumes, for one thing, that firms do not acquire money balances.

The real value of primary security issues during any period is expressed as $\frac{\dot{B}}{ip}$. $\dot{B}$ is the number of new bonds issued, each bond paying $1 of interest per period. It is also the nominal amount of interest payments on new bonds issued. p is the commodity price level, and i is the rate of interest. It follows that $\frac{\dot{B}}{i}$ is the nominal value of primary issues, $\frac{\dot{B}}{p}$ is the real value of interest payments on new bonds, and $\frac{\dot{B}}{ip}$ is the real value of these issues.

The budget deficit of firms is their real net investment expenditures ($\dot{K}$) less their real net saving (S^b). Primary security issues are equal to the firms' deficit. Their ratio to real national income (Y) is:

$$\frac{\dot{B}}{ipY} = \frac{(\dot{K} - S^b)}{Y}. \tag{1}$$

Dividing the numerator and denominator of the right-hand side of Equation 1 by the net saving of firms, we have:

$$\frac{\dot{B}}{ipY} = \left(\frac{\dot{K}}{S^b} - 1\right)\frac{S^b}{Y}. \tag{2}$$

In words, the issues-income ratio depends on the average propensity of firms to spend out of their income or saving $\left(\frac{\dot{K}}{S^b}\right)$ and on the share of national income received by firms $\left(\frac{S^b}{Y}\right)$.

Alternatively, we can look at the same phenomenon from the side of consumers by noting that the issues-income ratio is equal to consumers' budget surplus divided by national income, where this surplus is real consumer income (H) less real consumption expenditures (C). Proceeding in a manner similar to that above, we find that:

$$\text{(3)} \qquad \frac{\dot{B}}{ipY} = \left(1 - \frac{C}{H}\right)\frac{H}{Y}.$$

Again in words, the issues-income ratio depends on the average propensity to consume $\left(\frac{C}{H}\right)$ and on the share of national income received by consumers $\left(\frac{H}{Y}\right)$.

Consequently, considering these alternative formulations, we can say that the ratio of primary security issues to national income depends on the distribution of spending between the sectors relative to the distribution of income between them. When these distributions are the same, there is no specialization between sectors in spending and receiving income; both sectors have balanced budgets; and there is no financial growth. When the distributions are totally dissimilar, one sector does all the spending and the other receives all the income. Then one sector's budget deficit and the other's budget surplus are equal to national income, and financial growth during the period is also equal to national income.

The degree of specialization between sectors in spending and receiving income depends ultimately, in one way or another, on all variables and relationships of the second model. It depends, for example, on the determinants of firms' net investment expenditures, on those of consumption expenditures, and on those of the demand for bonds. But it is important to recognize that, however devious the channels, everything bearing on growth in financial assets works through the distribution of spending relative to the distribution of income between the two sectors.

PRIMARY SECURITY ISSUES IN BALANCED GROWTH

With this in mind, let us now inquire into the factors which lie behind sectoral income and spending distributions in the second model during balanced growth and which therefore lie behind the growth of primary securities. During balanced growth with stable prices, when flows and stocks are expanding at the uniform percentage rate, *n,* income shares and the average propensities to spend are constant, so the issues-income ratio is also constant. Financial assets in consumer portfolios and primary debt of business firms grow in each period by a constant proportion of that period's national income. What determines this proportion?

Starting with Equation 1, and recognizing that n is equal to the rate of growth of the capital stock $\frac{\dot{K}}{K}$, where K is the capital stock, so that $\dot{K}$ is equal to nK, it follows that the issues-income ratio is equal to $\frac{(nK-S^b)}{Y}$. Net saving of firms (S^b) is equal to the real rental rate $\frac{r}{p}$ *times* the capital stock and *minus* firms' real interest payments $\frac{B}{p}$, where B is the number of bonds outstanding, each paying \$1 of interest per period. Hence

$$(4) \qquad \frac{\dot{B}}{ipY} = \frac{nK - \left(\frac{Kr}{p} - \frac{B}{p}\right)}{Y}.^{1}$$

[1] In this equation $\frac{r}{p}$ represents the rental rate only when no dividends are paid by firms. If dividends were permitted, $\frac{r}{p}$ would represent the rental rate net of dividends.

This shows that the issues-income ratio is equal to the ratio of firms' real net investment less their real net saving to real national income.

We already know that, during balanced growth, $\frac{\dot{B}}{B}$ equals n. So substituting $\frac{\dot{B}}{n}$ for B in Equation 4, we can reformulate the issues-income ratio as:

$$(5) \qquad \frac{\dot{B}}{ipY} = \frac{\left(n - \frac{r}{p}\right)\frac{K}{Y}}{1 - \frac{i}{n}}.^{2}$$

That is to say, the issues-income ratio during balanced growth depends on:

the growth rate of output n,

the real rental rate $\frac{r}{p}$,

the capital-output ratio $\frac{K}{Y}$, and

the rate of interest i.

These are the determinants of the size of business firms' budget deficit relative to national income and, hence, of primary security issues relative to income. We shall first look at the relation between the growth rate of output and the issues-income ratio, assuming that the real rental rate exceeds the interest rate during the growth process.[3]

[2] This follows from the fact that $\frac{\dot{B}}{ipY} - \frac{\dot{B}}{npY} = \frac{\dot{B}}{ipY}\left(1 - \frac{i}{n}\right)$.

[3] This model of financial growth is not stable. A stock of primary debt in excess of its equilibrium level requires interest payments that increase business deficits and further stimulate growth in primary debt. Various stabilizers which we include in the complete model of Chapter III, and in the Mathematical Appendix, are excluded in the formulation of Equation

How does an increase in the growth rate of output affect the issues-income ratio? The answer is that a higher output growth rate will raise the issues-income ratio because it will increase firms' net investment expenditures relative to their net saving and thereby enlarge the business deficit as a proportion of national income. And a lower output growth rate will reduce the issues-income ratio.

One relationship between the output growth rate and the issues-income ratio is shown in Chart I by the curve labelled *A*. The growth rate of output is measured along the horizontal axis and the issues-income ratio along the vertical axis. The curve is drawn on the assumption that the capital-output ratio is equal to unity, and that the values of the real rental rate and the interest rate are as shown in the chart. The interest rate and the real rental rate are indicated by the broken vertical lines. The *A* curve shows that when the output growth rate is equal to the real rental rate the issues-income ratio is zero, a relationship that Equation 5 readily reveals, too. In this case business net investment and saving are equal to each other, both the consumer and business sectors have balanced budgets during the growth process, consumers accumulate no financial assets while firms incur no debt, and there are no interest payments.

Now consider a higher output growth rate, perhaps 10 per cent. The *A* curve shows that the issues-income ratio is about 3 per cent, which also measures firms' deficits and the surplus budget of consumers as a proportion of national income. The higher output growth rate increases the degree of specialization between sectors in spending and receiving income and leads to financial growth. Such specialization

5 above. They are the depressing effects of excess debt on investment, on business demand for money, and on dividends.

CHART I

Relation Between Issues-Income Ratio and Growth Rate of Output

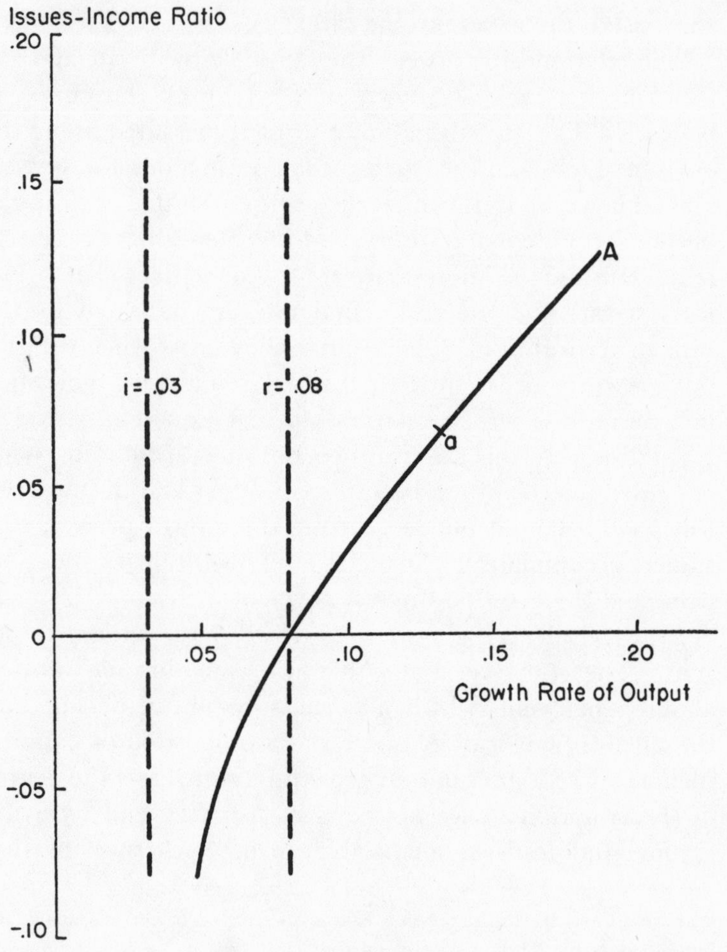

continues to increase at still higher output growth rates, and financial growth is accelerated.[4]

Suppose next that the output growth rate lies below the real rental rate and above the rate of interest, that is, between the broken vertical lines in the chart. The relevant part of the *A* curve shows that under these conditions the issues-income ratio is negative, that business firms have negative bond issues at each level of national income. The growth rate of output is not high enough to raise net investment expenditures of firms above their net saving, and so they have budget surpluses and consumers have budget deficits. This might be interpreted to mean that firms retire bonds in each period, while consumers finance their deficits by liquidating financial assets. But this could not continue forever. Consequently, it must be interpreted to mean that firms acquire financial assets while consumers incur debt; the tables are completely turned. Primary issues are positive, but they come from consumers and not from business firms. This state of affairs was assumed not to exist in our second model, which is to say essentially that the output growth rate in the second model was assumed to lie above the real rental rate.

What happens to the issues-income ratio if we change the values of the capital-output ratio, the real rental rate, and the rate of interest? We shall take them one at a time. A higher capital-output ratio during balanced growth raises the issues-income ratio at all growth rates of output that exceed the real rental rate—that is, at all growth rates to the right of the broken line indicating $\frac{r}{p}$ in Chart I. This is because a higher capital-output ratio raises the level of firms' net investment relative to national income and so raises their

[4] In the chart the slope of the *A* curve decreases asymptotically to the capital-output ratio.

deficits relative to income. On the other hand, a higher real rental rate during balanced growth lowers the issues-income ratio, for the reason that it raises firms' net saving and in this way reduces their deficits at each level of national income. Finally, a higher interest rate raises the issues-income ratio at each growth rate of output that is higher than the real rental rate, because it reduces firms' net saving by increasing their interest payments.[5]

STOCK OF PRIMARY SECURITIES IN BALANCED GROWTH

The stock of primary securities at the beginning of any period in the balanced growth process is the accumulation of all primary security issues in past periods. This stock of securities as a ratio of national income—which we shall call the debt-income ratio—is stable during balanced growth, since the stock of securities and national income both grow at the uniform percentage rate, n. The debt-income ratio is equal to $\frac{1}{n}$ *times* the issues-income ratio, because in balanced growth $\frac{\dot{B}}{B}$ is equal to n. For example, if the issues-income ratio is 10 per cent when n is 5 per cent, then the stock of securities is twice the level of national income $\left(\frac{.10}{.05}\right)$.

[5] In the first and third cases, the A curve in Chart I rotates leftward around its intersection with the horizontal axis. In the second case, it shifts downward and to the right, cutting the horizontal axis at the higher value of $\frac{r}{p}$.

Multiplying both sides of Equation 5 by $\frac{1}{n}$, we can develop a statement for the debt-income ratio:

$$\text{(6)} \qquad \frac{B}{ipY} = \frac{\left(n - \frac{r}{p}\right)\frac{K}{Y}}{n-i}.$$

Thus the stock of primary securities at each income level depends on the same variables as did the issues-income ratio, namely the growth rate of output, the real rental rate, the capital-output ratio, and the rate of interest.

The *A* curve in Chart II gives the relation between the debt-income ratio and the growth rate of output, assuming that this growth rate is equal to or exceeds the real rental rate and that the latter exceeds the rate of interest. It is clear that the debt-income ratio is higher at higher output growth rates, but the ratio asymptotically approaches the capital-output ratio. That is to say, at extremely high rates of output growth almost all net investment expenditures are externally financed by primary security issues, so that accumulated securities tend to equal the capital stock. At the other extreme, when the output growth rate equals the real rental rate, all net investment expenditures are internally financed out of business net saving, so that the stock of securities is zero during the growth process. In between, net investment expenditures are financed partly internally and partly externally, with the result that the stock of primary securities at any time is positive but less than the capital stock.[6]

[6] When the growth rate of output lies between the interest rate and the real rental rate, Chart II shows a negative debt-income ratio. This means that business firms have a positive stock of financial assets and consumers a positive amount of debt outstanding.

CHART II

Relationship Between Ratio of Accumulated Securities to Income and Growth Rate of Output

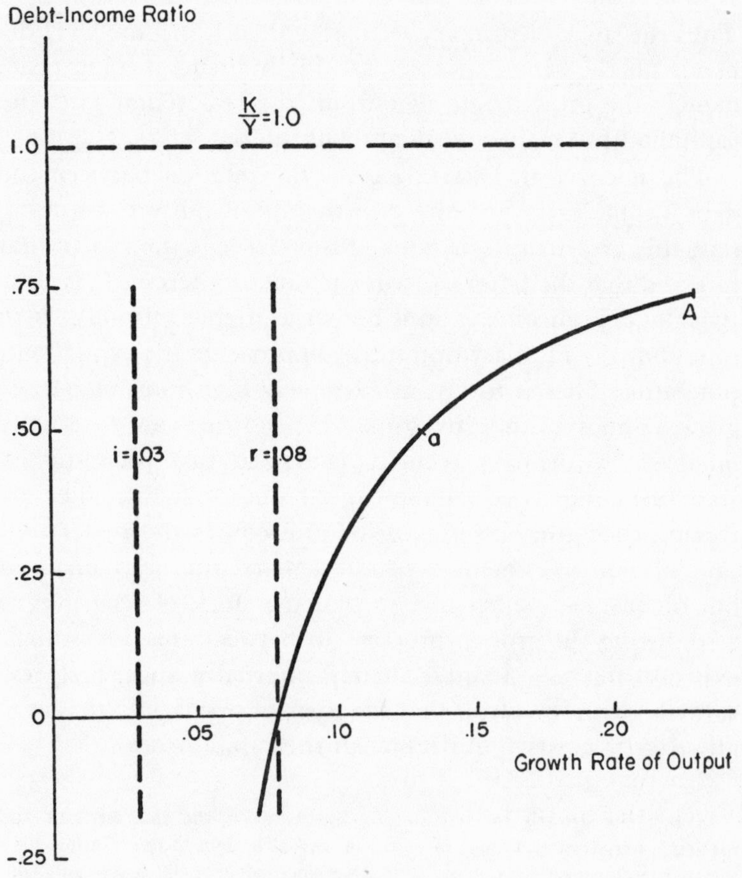

There is a simple relationship between the *A* curves in Charts I and II: the height of the latter is $\frac{1}{n}$ *times* the height of the former. To illustrate, suppose that the growth rate of output is 13 per cent. Then, from Chart I, the issues-income ratio is 6.5 per cent, shown by point *a*. Now moving to Chart II, we find that at this growth rate the debt-income ratio is 50 per cent (at point *a*)—that is, $\frac{.065}{.13}$.

The foregoing discussion assumes, of course, that the values of the capital-output ratio, the real rental rate, and the interest rate are constant during the growth process, as they would be during balanced growth. Consider now how a different value for each of these would affect the debt-income ratio. First, a higher capital-output ratio during the growth process would raise the stock of securities relative to income, because it would raise net investment and make external financing more imperative. Second, a higher real rental rate would lower the debt-income ratio by raising business net saving and, thus, internal financing. Third, a higher interest rate would raise the debt-income ratio, because it would increase interest payments and so cut into firms' net saving, increasing external relative to internal financing.

PRIMARY SECURITIES AND FINANCIAL IMMATURITY

So far we have discussed financial growth when the stock of primary securities and real output are growing at the same rate. Suppose now that the real growth process begins with a zero or very small stock of primary securities—that is, a stock of securities that is below its long-run, balanced relationship with real output—and that our other assumptions are retained. What are the contours of financial growth under these conditions?

In answering this, we shall glance back to Charts I and II. In Chart I, the issues-income ratio *during balanced growth* is 6.5 per cent if the output growth rate is 13 per cent (point *a*). And according to Chart II, the debt-income ratio *during balanced growth* is 50 per cent. Now each of these values is shown by a horizontal broken line in Chart III, where time is measured along the horizontal axis and the above two ratios are plotted along the vertical one. If primary security issues and the stock of these securities are already attuned to the growth of real output at 13 per cent per period, then the ratio of each to national income would be stable over time. Each ratio would simply move along its horizontal line over time. This is familiar ground.

But suppose, at the start of the growth process, that the issues and stock of primary securities are not attuned to a steady growth rate of output. Suppose, in particular, that the initial stock of primary securities is zero. During the growth of output, the stock of primary securities builds up rapidly relative to national income; the debt-income ratio starts at zero and eventually builds up to its long-run, balanced level. In Chart III, it starts at zero and rises asymptotically to 50 per cent. Thus, the stock of primary securities grows very much faster than output at first, but the growth rate of securities gradually falls to the stable growth rate of output, so that eventually the two are approximately the same. At this point balanced growth has been restored. These trends would be substantially the same if we had started with any initial stock of securities below its balanced relationship with national income.

The relatively low stock of primary securities in the early stages of output growth means that firms have relatively low interest payments and relatively low deficits as well. Consequently, the issues-income ratio is quite low during these

CHART III

Growth of Primary Securities During Financial Immaturity

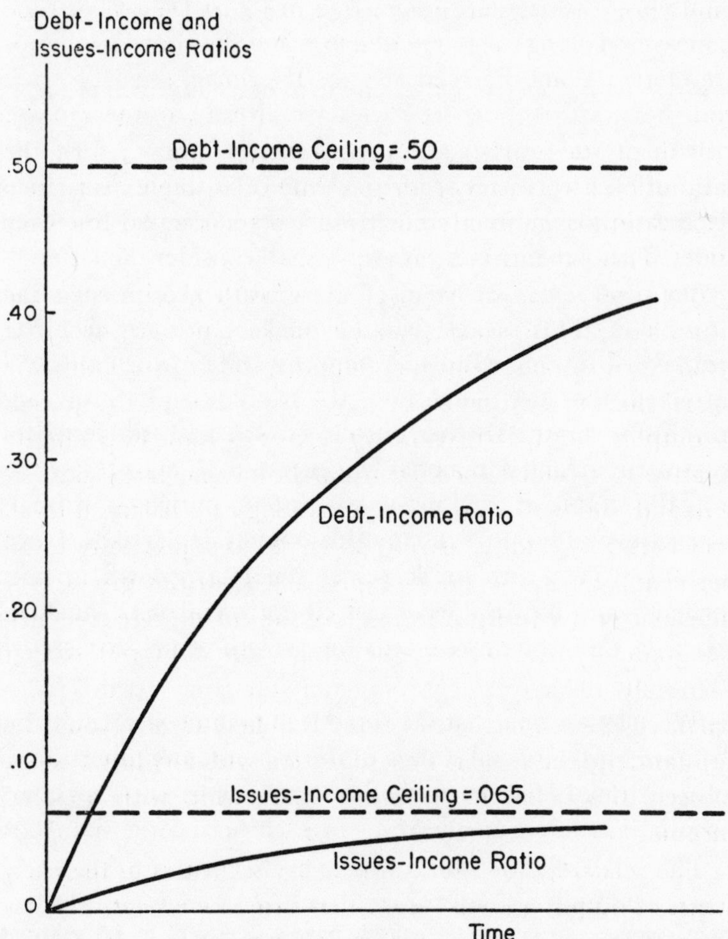

stages of "financial immaturity." But as the stock of primary securities builds up to a level that is balanced with national income, firms' interest payments also mount, which raise their deficits relative to income. This is why the issues-income ratio, shown by the lower curve in Chart III, starts from zero and rises gradually to its long-run, balanced level.[7]

GROWTH OF PRIMARY AND INDIRECT SECURITIES

We mentioned earlier that financial growth may refer to the expansion of primary securities only or to the expansion of primary plus indirect securities. Up to now we have considered only the former. Now we shall consider the latter.

Suppose, first, that balanced growth at stable prices is taking place. This means that the stock of primary securities relative to income will depend on the rate at which output is growing, the real rental rate, the capital-output ratio, and the interest rate. During output growth with stable prices, nominal demand for money is generated. The interest rate remains stable if the monetary system purchases primary securities and supplies the nominal money demanded. Hence, output growth with stable prices generates growth in both primary and indirect securities; the growth of all financial assets in the economy exceeds the growth of primary securities alone.

We may assume that, at some stable interest rate during balanced growth, consumers desire a constant proportion m of their financial-asset portfolios in money balances, primary securities making up the rest. In each period the monetary

[7] Over the same time, the budget surpluses of consumers relative to national income rise during the growth process from zero to 6.5 per cent. Consumers build up their financial assets relative to income in the same way that firms build up their debt.

system must purchase this proportion of primary security issues and create an equivalent amount of money. Consequently, during any period, the growth of all financial assets in the economy is equal to the primary security issues *plus m times* these issues, the latter representing the creation of indirect securities, in the form of money. Furthermore, the stock of all financial assets at any time during balanced growth is the stock of primary securities *plus m times* this stock, the latter representing the amount of money balances outstanding—that is, the amount of primary securities owned by the monetary system.

It follows that total securities, primary and indirect, grow at the same percentage rate as real output during balanced growth. It is also apparent that the ratio of money to income, or its reciprocal, the income velocity of money, is constant during balanced growth. Given the proportion of their financial assets that consumers desire to hold in money balances at each rate of interest, income velocity depends on how high the stock of primary securities is relative to national income; and this, in turn, depends on the output growth rate, the real rental rate, the capital-output ratio, and the interest rate. Thus, income velocity depends ultimately on these four variables. To give just one example, a higher growth rate of output, by raising the stock of primary securities relative to income, increases the amount of money demanded at each income level, and so lowers income velocity.

When real growth, at a steady rate, occurs with an initial stock of primary securities that is below its long-run, balanced relationship with income, the debt-income ratio rises during the growth process. Hence, the ratio of money to income also rises gradually to its long-run, balanced level. This means that income velocity falls during the growth process, but it falls asymptotically to a lower plateau. Further, total financial assets in the economy rise relative to income during this process. Once balanced growth is reached, or rather very closely approached, income velocity is virtually stabilized, and total financial assets grow almost in proportion to real output.

FINANCIAL GROWTH AND MIXED ASSET-DEBT POSITIONS

Spending units and sectors of spending units have *pure* asset-debt positions when they hold financial assets or have debt outstanding and not both. They have *mixed* asset-debt positions when they have both. In our analysis of the second model in Chapter III, we assumed a pure asset-debt position for consumers and a mixed asset-debt position for business firms. The former held financial assets and had no debt outstanding; the latter incurred debt and acquired money balances. However, in our present discussion, for purposes of simplification, we have assumed that both sectors have pure asset-debt positions, consumers acquiring financial assets and firms incurring debt. We must now analyze the consequences for financial growth of relaxing this assumption.

Suppose that business firms desire to acquire money balances during output growth, as in our second model, and that there is balanced growth with deficits in the business sector and surpluses in the consumer sector. Then firms issue primary securities in each period not only to cover deficits but also to increase holdings of money balances. Hence, the issues-income ratio is higher during balanced growth, and so is the stock of primary securities and financial assets relative to national income. The money-income ratio is also higher, and income velocity is lower. Mixed asset-debt positions in the business sector tend to speed up financial growth.

Next, consider the consumer sector. Though this sector

has a budget surplus during balanced growth, it may desire to issue debt of its own to acquire business bonds, money, or both. If so, the issues of all primary securities as well as stocks of primary securities and financial assets are higher relative to income in the growth process. Furthermore, since consumer debt is unlike business bonds, firms may want to issue bonds for the purpose of acquiring not only money balances but consumer debt, too. Finally, if consumer debt is not homogeneous and if business bonds are not homogeneous, both the consumer and business sectors may rationally hold some of their own issues.

The point is that mixed asset-debt positions tend to increase with the differentiation of financial assets. If all financial assets were perfectly homogeneous—something that is really impossible in a deconsolidated economy—surplus units would be indifferent to the choice of acquiring financial assets or retiring debt, and deficit units would be indifferent to the choice of disposing of financial assets or incurring debt. While mixed asset-debt positions would be possible in this case, there would be no reason for them. It would be perfectly rational for each spending unit to maintain a pure asset-debt position. But financial assets are not perfect substitutes for one another. Some spending units may decide rationally to conserve, say, money balances while financing deficits with primary security issues. Others may decide rationally to accumulate money instead of retiring debt. Moreover, since primary securities themselves are heterogeneous, some spending units may want to issue debt rather than give up certain types of these securities, and others may prefer to acquire certain types of primary securities rather than retire their own debt. An increasingly variegated structure of financial assets tends to diminish the importance of pure asset-debt positions; it has the effect of increasing the growth of primary securities and financial assets.

FINANCIAL GROWTH, CYCLES, AND DEFICIT ROTATION

During steady or balanced growth, when the growth rate of output exceeds the real rental rate, business firms have chronic deficits—that is, deficits in each period of the growth process—and consumers have chronic surpluses. However, the tables are turned when the growth rate of output lies below the real rental rate (but above the interest rate). Then the low rate of output growth depresses firms' net investment expenditures below their net saving, giving them surplus budgets. Deficits are in the consumer sector.

It must be noted that in a balanced growth context we cannot legitimately speak of the growth rate rising or falling. There are two alternatives: either the growth rate is above the real rental rate or it is below. Therefore, deficit rotation—that is, the rotation of deficits from one sector to another—does not really occur in balanced growth; it occurs, rather, in a context of business cycles or short-period fluctuations. Nevertheless, the different deficit-surplus patterns that are associated with alternative output growth rates in balanced growth are highly suggestive of what happens in an "unbalanced world."

During a sharp downturn of business activity, for example, business firms may shift from deficits to surpluses as they cut back investment spending relative to saving. At the same time, if consumers are reluctant to give up former consumption levels, consumer spending may exceed consumer income, throwing this sector into the deficit column. During the upswing, especially if it is pronounced, the deficit-surplus wheel may be twirled again as consumers spend less than their incomes and investment spending of firms overtakes their saving.

Deficit rotation may also occur as a result of spending

fluctuations in other sectors. A sharp increase in government expenditures during war periods, for instance, often leads to a large deficit in that sector, creating surpluses in both of the private sectors, usually with the aid of direct controls. Thus, the business sector may be swung from the deficit to the surplus side. When government spending is cut back in the immediate postwar period, the previous relationships tend to be re-established, so that rotation again occurs.

Deficit rotation is a drag on the growth of primary securities and financial assets. A sector that incurs debt when it has deficits tends to retire debt when it has a surplus, and a sector that accumulates financial assets when it has surpluses tends to dispose of financial assets when it has a deficit. Another way of putting this is that over a series of fiscal periods the rotation of deficits among sectors reduces the sum of their *net* deficits and surpluses (that is, the algebraic sum of each sector's positive and negative budget imbalances over several periods), and so tends to slow up primary security issues and acquisitions of financial assets. Such rotation reduces the degree of specialization among sectors in spending and receiving income.

FINANCIAL GROWTH AND THE FOREIGN SECTOR

The presence of a foreign sector means that the deficits of some domestic sectors need not be balanced by surpluses of other domestic sectors: the difference is the deficit or surplus of the foreign sector. The foreign sector's deficit is the domestic economy's excess of exports over imports on current account, or its net foreign investment. The foreign sector's surplus is the domestic economy's excess of imports over exports, or its net foreign disinvestment.

When the foreign sector has a deficit, the primary security

issues of domestic sectors are less than the increase in the financial assets of domestic sectors—less by the amount of gold and financial assets coming from the foreign sector. That is to say, the domestic sectors gain financial assets in an amount equal not only to the primary security issues of the community but to those issues plus the financial assets gained from the foreign sector. When the foreign sector has a surplus, primary security issues of domestic sectors exceed their gain in financial assets by the amount of financial assets acquired from the domestic economy by the foreign sector—that is, by the amount of securities and gold sold abroad.

Differentiation of Primary Securities

Our second model contained only one type of primary security, a homogeneous business bond. In discussing financial growth, however, we have introduced other types of primary securities—consumer debt, government debt, and foreign securities. An economy that contains a wide variety of securities generates a different demand for money than one that includes only homogeneous business bonds, all other things the same. This is a point that will be dealt with in Chapter V. In the meantime, we can prepare the way for that discussion by showing how security differentiation fits into our analysis and by pointing out some of its historical and institutional aspects.

REASONS FOR SECURITY DIFFERENTIATION

Primary securities differ one from another: the issue of each borrower is unlike the issue of any other borrower; no two borrowers can give the same degree of assurance to creditors that loan contracts will be fulfilled. Successive issues of a given borrower are necessarily different "products" since the first issue, unlike the second, is not prejudiced by existing claims against the borrower's sources of repayment.

Markets for primary securities are by nature imperfectly competitive markets; they are compartmentalized markets. In and among the compartments one finds the telltale marks of imperfect competition. Many interest rates are inflexible in short periods, and excess demands for funds are resolved temporarily by rationing techniques, changes in requirements for collateral, or adjustments in other non-price terms of exchange. There are notable inequalities in bargaining power on the security markets, so that it is easy to find manifestations of monopoly or monopsony, oligopoly or oligopsony.

Individual spending units diversify primary issues. They issue both debt and equities, debt of various maturities, equities with different ownership rights, and so on. The ultimate motive for such diversification is essentially the same as the motive for holding money, to set up a defense against the hazards of specialization in saving and investment. These risks are divisible into general and specific ones.

Each spending unit, debtor or creditor, is subject to general risks involved in the aggregative aspects of growth. An unforeseen change in the growth rate of output and employment puts everyone into an unexpected debt-wealth or asset-income position. An unforeseen change in the distribution of wealth and income shifts everyone's target of debt accumulation or asset accumulation. An unforeseen change in the price level on either the market for goods or the market for primary securities implies windfall rewards or penalties for decisions based on anticipation of different price levels. Investors who have reached a desired relation of debt burden to real wealth and its yield are thrown off balance. Savers who have reached a desired relation of financial assets to income are compelled to reassess their financial plans and their preferred rates of financial accumulation. The ultimate penalties for misjudging contours of aggregative growth are bankruptcy for debtors and destruction of saved net worth for creditors.

Each spending unit is subject to specific risks that may discredit debtors' estimates of debt burden or creditors' forecasts of the real value of financial assets. Impulses of real growth are not distributed evenly through the community, and creditors or debtors who are trapped in stagnant sectors or who step out too far beyond the general pace can be penalized harshly by depreciation in real value of financial assets or appreciation in real value of debt.

Diversification of primary issues by borrowers and diversification of financial assets by lenders are one defense against these general and specific risks. Anyone accumulating stocks in a world where flows and prices may change unexpectedly can protect himself, to a degree, by diversifying his stocks—of debt, or financial assets, or tangible assets. Economic analysis that consolidates stocks of domestic claims and counterclaims, concentrating on flows and prices, blinds itself to the effects on flows and prices of spending units' maneuvers to minimize risks on assets and debts.

In formal analysis of security differentiation, one can imagine that each debtor, by his own more or less meticulous methods, tries by diversifying issues to minimize a "disutility function" of debt burden. He mixes his issues, at each given level of debt burden, to minimize the expected value of the real expenses and losses he can incur from the general and specific hazards he confronts. And most debtors come to the conclusion that the disutility of a given amount of *net* debt (that is, gross debt less financial assets) may be lightened not only by issuing debt in various forms but also by issuing some debt for the purpose of acquiring some financial assets. That is, to minimize the risks of a given net debt position, they show a mixed asset-debt position on their balance sheets—some debt and some financial assets.

One can imagine, too, that each creditor, more or less carefully and rationally, tries by selecting a mix of assets to maximize a "utility function" of his portfolio. Given the amount of his *net* assets (that is, gross assets less debt), his objective is to achieve the maximum prospective net yield. The portfolio that suits his taste depends partly on the assets that are accessible and their relative prices, the range of expectations concerning their real convertibility in financing future deficits, and his own emotional bias in facing up to risk or running away from it.

At any level of debt, a debtor may be deterred in various degrees from new investment and encouraged in various degrees to step up saving—to depend more on internal finance and less on external—by the mix of his debt. At any level of financial assets in relation to income, a creditor may adjust his goal of asset accumulation or regard a given goal as exceeded, equalled, or still ahead of him, depending on his mix of financial assets. The debtor has minimized the disutility of debt, at given interest rates, when no further change in mix among accessible options will stimulate his investment relative to his saving. The creditor has maximized his portfolio's utility when no further change in mix, at given interest rates on accessible options, will either raise his goal of accumulation or bring him closer to a given goal. One can visualize a socially optimal mix of securities when, with given tangible and financial resources and distribution of income and wealth, no further change in relative rates of interest on existing types of securities will change the proportion of investment to income. Then the restraint upon growth, imposed by risks that are coincident with the division of labor between saving and investment, has been whittled away as much as it can be.

At any moment, with stocks of securities given, bargaining between debtors and creditors toward a harmony of their preferred mixtures of debt and assets is reflected only in the structure of interest rates. Over time, the mutual adaptation of debtors and creditors shows up not only in the interest rate structure but in the pattern of issues and of accumulated securities. This process of adaptation is never completed. One reason is that the asset-debt utility functions of individual spending units shift as risks are revalued, as the scale of portfolios increases, as new forms of debt and assets become accessible. Another reason is that there is a constantly changing distribution of deficits and surpluses among spending units whose utility functions are dissimilar. Now consumers are heading the list of borrowers, now firms or government or the foreign sector. These sectors take their turns in dominating total issues of primary securities.

As deficits and surpluses rotate through the community, new optimal mixes of debt and assets result not only because asset-debt utility functions differ among spending units but also because all debtors do not have access to all varieties of security issue nor all creditors to all varieties of asset. Sharecroppers cannot issue commercial paper, or farmers corporate bonds, or business firms Treasury bills. On the side of creditors, a state treasurer is unlikely to buy accounts receivable, and a manufacturing corporation seldom invests in small residential mortgages. As deficits and surpluses rotate among these and other sectors, the optimal patterns of debt and assets must change, too, because asset-debt contracts are adapted to the kind and stock of wealth, the level and stability of income, and other characteristics of sectors that are active on the security markets.

In brief, the demand for money, the demand for diversification among other financial assets, offers of differentiated primary securities, and the demand for mixed asset-debt positions are to be explained by a common principle. They are tactics of risk-avoidance by spending units in a society where division of labor between saving and investment creates stocks of claims and counterclaims. The monetary system eases the burden of risk upon growth by supplying money to satisfy diversification demand. Public-debt management regulates impulses to growth by providing bills to alleviate risk in asset accumulation or by providing bonds to aggravate risk in asset accumulation. Governmental guarantees and insurance of primary securities diminish private risk in accumulating debt and assets.

HISTORICAL-INSTITUTIONAL ASPECTS

We shall now analyze some historical and institutional examples of security differentiation. In the real world there is a variety of primary securities—short-term debt, bonds, equities, mortgages, and so on. One or more types are issued by each of the five sectors of the economy—consumers, nonfinancial corporate business, federal government, state and local governments, and foreign. Short-term debt in one form or another (for example, consumer debt, trade debt, and Treasury bills) is issued by all sectors. Bonds are issued by all sectors except the consumer. Equities come mainly from corporate business, both domestic and foreign. Mortgages are primarily consumer mortgages, but there are also business mortgages. The relative importance of the various types has changed markedly over time.

Changes in the mix of primary securities are associated with changes in the rate and pattern of real economic activity over periods that vary from the long sweep of a century to the seasons of a single year. For decades governmental units may play so large a role in economic activity that federal, state, and local government issues dominate the security markets. Over other long stretches of time the corporate business sector may be bidding for the lion's share of loanable funds, so that corporate bonds, equities, and short-term business debt take precedence. Mortgages are issued in heavy volume during the rising phases of the building cycle, and then dry to a trickle when construction activity is at low ebb.

Over the shorter periods of business cycles, the composition of primary issues seems to vary systematically. During early recovery years, the flow of issues tends to be most heavily weighted with short-term business borrowing, and long-term flotations feature bonds rather than equities. In the later phases of the upturn, corporate bond issues may decline as equities appear in heavier volume. Recession and depression minimize private short-term issues; bond financing becomes more attractive; and the federal government often succeeds state and local governments on the security markets. There is variation in the composition of primary issues, too, between intervals of war and peace and between periods of net foreign investment and disinvestment.

For every change in conformation of aggregate real output and in distribution of aggregate real income, there are allied changes in the complex of primary security issues: compartments of the security market tend to have boundaries in common with sectors of the goods market. Indeed financial development is incomprehensible apart from its context of real development. Markets for goods and markets for securities (including money) are simultaneously the media through which spending units seek optimal adjustment between income and spending, net worth and wealth. Excess demands, positive or negative, for current output are of necessity excess supplies of securities, and the sectoral location of excess demands partly determines the types of primary securities that will be issued. The real world and the financial world are one world.

The mix of primary issues is affected too, by the development of financial technology. In a primitive society, loanable funds trade between ultimate lenders and ultimate borrowers by elemental negotiation on a face-to-face basis, in highly imperfect markets. In a more mature society, such personal loans on minutely compartmentalized markets are a smaller share of total issues. Development of financial techniques creates alternatives to face-to-face loans that increase, for borrowers and lenders or both, the gains from trade in loanable funds.

There are two principal types of financial techniques. Distributive techniques increase the efficiency of markets on which ultimate borrowers sell and ultimate lenders buy primary securities. Intermediary techniques bring financial institutions into the bidding for primary securities and substitute indirect financial assets for primary securities in the portfolios of ultimate lenders. Both techniques play a major role in determining the structure of primary securities.

Distributive techniques include the broadcast of information to borrowers regarding the asset preferences of lenders and to lenders regarding the issues of borrowers. They include a widespread network of communication that tends to overcome regional market barriers. Facilities for rapid contract and settlement of loan transactions—security exchanges—increase the resemblance of security markets to competitive commodity exchanges. Facilities for brokerage, for market support and seasoning of new issues, for dealer inventories, for future as well as spot deliveries are other familiar distributive techniques.

Distributive techniques enhance freedom of entry to security markets. They tend to break up "customer markets" of very limited breadth and to replace them with "open" markets on which borrowers and lenders or both are individually of small importance relative to the market as a whole. They promote flexibility of security prices; they make supply and demand more responsive to price changes. Briefly, they increase the competitiveness of security markets and standardize groups of security issues.

The effect of distributive techniques in widening security markets is to permit each borrower and lender a higher degree of diversification in his debt or financial assets than he could otherwise achieve. On balance, security differentiation is reduced, but each spending unit has access to a wider range of borrowing and lending options. Investing in primary securities alone, each ultimate lender can spread his budget of financial assets over a greater variety of claims than he could acquire on local markets. He can obtain liquidity in varying degree, or safety, or prospect of price appreciation, or participation in management, or exemption from taxation. He can enrich the packet of real advantages associated with the marginal dollar's worth of "consumption" of primary securities. Efficient distributive techniques tend to reduce the demand of investors for such alternatives to primary securities as claims on intermediaries, monetary and nonmonetary. In particular, efficient distributive techniques tend to reduce the demand for money.

Efficient distributive techniques, then, increase the breadth of markets for loanable funds and, as a result, increase efficiency of funds allocation. By providing the individual saver with opportunities for asset diversification, they increase the marginal real return to given budgets of net financial assets. But they have their obvious and familiar disadvantages as well. Because they depend on economies of scale, distributive techniques do not work out to the equal benefit of large and small producers of primary securities, of borrowers in established lines of industry and borrowers in industries on the frontier of development, or of large and small consumers of primary securities. Moreover, the price flexibility on open markets that tends to more efficient allocation of loanable funds makes these markets vulnerable to waves of bullishness and bearishness that can interrupt steady real growth. Price flexibility increases the risk of market loss for asset holders. While distributive techniques reduce the demand for money and its substitutes by providing to savers opportunities to diversify portfolios through investment in primary securities alone, they also stimulate the demand for indirect financial assets by adding the hazard of market losses to other risks of asset holding.

The development of financial intermediation has also had profound effects on the composition of primary securities. On balance, it has resulted in a more homogeneous debt structure, in more competitive markets, in greater flexibility of interest rates. Intermediaries have discovered and exploited economies of scale in consumer and mortgage credit, farm loans, commercial paper, and other forms of primary securities. They have been able to transform the heterogeneous issues of small borrowers into a homogeneous, standardized form of security that is marketable far outside the local market areas of the borrowers. The intermediary, too, has been capable of arbitrage between security markets on such a scale that regional differences in primary securities and in interest rates have been significantly reduced. By exploiting economies of scale and opportunities for arbitrage, intermediaries have been able to increase returns to their own creditors and increase the attractiveness of their own debt at given levels of interest cost to primary borrowers.

Distributive and intermediating techniques tend to produce homogeneity within each security type. It is equally true, though, that any particular mixture of primary issues favors the development and growth of some security markets and intermediaries over others, so that the structure of distribution and intermediation tends to adapt to the security outflow. There is mutual adaptation between the composition of primary securities and the markets of distribution and intermediation.

Distributive techniques for United States government securities developed most rapidly, for example, when these securities dominated total primary issues, as during the Civil War and the two World Wars. Distributive techniques for corporate equities and bonds were largely perfected in the latter part of the 19th century when these securities were issued in heavy volume. Particular mixtures of primary issues create a favorable environment for some intermediaries and an unfavorable one for others. Savings and loan associations grew especially fast during the residential construction boom of the 1880's which "threw off" heavy issues of mortgages. They again spurted ahead just before World War I, in the 1920's, and in the present postwar period for the same reason. Between these periods of rapid growth, the associations languished along with construction activity. To a lesser extent mutual savings banks have responded in much the same way. The rise in consumer debt in the decade prior to World War I was the impetus behind the creation of intermediaries catering to consumers—credit unions, sales finance companies, and personal loan companies. Sales finance companies have recently shown a particularly fast rate of growth, paralleling the growth rate of consumer installment debt. Investment companies gained prominence during the 1920's and 1950's when corporate equity issues were heavy and when market activity especially favored this type of primary security. Government lending institutions sprang up after 1915 to intermediate in farm mortgages at the very time when farm mortgage issues were heaviest.

SECURITY DIFFERENTIATION AND DEMAND FOR MONEY

The stockpiling of debts and financial assets is a necessary part of a society whose economic units specialize in spending income and in earning it, in saving and investment. Such stockpiling, however, increases the vulnerability of spending units to instability in the growth and distribution of output and income as well as in prices of labor, goods, and bonds. There are debt burdens to be minimized and assets to be conserved.

Differentiation of primary securities is one defense of deficit spenders against debt burden. Presumably it is wise for each debtor to spread his total issues over the various kinds of issues accessible to him so that the marginal increment of debt burden is the same for all issues. Diversification of financial assets is one defense of savers against depreciation in the real value of assets, and we suppose that each saver spreads his portfolio over assets accessible to him so that marginal yield, after allowance for risk, is the same for all assets. Though it takes place on imperfectly competitive markets, bargaining between borrowers and lenders tends to the limit at which relative terms of lending on various financial assets reflect both debtors' marginal debt burden and creditors' anticipated marginal yield.

Money is free from some but not all risks associated with other assets in savers' portfolios. Acquisitions of money balances also relieve debtors of some risks of indebtedness and reduce the marginal debt burden associated with any level of real capital and external finance. By supplying nominal money, the monetary system may reduce the burden of accumulated debt and assets upon new financing of economic growth. The easing of the past's dead hand upon the present, by nominal monetary expansion, works itself out, in a world where money is not neutral, through the interest rate and through rates of real saving and investment.

There can be expansion of real money without expansion of nominal money: a falling price level can "create" real money. But there is usually a substantive basis for choice between creation of money by price deflation and creation of money by the monetary system. The latter satisfies diversification demand for money at a given interest rate, and so may the former. However, when money is non-neutral, the choice may favor nominal growth in money not only because of short-period considerations but also because nominal growth in money affects in the long run the real composition of spending units' financial assets.

The next chapter explores the effect of differentiation of primary securities upon the demand for money by anyone holding financial assets, whether he is debtor or creditor on balance. Chapter VI will look into the effect of differentiation of indirect debt upon demand for money. In the growth process economic systems constantly experiment with ways of mitigating the restrictive effect of risk upon saving by some sectors and upon investment by others. Monetary expansion is one way; differentiation of primary securities is another; differentiation and expansion on the part of nonmonetary intermediaries is a third way. There are still other ways, including public-debt management, debt insurance and guarantees, and devices of taxation.

Summary

The private sectors' holdings of real financial assets and their real indebtedness grew with real output in our second economy. At a stable price level during output growth, the nominal amounts of financial assets and primary debt expanded, too. This chapter concentrates on the determinants of growth in financial assets and primary debt. It is concerned both with the quantity of financial growth and with development in differentiation of financial assets.

It is assumed, to begin with, that there is balanced growth in the economy at stable prices and that only consumers acquire financial assets. In each fiscal period the issues of primary securities by firms are equal to the acquisitions of financial assets (bonds and money) by consumers. The ratio of primary security issues (or financial-asset accumulation) to national income during balanced growth depends on the distribution of spending between the two private sectors relative to the distribution of income between them. The degree of specialization between sectors in spending and receiving income—in saving and investing—depends in one way or another on all the variables and relationships in the second economy.

The issues-income ratio can be related, however, to four variables: the balanced growth rate of output, the real rental rate, the capital-output ratio, and the interest rate on business bonds. Assuming that the growth rate of output is higher than the real rental rate and that the latter exceeds the interest rate, the issues-income ratio is higher during balanced growth at higher levels of the output growth rate, at a higher capital-output ratio, and at a higher interest rate. On the other hand, the issues-income ratio is lower at higher levels of real rental rate. Since primary security issues are equal to accumulations of financial assets by consumers, these relationships also apply to the ratio of consumers' acquisitions of financial assets to national income.

The stock of primary securities at any time in the balanced growth process is the accumulation of primary security issues in the past. This stock as a ratio to national income is equal to $\frac{1}{n}$ times the issues-income ratio, where n is the balanced growth rate of output. The ratio of the stock of primary securities to national income depends on the same variables as the issues-income ratio does; anything that raises the latter also raises the former. Both ratios are constant during balanced growth.

However, when the growth process commences with a zero (or relatively small) stock of primary securities and financial assets, both ratios rise at first during output growth and then ultimately reach plateau levels. That is, issues of primary securities and the stock of these securities both build up rapidly relative to national income, but eventually stable relationships are established. If consumers desire to hold a constant proportion of their financial assets in money balances during output growth, the ratio of money to national income rises during the earlier stages of growth and then eventually levels off.

Our assumption has been that each sector has a pure asset-debt position—that each has either debt or financial assets, not both. An increasingly variegated structure of financial assets tends to diminish the likelihood of such positions; it becomes increasingly rational for each sector to be in debt and to hold financial assets at the same time, to have a mixed asset-debt position. Consequently, development of financial-asset differentiation tends to increase primary security issues and acquisitions of financial assets at each level of national income.

Up to this point, we have also assumed steady growth of output. However, when national output is subject to cyclical disturbances, budget deficits and surpluses tend to rotate among sectors of spending units, each sector having surpluses for a time and then deficits. Deficit rotation is a drag on the growth of primary securities and financial assets because it reduces the degree of specialization among sectors in spending and receiving income over a succession of fiscal periods.

The stockpiling of debts and financial assets is a necessary part of an economy whose spending units specialize in spending income and in earning it, in saving and investing. Such stockpiling, however, increases the vulnerability of spending units to instability in the growth and distribution of output and income as well as in prices of labor, current output, and bonds. It is rational, in view of this, for borrowers to differentiate their primary debt and for lenders to diversify their holdings of financial assets. Both are tactics of risk-avoidance in a society where there is division of labor between saving and investment.

Changes in the composition of primary securities are associated with changes in the rate and pattern of real economic activity over periods that vary from the long sweep of a century to the seasons of a single year. The mix of primary securities is affected, too, by the development of financial technology—by the development of distributive and intermediating techniques. The former increase the efficiency of markets on which borrowers sell and lenders buy primary securities. The latter take primary securities off the market and substitute indirect securities for them. Though these techniques have tended to produce homogeneity within each broad type of primary security, they have permitted each spending unit access to a wider range of borrowing and lending options.

CHAPTER V

Money in a Complex Financial Structure

IN THIS CHAPTER we come back to the money market—to the demand for money, the stock of money, monetary equilibrium, and monetary policy. Since our last excursion into this market, the analysis of Chapter IV has provided a more realistic context for the study of money. It showed that the growth process includes accumulation by spending units of primary debt and financial assets. This financial accumulation proceeds along a path related to trends in real income and tangible wealth. There is not only growth in the mass of finance but also increasingly intricate differentiation in the quality of debt and assets. Our purpose now is to explore monetary growth against this backdrop of development in nonmonetary finance.

The monetary system continues to be the governmental Policy and Banking Bureaus. The Banking Bureau manipulates the nominal stock of money, on instructions from the Policy Bureau. For the most part, the Banking Bureau changes the nominal stock of money by open-market operations in primary securities, but we will examine briefly the consequences of allowing the Banking Bureau to finance government deficits by money-issue. Money so created gravitates to financial portfolios of consumers and firms, helping to satisfy the demand for protection against risk in a hazardous world. Financial development in a maturing economy generates growth in the demand for money, by both consumers and firms, as one component of diversified portfolios. The Policy Bureau's choice between alternative ways of satisfying growth in the demand for money may affect the contours of growth in real income and wealth.

The first section below reverts to the distinction drawn in Chapter III between "inside" and "outside" money—that is, between money created on the basis of private domestic primary debt in the Banking Bureau's portfolio and money based on net claims of consumers and firms against government and foreign sectors. It is often argued that inside money and all other financial assets with counterparts of private domestic debt can be consolidated against their counterparts and excluded from aggregative analysis without affecting the results of that analysis. Our belief is that financial analysis cannot be narrowed down to a concentrated residue of outside claims. It is the purpose of this section to explain why.

The next four sections deal with the theory of demand for money when the economy has only one kind of nonmonetary financial asset, the modifications that are necessary when there is differentiation of primary securities, the impact of monetary policy on the real variables of the economy when there are differentiated securities, and some of the factors that have affected the money-income ratio in this country over the past century and more. The final section discusses the choice between expansion in nominal money and price deflation as means of satisfying growth in the real demand for money.

Money and Finance: Alternative Approaches

One approach to monetary theory nets out all private domestic claims and counterclaims before it comes to grips with supply and demand on the money market. This is "net-money" doctrine. Another approach—the one we use—avoids such consolidation of financial accounts. It may be termed "gross-money" doctrine. The two approaches measure the stock of money in different ways. This is the first point we discuss below. The two approaches are also at odds on measuring the demand for money. This is the second topic we take up. Finally, we shall explain the implications of the net-money approach for financial analysis and indicate why we prefer gross-money over net-money doctrine regarding behavior on the market for money.

THE STOCK OF MONEY

We count as money any debts of the monetary system that are means of payment generally accepted on markets for labor services, current output, and primary securities. Thus we regard the nominal stock of money in the United States as the sum of currency held by spending units and demand deposits subject to check after adjustment for checks drawn but not yet charged against deposit accounts.[1]

[1] Various other ways of measuring money are in use. Some of them are more inclusive than ours, counting in the money stock virtually any type of indirect financial asset that bears the title "deposit," including time and demand deposits of commercial banks, deposits of mutual savings banks, and Postal Savings deposits. Such measurements count as money various items that we shall consider, in Chapter VI, as money substitutes.

Net-money doctrine measures money less inclusively. To illustrate with the combined partial balance sheets in Table 7, we would say that the money stock is 200, comprised of 170 of demand deposits and 30 of currency owed by the monetary system and owned by private domestic sectors. Total

TABLE 7

Combined Partial Balance Sheets of the Monetary System and Private Domestic Economy

Monetary System				Private Domestic Economy			
Assets		*Liabilities*		*Assets*		*Liabilities*	
Gold	20	Demand deposits	170	Money	200	Primary debt	170
Foreign securities	10	Currency	30	Foreign securities	20	Nonmonetary indirect debt	40
Government securities	50			Government securities	30		
Private domestic primary securities	120			Private domestic primary securities	50		
				Nonmonetary indirect financial assets	40		

money of 200 includes 120 of inside money, based on the monetary system's portfolio of private domestic primary securities, and 80 of outside money, based on the monetary system's holdings of gold, foreign securities, and government securities. Net-money doctrine would recognize only the 80 of outside money, consolidating inside money against its counterpart in private domestic primary debt.

Thus, from Table 7 outside money balances can be measured in either of the following two ways:

(1)	Outside money balances	=	Gross money	−	Private domestic primary securities of monetary system
	(80)	=	(200)	−	(120),

or,

(2)	Outside money balances	=	Monetary system's gold	+	Monetary system's foreign securities	+	Monetary system's government securities
	(80)	=	(20)	+	(10)	+	(50).

In the net-money approach, outside money balances are part of the private domestic economy's margin of accumulated saving over accumulated private domestic investment in tangible assets, the other part being securities issued from the outside sectors—government and foreign. With reference to Table 7, the private domestic economy's net financial assets consist of outside money balances (80), foreign securities (20), and government securities (30). Consolidation eliminates all private domestic financial assets and their offset in private domestic primary debt. When consolidated, the community's balance sheets appear as in Table 8.

While net-money doctrine consolidates private domestic accounts, it stops short of all-out consolidation and keeps a truncated "outside" sector, with "outside" construed to include the government as well as economies literally on the other side of political boundaries. It must do this, of course, to avoid reverting completely to economic analysis in terms of a barter society where there is neither money nor demand for money, neither bonds nor demand for bonds. If there are to be financial markets, somebody must escape the consolidation process. All financial assets and debt cancel out in complete consolidation, leaving nothing in the financial sphere to analyze.

TABLE 8

Partial Balance Sheets Consolidated According to Net-Money Approach

Monetary System				Private Domestic Economy			
Assets		*Liabilities*		*Assets*		*Liabilities*	
Gold	20	Outside money	80	Outside money	80		
Foreign securities	10			Foreign securities	20		
Government securities	50			Government securities	30		

THE DEMAND FOR MONEY

Net-money doctrine measures the stock of money one way, we another. Net-money doctrine also puts a different twist on the money-demand function. It would say that the real demand for money depends on real income, the amount and yield of real wealth, including the outside bonds and outside money held by the private sectors, and the bond rate of interest. It would deny that aggregative real demand for money depends on accumulation of private domestic securities. Growth in the stock of such securities would be considered irrelevant, except in short periods, to aggregate demand for money, just as growth in the monetary system's holdings of such securities would be considered irrelevant to the stock of (outside) money.

The alternative approach is to measure the stock of money in gross terms, including both inside and outside money, and to measure the demand for money as demand for existing stocks of inside and outside money together. And among the determinants of demand one finds both savers' portfolios of private domestic primary securities and investors' primary debt.

In the basic model of Chapter III, there were no outside money and outside securities—only inside money and private domestic primary securities (business bonds). In such a situation, we said, spending units' real demand for money depends on their real holdings of financial assets, divided into money and business bonds, the level of real income, the bond rate of interest, the real rental rate, and the relation of investors' primary debt to their tangible assets (the debt burden). In this same situation, however, net-money doctrine would delete all financial variables from the money-demand function, consolidating debt against bonds held by spending units and the Banking Bureau. For net-money doctrine, this kind of economy would be money-less and bond-less. Only the real variables of tangible wealth, income, rental rate, and interest rate would remain in demand functions. It should be noted, though, that both the gross and net approaches would include in the money-demand function real outside money and real outside bonds, if such existed, counting them as part of the community's wealth.

For short-period analysis, as distinct from analysis of equilibrium during growth, net-money doctrine would not consolidate internal claims and counterclaims. In the short period, aggregate real demands on any or all markets may be influenced by temporary windfalls in income and wealth to private domestic creditors at the expense of debtors or to debtors at creditors' expense. There may be distribution effects on real demands, say from a change in the price level, that may swing real demands away temporarily from their trends by affecting debtors and creditors unsymmetrically.

But net-money doctrine imposes the neo-classical rule that the economy manages in time to dissipate distribution effects associated with private domestic debtor-creditor relationships. For the long run, the supposition is that negative effects of debt on real demands balance out against the positive effects of creditor status.

In net-money doctrine, there is a market for private domestic securities, and the rate of interest on this market does enter all aggregative demand functions. Any rise in the interest rate tends to reduce the demand for money, and any fall in the interest rate tends to increase the demand for money. Private domestic bonds themselves are deleted from the explanation of aggregate behavior, but the market price of these bonds is considered to be a real phenomenon, a relative price that may influence behavior on all markets.

IMPLICATIONS OF NET-MONEY DOCTRINE

The implications of net-money doctrine for financial analysis are far-reaching. Primary securities, including corporate equities, are merely a device for distributing among spending units the private domestic economy's net worth in its real wealth. These securities permit accumulation of real wealth among one array of spending units and accumulation of saving among another array of spending units. But they do not change the aggregate of real wealth. It is supposed to be the private domestic economy's aggregate of real wealth, not the array of equity in it, that determines real demands on various markets, including the money market. The conclusion follows that, for analysis of market behavior, private domestic debt cancels out against equivalent private domestic financial assets in both monetary and nonmonetary form. Government debt and government debt management do affect market behavior. But the changing quantity and quality of private domestic debt are irrelevant to aggregative analysis, according to this doctrine.

Financial institutions disappear as by magic in net-money analysis. Savings and loan shares cancel out against the mortgage debt of borrowers at savings and loan associations. Policy reserves of insurance companies cancel out against, say, corporate bonds in the companies' portfolios. The bulk of demand and time deposits in commercial banks cancels out against bank investments in such domestic securities as municipal warrants or business term loans or consumer credit. In all of the froth of finance and financial institutions, there is a fractional residue of real economic substance—the net asset counterpart of governmental and other outside debt. Following this line of reasoning, our own emphasis on growth of primary debt and of financial institutions as aspects of real growth would be said to be a myopic failure to distinguish between the froth of finance and the economic reality it conceals.

THE CHOICE BETWEEN NET AND GROSS MONEY

What can be the rejoinder of gross-money doctrine? It comes to the conclusion that money should be studied in the context of a sectored society, that disaggregation is the essence of monetary theory. Money is supplied and demanded only in a sectored society. It is one financial phenomenon among the many that co-ordinate the activities of spending units. It is a device for communication between autonomous spending units, and a means for the self-preservation of individual spending units in a risky world. The result of consolidating spending units into a monolithic solidarity must be to eliminate money as well as other financial phenomena from aggregative economic analysis.

If one pushes the whole way with consolidation, all

markets disappear and economics becomes a study of Robinson Crusoe's personal accounts. Consolidation may stop short of this limit and assume a barter society, where co-ordination between spending units is nearly as efficient as though they were one, where the unseen hand manipulates relative prices to allocate resources and distribute output efficiently. This is the world of Say's Law, where excess demand for money is always identically zero and where, hence, there is no rational explanation of either absolute demand for or stock of money balances. Net-money doctrine does not fuse all spending units into one. Nor is it an alias of Say's Law. But it approaches these limits of consolidation quite closely.

The first objection to be made against net-money doctrine is that it consolidates and deconsolidates social accounts capriciously; it occupies an irrational no-man's land between gross money and no money. It tolerates a market in private domestic securities, and it retains the market price—the bond rate of interest—in analyzing aggregative behavior. But it washes out the securities that are traded at the bond rate of interest on the bond market. That is to say, borrowers and lenders are consolidated in order to eliminate their claims and counterclaims, and then they are deconsolidated so that they may haggle over a price for these nonexistent securities.

Net-money doctrine consolidates private domestic spending units to eliminate their debtor-creditor relationships. But then it turns right around and deconsolidates them in order to rationalize their demand for money. In effect, Crusoe may not borrow from himself, lend to himself, or set up a bank to buy his promissory notes and issue money to him. But *Cru* may be so uncertain of *Soe's* behavior on various markets as to desire a protective stock of money balances. He may elect to hold money because he fears *Soe* may force down the price of bonds—the stock of which is zero. Or he may elect to hold money because he has not arranged with *Soe* an exact coincidence of payments and receipts in their market dealings. *Cru* and *Soe* have minds of their own —part of the time.

Net-money doctrine consolidates far enough to eliminate one body of financial assets. But having admitted a demand for money, it must not consolidate far enough to eliminate all financial assets—for there must be a stock of money. So net-money doctrine allows an external sector to escape the consolidation process. This external sector—the government, economies abroad, or even a *deus ex machina*—may borrow from the domestic economy, and its borrowings will be attested by securities in monetary and nonmonetary form. Net-money doctrine cannot escape the principle that disaggregation in some degree is prerequisite to both the demand for and the stock of money. But, as noted above, it seems to be an inconsistent compromise between the two extremes of gross money and no money.

Net-money doctrine, as we have said, cancels out all private domestic debt against its counterparts in monetary and nonmonetary form, so that when an economy contains no outside money or "foreign" securities it becomes money-less and bond-less. It is in effect a barter society, without a determinate price level. Our second objection pertains to this conclusion. We have already given some attention to this point, in Chapter III.[2] There it was demonstrated that, even in the long run and under the ground rules of neo-classical analysis, an economy with only inside money and private domestic primary debt is a money economy with a determinate price level, a real aggregate demand for money, and a real stock of money. Such an economy is definitely not a barter system, so that consolidation of inside money against

[2] Pp. 72-75.

private domestic primary debt misrepresents behavior patterns.

The proof that there is a determinate price level, given nominal inside money, in such an economy can be restated as follows. Assume an initial state of equilibrium on all markets. Then double commodity prices, money wage rates, and nominal bonds, while holding nominal money constant. This will keep real primary debt of firms constant. However, since private spending units hold both money and primary securities in their portfolios and since nominal money is constant, there will be an increase in the real value of bonds in these portfolios and a decrease in the real value of money. The outcome is the creation of an excess demand for money and an excess supply of bonds at the new price level and the initial rate of interest.[3] The economic system can be counted upon to reject the arbitrary inflation of prices, along with the rise in the bond rate of interest that follows from an excess supply of bonds, and to re-establish the initial constellation of price level and interest rate. Only one price level is compatible with general equilibrium. Inside money is a claim by private sectors against the monetary system, and the private sectors demand this claim in real value that they consider appropriate to their own portfolio balance.

The net-money interpretation of our exercise with the price level would be that the private sectors' claim on the monetary system has been reduced in real value, that the pri-

[3] If nominal money is constant, nominal liabilities of the money-creating entity must be constant, which implies its assets in the form of nominal primary securities must also be constant. This means that the entire increase in the nominal amount of primary securities is concentrated on the money-holding sector. Thus, if business nominal debt was first 100, with the banking system holding 30 and consumers holding 70, and then the total goes to 200, with the banking system's holdings remaining at 30, consumer holdings must rise from 70 to 170, which exceeds the rise in the price level.

vate sectors' debt to the monetary system has been reduced in the same degree, hence that real net wealth in the private sectors is unaffected. From this it follows that the change in the price level would have no real consequences on markets for labor, current output, and bonds, that any price level is compatible with equilibrium. Therefore, our economy is a barter economy and not a money economy.

What net-money doctrine misses is that private debtors are indifferent to the distribution of their bonds between private creditors and the monetary system, while private creditors are not indifferent to the distribution of their portfolios between bonds and money. Net-money doctrine overlooks the bearing of portfolio balance on real behavior.

Our second objection to net-money doctrine concerned its implication that the price level is indeterminate when all financial assets are of the inside variety. Our third objection is that net-money doctrine implies that a change in nominal money, of the inside variety, cannot affect the real variables of the economy in the long run, within the neo-classical framework. The second objection has to do with price-level determinancy, while the third bears on money's neutrality.

We have previously discussed the issue of neutrality in Chapter III.[4] There we demonstrated that a change in nominal inside money can have real effects when there is a combination of inside and outside money. When, on the other hand, the economy contains only inside or only outside money, a change in nominal money has no real effects, within the models of Chapters II and III. Hence, by washing out inside money (and debt), net-money doctrine misses the effects on real behavior emanating from a combination of inside and outside money.

This may be shown in the following way. Suppose that an

[4] Pp. 75-86.

initial equilibrium exists and that the combined financial position of private domestic spending units is as described in *Balance Sheet A* of Table 9. The entire money stock is outside money, and all primary debt is in the portfolios of spending units. The monetary system now doubles the nominal stock of money, entirely by open-market buying of private domestic primary debt. This transforms *Balance Sheet A* into *Balance Sheet B,* which is also shown in the table.

The first consequence of the open-market buying operation is that creditor spending units have reduced their primary security holdings and increased their money balances; monetary intermediation has changed the mix of creditors' portfolios. Debtor spending units are in the same position as before, with primary debt of 50. The transfer of primary securities to the monetary system cannot affect the real demands of debtors. But there is an effect on real demands of creditors, whose portfolios contain fewer primary securities and more money. Since the inside money must be a perfect substitute for outside money, creditors now have an excess stock of money, given the initial price level and rate of interest. The creation of inside money results in an excess stock of money and excess demands on markets for labor services, current output, and bonds.

Such a situation would culminate, if we followed quantity theory, in a new equilibrium at doubled levels of commodity prices, money wage rates, and nominal primary securities—with the rate of interest unchanged. The quantity-theory solution is shown in *Balance Sheet C.* Nominal primary debt has doubled from 50 to 100, and the additional debt of 50 has found its way into the portfolios of creditors, who now hold nominal securities of 80. The nominal value of capital goods has doubled, too. But it is clear, that this position cannot be the new equilibrium. While the doubling of

TABLE 9

Combined Balance Sheets of Private Domestic Spending Units

BALANCE SHEET A

Assets		*Liabilities*	
Outside money	20	Private domestic primary securities	50
Private domestic primary securities	50	Net worth	45
Capital goods	25		

BALANCE SHEET B

Assets		*Liabilities*	
Outside money	20	Private domestic primary securities	50
Inside money	20	Net worth	45
Private domestic primary securities	30		
Capital goods	25		

BALANCE SHEET C

Assets		*Liabilities*	
Outside money	20	Private domestic primary securities	100
Inside money	20	Net worth	70
Private domestic primary securities	80		
Capital goods	50		

nominal money has not altered the real position of debtors, it has altered the real position of creditors. They have suffered a capital loss in real primary securities, and the proportion of money to primary securities in their portfolios has risen, from 40 per cent in *Balance Sheet A* to 50 per cent in *Balance Sheet C*. Their response will be to demand less of both money and current output, more of primary securities. In the new equilibrium, the rate of interest will be lower than at the beginning of our experiment; the price level will be higher but not in proportion to monetary expansion; real capital will become more plentiful; and, with more capital applied to the same labor force, real income will exceed its initial level. Expansion solely in inside money, by way of an open-market operation in private domestic primary securities, has not been the hollow gesture that net-money doctrine would allege it to be. On the contrary, it has stimulated real growth of capital and income.

This suggests that consolidation of financial accounts in obedience to net-money doctrine conceals important aspects of real behavior. Such doctrine implies that management of inside money cannot come to grips with the rate of interest, real stocks of financial and tangible assets, or the level of real income, and it is in error. The real effects of inside money and private domestic primary debt are not symmetrical, as between debtors and creditors, even in general-equilibrium models built to neo-classical specifications.

Furthermore, in models that admit short-period effects and tolerate some imperfection of competition, price inflexibility, money illusion, distribution effects, and unstable price expectations, the net-money principle of disregarding inside claims and counterclaims may lead to serious error in describing adjustments to monetary policy. Then the division of labor between saving and investment and the division of spending units between creditors and debtors become structural characteristics that condition the responses of relative prices, real income and wealth to changes in growth rates of inside money, other inside indirect debt, and private domestic primary debt. Then inside financial stocks and flows are clearly not excess baggage in aggregative analysis.

Net-money doctrine implies that the quantity of private domestic primary debt and its counterparts in financial assets in both monetary and nonmonetary form have no net effects on the aggregate real demand for money. It implies that the growth of primary debt reduces the debtors' real demand for money to the same degree that the growth in holdings of inside financial assets increases it for creditors. Hence, the aggregate real demand for money is unaffected by the accumulation of inside claims and counterclaims. This implication of net-money doctrine gives rise to our fourth objection.

In the model of Chapter III, we assumed that business management had a definite desire to reach an optimal asset-debt position that involved an optimal mixture of real capital goods, money, and primary debt. Firms attempted to reach this optimal position by equating the marginal rental rate on capital goods, after allowance for risk, to the marginal implicit deposit rate on money and to the rate of interest on primary debt. Such a position involved positive holdings of capital goods and real money balances and a positive level of outstanding primary debt. During output growth, firms desired to expand their capital goods and to attain diversified portfolios by accumulating money balances and primary debt. They demanded a certain net debt position at each level of capital goods, with net debt taking the form of positive gross debt and money holdings.

At the same time, consumers wanted to diversify their portfolios between primary securities and money, so that as their portfolios expanded during output growth they increased their real demand for money balances. The considerations that induced consumers to diversify their portfolios by demanding additional money and primary securities also stimulated firms to incur additional debt and add to money balances, along with their capital stock, during the growth process.

Thus, the aggregate real demand for money grew during the growth process partly because of the growth of firms' net debt position and consumers' financial-asset portfolios. This financial growth in turn depended on the distribution of income relative to the distribution of spending between the two sectors—on the division of labor between saving and investment. As this division of labor increased, the growth of primary debt and financial assets became more rapid, stimulating the aggregate real demand for money. It seems to us that the aggregate real demand for money is not independent of the quantity of claims and counterclaims between consumers and firms.

Our final objection to net-money doctrine, though it applies as well to the models in Chapters II and III, is that it distinguishes too sharply between private domestic and other or outside sectors, the latter including both government and countries abroad. It alleges that private domestic claims against these foreign sectors have the effect only of increasing real demands by the private domestic sectors, never of decreasing real demands by the foreign sectors in the domestic economy's markets. This implies that neither the government nor its taxpayers economizes in order to limit government debt and that economies abroad do not retrench in their demand for the domestic economy's exports due to a loss of gold or incurrence of debt to the domestic economy. So private domestic claims on the foreign sectors, or debts to them, are admissible into private domestic demand functions, while private domestic inside claims and counterclaims are excluded. As sharp a delineation as this between inside and outside claims is not completely realistic.

Demand for Money in Diversified Portfolios

The accumulation of assets is a central feature of the growth process. Tangible assets embody the savings of the community and provide the technological basis for rising standards of production and consumption. There is stockpiling, too, of financial assets. Primary securities are offered upon the security markets by spending units wanting funds to dispose of either on current output or financial assets. An equivalent amount of financial assets is taken into spending units' portfolios as a use of funds saved or borrowed.

In dealings directly between spending units, there is a chronic excess supply of primary securities. The reason is, of course, that spending units who lend desire a diversified portfolio. They demand a form of financial asset that other spending units cannot create and supply. This form of asset is money, either of the inside or outside variety.

The excess supply of primary securities in dealings directly between spending units can be, and in the long run is likely to be, eliminated by an increase in the real stock of money balances. This monetary expansion may come about by a fall in prices on markets for current output and labor services that raises the real value of a given nominal stock of money. If the Policy Bureau prefers a stable price level, the expansion in real money that is the desired complement of expansion in primary securities, at a given interest rate, is achieved by growth in nominal money. Then the Banking Bureau absorbs the excess supply of primary securities and creates money to fill the corresponding gap in spending units' portfolios of financial assets.

The governmental monetary system equates supply and

demand on the primary security market during the growth process by adding continuously to its own holdings of primary securities. Simultaneously it may balance supply and demand on the *money* market, at a given interest rate and price level, by paying for its purchases of securities with new issues of the money that spending units desire for diversification. Aside from providing an efficient payments mechanism, it is the function of the monetary system in a growth context to clear the primary security market of excess supply and the money market of excess demand.

THE IMPLICIT DEPOSIT RATE

Why do spending units want a diversified portfolio—some primary securities and some money? Why is growth in real money a common, even a necessary, part of the growth process? Why must banks grow in real and, usually, in nominal size?

In answering these questions, we suppose that each spending unit manages its portfolio of financial assets with a view to maximizing the expected rate of return, net of allowance for risk, up to the spending unit's planning horizon. Spending units are on the watch for opportunities to replace any one variety of financial asset that bears a relatively low yield at the margin with another financial asset bearing a higher return. The objective of portfolio policy is to equalize marginal expected rates of return.

Money is judged in terms of its marginal pay-off, just as other assets are. Demand for money in a given amount implies that the marginal return anticipated from such a stock of money is higher than the return to be realized by exchanging one dollar of money for a dollar's worth of alternative assets. The incentive to hold money is money's marginal return. This return is the "deposit rate."

In current American practice the *explicit* deposit rate on money is nil. In fact, service charges on demand deposit accounts amount to a negative deposit rate which may or may not be offset by "free" banking services of various kinds. How, then, can there be some positive deposit rate which induces a demand for money in the face of positive rates of interest and rent on alternative assets?

Consider the nature of money. The price is fixed in terms of the accounting unit. No other asset can make this claim. So one may impute to money, as its *implicit* deposit rate, the losses and expenses that lenders would incur by holding some other asset that is not fixed in price.

Money is protection against real capital loss as interest rates rise. Bonds promising fixed nominal payments are not. Money balances held in preference to bonds may be credited with implicit earnings equal to the amount of prospective capital losses avoided. The protection that money gives against rising interest rates can be counted as an element of the implicit marginal deposit rate.

Money is also protection against capital loss as goods prices decline. Primary securities such as business equities are not. Consequently, money balances may be credited with a yield equal to prospective capital losses that are avoided by holding money rather than equities. Money is not the asset to hold when there is little doubt that interest rates will fall or that goods prices will rise. Then money is vulnerable to capital loss in real value. The marginal deposit rate on any given stock of money balances is lower as probabilities of capital loss on money balances increase.

There are ingredients of the deposit rate other than the prospective capital loss avoided on alternative assets. One of them is brokerage fees and other turnover expenses involved in substituting primary securities for money balances. Another is any savings in the cost of borrowing that can be realized by maintenance of a strong cash position. Still another is savings realizable when cash discounts are taken or when bargain opportunities are seized by a quick purchase on any market.

In short, there are marginal returns that can be imputed to money and expressed as the implicit deposit rate. The demand for money is based upon a comparison marginally of the deposit rate with yields on other uses of funds saved or borrowed. Taking into account only financial dispositions of spending units' funds, there is chronic excess supply of primary securities in dealings between spending units during the growth process because the marginal return to portfolios consisting only of primary securities is below the marginal return on portfolios comprising both primary securities and money. By virtue of its implicit deposit rate, money is a desired component of the diversified or balanced portfolio.

MONEY VS. HOMOGENEOUS BONDS

The matter that principally concerns us in this chapter is the effect on the money market of differentiation of primary securities. We intend to emphasize that such differentiation affects the demand for money in spending units' portfolios. There is differentiation that reduces the demand for money, and there is also differentiation that increases it, all other things equal. Changes in the demand for money ordinarily imply changes, too, in demands for labor services, current output, and primary securities, but we shall limit ourselves to partial analysis of the money market as mutations are introduced in primary securities. However, before we experiment with effects of differentiation on the demand for money, it may be helpful to review some of the factors underlying the demand for money when the only financial alternative is a homogeneous business bond (perpetuity), as in our second model of Chapter III.

In *Panel A* of Chart IV below, the given nominal stock of

CHART IV

The Market for Money

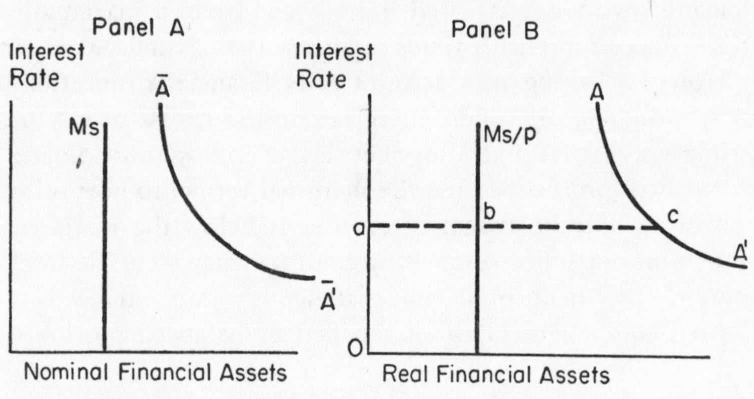

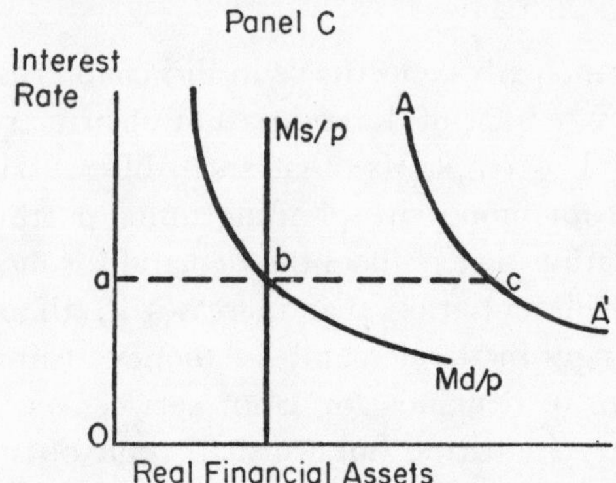

money is shown by the vertical line, *Ms*. This money stock is held by both consumers and firms. The "portfolio schedule," $\overline{AA'}$, measures the nominal present worth of spending units' financial-asset portfolios at alternative rates of interest, which are plotted on the vertical axis. The horizontal distance between the money-stock line and the portfolio schedule is the nominal present worth of business bonds held by consumers.

In *Panel B,* the equilibrium levels of the interest rate and prices of current output are introduced. Money and business bonds are now valued in real terms. The real stock of money is shown by $\frac{Ms}{p}$. The portfolio schedule, *AA′,* gives the real value of financial assets that is compatible with equilibrium on markets for current output and labor services, given real values of tangible assets and national income. The equilibrium rate of interest is *Oa,* and *ac* is the corresponding real value of financial assets.

Panel C adds a demand schedule for real money balances, $\frac{Md}{p}$. Since equilibrium is assumed on all other markets, the demand schedule must intersect the money-stock line at the rate of interest, *Oa.* At this interest rate, the real demand for money by consumers and firms is equal to the real stock of money: there is equilibrium on the money market. At any higher rate of interest, there is an excess stock of money; at any lower rate of interest, there is an excess demand for money. Either excess stock or excess demand on the money market is incompatible with equilibrium levels of demand and supply on the other markets.

We are interested in the general conformation of the demand schedule for money, even though only one point on it is relevant to the given case of general equilibrium. The rate of return applying to each point along the schedule measures not only the rate of interest on bonds but also the marginal deposit rate on the indicated stock of money balances. The schedule suggests that the marginal return on money balances varies inversely with the stock of these balances. If spending units are to be content with a smaller proportion of money in their portfolios, with money bearing a higher marginal utility or deposit rate in their estimation, they must be rewarded with a higher market rate of interest on bonds. If spending units are to be satisfied with a larger proportion of money in their portfolios, and so with a lower marginal utility for money, they must be faced with a lower interest rate on bonds. The ratio of desired money balances to total financial-asset portfolios varies inversely with the rate of interest.

Given real income and real stocks of assets, there is some virtually irreducible minimum of real money balances below which balances desired will not fall as the interest rate rises indefinitely high; some minimum amount of liquidity is regarded as indispensable. This means that the demand schedule for money is vertical in its upper reaches. At the lower end of the schedule, spending units resist converting portfolios wholly to money at the sacrifice of all interest income. We are not really interested in neurotic economic systems where bonds might replace all money or where money might supplant all bonds.

The demand schedule is a profile of spending units' preferences between real money and real bonds. The real demand for money is relatively low at a high present rate of interest because such a rate implies the maximum chance for a future fall in the interest rate, with capital gains for bonds. The real demand for money is relatively high at a low present interest rate because the low rate implies the maximum chance of a future rise in the interest rate, with capital losses for bonds. For both consumers and firms, it is rational to conserve on money-holding when bonds are cheap and splurge on money-holding when bonds are dear.

Money as an asset fixed in price in terms of the accounting unit and bonds with a fixed nominal yield are both vehicles for speculation on prices for current output and labor services. Given real wealth, real income, and nominal money and bonds, a prospect of price inflation implies a higher market rate of interest now to repress excess demand for current output and prevent an immediate rise in the price level. One expects a shift in demand from both bonds and money to current output that will be brought under control by an increase in the interest rate.

But how can an interest rate above *Oa* in *Panel C* be consistent with equilibrium on the money market? The answer is that both business borrowers and consumer lenders become more wary than before of further advances in the interest rate, and so shift their preferences from bonds to money. Given the portfolio schedule in *Panel C,* the demand schedule for money shifts to the right to a higher intersection with the money-stock line, so that the rate of interest which restrains the demand for current output does not imply an excess stock of money. Expected deflation will have opposite effects, of diverting demand from current output to financial assets and from money to bonds; the equilibrium interest rate will be lower. The implicit deposit rate associated with each amount of real money balances, then, depends in part on expected price behavior on markets for both current output and primary securities.

The demand schedule for money is a profile of spending units' preferences between money and bonds at only one level of real income. All else the same, a higher level of real income shifts demand from bonds to money at each rate of interest, so that the demand schedule shifts to the right. The transactions motive for money-holding is strengthened by the rise in real income, and the immediate result for the money market is a higher rate of interest to repress excess demand for money. The ultimate result, in a quantity-theory world, would be that the higher real demand for money is met by a fall in the price level of current output, which expands the real stock of money, and by a fall in nominal bonds outstanding, which permits existing and desired money balances to rise in proportion to real bonds.[5] In the long run, with money neutral, both the supply and demand schedules move rightward relative to a new *AA′*, with their intersection at the original rate of interest, *Oa*. The increase in demand for money would narrow the distance, *bc*.

We know from Chapter IV that the portfolio schedule, *AA′*, tends to move steadily rightward in a developing economy, the real value of primary debt and financial assets sharing the upward trend of tangible wealth and income. Our money-demand function specifies that the rightward drift of the portfolio schedule draws the demand schedule for money in its wake, reflecting the determination of both firms and consumers to maintain a diversified financial position. Given the real stock of money, growth in the desired stock implies an excess supply of bonds and a rise in the interest rate. If money is neutral, of course, an excess supply of bonds and an excess demand for money may be resolved by price deflation that shifts the money-stock line to the right along with both the money-demand and portfolio schedules. Or the solution may be continuous growth in nominal money. In either case, the requirement for monetary equilibrium is that the monetary system expand in real terms as the accumulation of financial assets intensifies the real demand for money balances.

[5] Long-run analysis based on comparative statics is not concerned with the techniques employed by the private domestic economy in adjusting the nominal stock of bonds to change in the price level. For short-run analysis of the adjustment process, it might be demonstrated that the business community of our model would apply depreciation reserves to debt repayment, during price deflation, and permit the rate of growth in real capital to fall temporarily below its trend. With their nominal debt adapted to a lower price level, firms would repair the deficiency in capital goods. Of course, the adjustment process might be a disorderly one, with nominal debt being contracted by business failures and bankruptcies.

Differentiation of Primary Securities and Demand for Money

Financial growth is not exclusively quantitative, involving growth only in the real value of primary debt and financial assets. It is qualitative, too. The mix of primary securities emanating from spending units is constantly changing in ways closely related to the community's growth experience—according to the sectoral distribution of saving and investment, to the degree of stability in real growth and the price level, and to the vigor of innovation in financial contracts and financial markets. We considered evolving patterns of security differentiation in Chapter IV and turn now to their effect on the demand for money and on the growth of the monetary system.

No simple scheme for classifying primary securities can do full justice to their differences in quality. For our purposes, however, a simple scheme will have to do, based on five criteria of distinction. The first criterion is maturity. The second sets apart those securities that contain an implicit or explicit purchasing-power clause, allowing for changes in the price level of current output, from securities that promise nominal payments unadjusted for price inflation or deflation. The third creates a special class for securities with an implicit or explicit productivity clause that permits savers to share with investors gains or losses in the real productivity of tangible assets. The fourth criterion distinguishes between gilt-edge securities and non-gilt-edge issues according to the degree of certainty regarding the debtor's fulfillment of his contract. The fifth criterion is a catchall for classifying securities according to their marketability.

In the present section, each class of security is considered in turn as a component of spending units' financial-asset portfolios. We explore briefly its effect on the real demand for money and hence, given the objectives of the Policy Bureau, on the nominal stock of money. We continue to use partial equilibrium analysis of the money market.

MATURITY

In a financially mature economy, there may be virtually a continuous curve or spectrum of maturities on outstanding primary debt, with a corresponding curve of yields. For our purposes, it is sufficient to pick out two points on the curve, one for perpetuities and one for short-dated bills.

Suppose, to begin with, that all primary securities are bills rather than perpetuities. The aggregate issue price of bills is assumed to be the same as that of the bonds which would have been outstanding in our earlier models. And the nominal stock of money is not affected by this transformation in primary debt. The question arises whether spending units' money-demand schedule, as in Chart IV, is insensitive to this transformation, whether there is monetary equilibrium at the rate of interest and price level that previously cleared markets for bonds, current output, and labor services.

The answer is a qualified "no." The unfunding of primary debt, replacing bonds with bills, is likely to reduce the real demand for money when the primary debt is inside debt of business firms. On the other hand, one can be much more confident that unfunding reduces the real demand for money when the debt is a Treasury bill or some other outside issue at short term. In both cases, unfunding reduces creditors' demand for money. In the first case, though, it may be argued that unfunding increases debtors' demand for money so that the net effect on aggregate demand, taking into account both creditors and debtors, is ambiguous. We put aside this question for the moment, assuming that the short-term debt is of outside origin.

There are two effects of such unfunding on money's implicit deposit rate. First, relatively frequent turnover of bills in creditors' portfolios may involve management costs. This effect adds to the advantage of holding money, increases the deposit rate of money, and so stimulates the demand for money. There would be the same result, without an unfunding operation, if a tax were imposed on bonds in an amount equal to the turnover costs on bills.

The second effect of unfunding is to increase the degree of certainty with which spending units can forecast future values of existing portfolios. There is no uncertainty at all about maturity values of bills, and for dates other than maturity dates uncertainty is diminished by the comparative inflexibility of bill prices. There would be the same result, without an unfunding operation, if spending units' expectations about bond rates of interest could be pegged within sufficiently narrow limits.

This second effect of substituting bills for bonds tends to reduce the demand for money at every rate of interest, since it shrinks the capital loss that could result from any rise in interest rates. On the other hand, bills do not have as high potentialities as bonds for capital gains. Since capital losses are most to be feared at low rates of interest, and capital gains are most to be hoped for at high rates of interest, the replacement of bonds by bills steepens the demand schedule for money and shifts it to the left. The demand for money is lowered relatively little at the top of the curve, but it is lowered significantly at the bottom.

Unfunding, on balance, is likely to reduce the demand for money. If the economy's system of markets was in equilibrium before bills replaced bonds, it is no longer in equilibrium. There is now an excess stock of money, and the excess stock is larger at interest rates that are low relative to the mean expectation of future rates. Unfunding has inflationary consequences on the markets of the economy, the price level rising to dissipate unwanted real balances. If inflation is averted by a reduction in the nominal stock of money, unfunding is responsible for contraction in both the real and nominal size of the monetary system that is appropriate to given real levels of income, wealth, and financial assets. A Treasury issuing bills is a competitor of the monetary system.

In Chart V, to illustrate the point, unfunding shifts the demand schedule for money to the left from D to D'. If the unfunding operation occurs when the monetary authority wishes to raise the interest rate in the short run from Oa to Ob, the nominal stock of money must be reduced by the amount CA, given the price level. In the absence of unfunding, the reduction in the money stock need be only CB to achieve the same goal. Consequently, if unfunding always takes place as the rate of interest rises and if funding always occurs as the rate falls, the "demand schedule" for money is in effect the broken line D''; it is relatively elastic. We shall show in Chapter VI that the activities of nonmonetary intermediaries, such as savings banks and life insurance companies, also tend to produce such a schedule. That is, unfunding by the Treasury is analogous to the growth of nonmonetary indirect financial assets—of claims on these intermediaries. It is analogous to unfunding through nonmonetary intermediaries.

The money-demand schedule tends to be relatively elastic when a given stock of financial assets includes both bills and bonds as well as money—when there is partial unfunding. There are now two rates of interest, a bill rate and a bond rate. For each bond rate and each pattern of spending units' expectations regarding the future bond rate, there is a bill rate that equalizes expected returns on bonds and bills. The bill rate is high relative to the present bond rate if the weight of expectations favors a fall in the bond rate, and it is low relative to the bond rate if a rise in the latter seems most

CHART V

Demand for Money and Unfunding

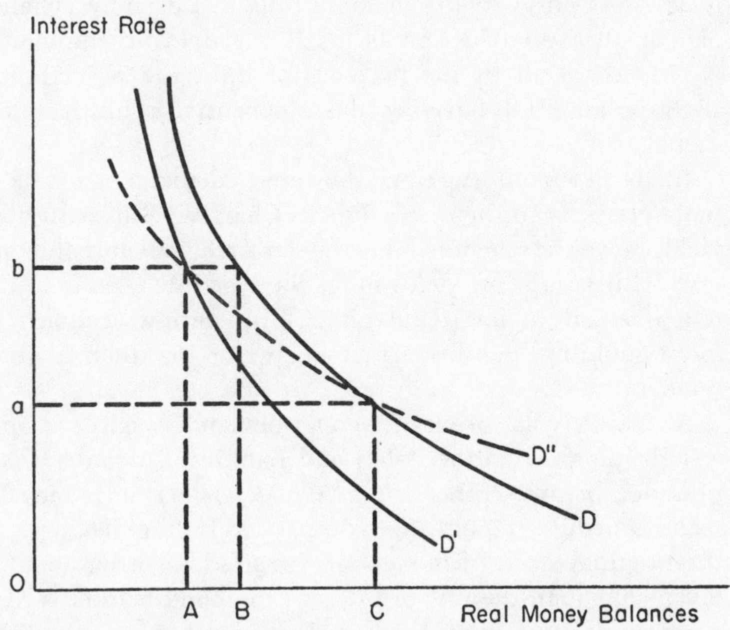

probable. It is the same as the bond rate if extra management costs for bills exactly offset an expected small rise in the bond rate.

At each bond rate, spending units may now choose among money, bonds, and bills—at the bill rate that is appropriate to the bond rate. At all bond rates that are high relative to the mean expectation of the future bond rate, the combination of a high yield on bonds, favorable prospects for capital gains on bonds, the bill rate higher than the bond rate, and a chance for modest capital gains even on bills will shift the money-demand schedule *D* in Chart V to the left. The order of the day, under such circumstances, should be economy in the demand for money.

As the bond rate falls, demand is diverted to money by the low yield on bonds, relatively strong prospects for capital losses on bonds, very low yield on bills, and even by a chance of a small capital loss on bills. If the demand for money is reduced at all by the presence of bills, the reduction is slight because bills have become so expensive a substitute for money.

In its new conformation, the money-demand schedule is more elastic than the *D*-schedule in Chart V. Bills with high yields move the schedule relatively far to the left at high bond rates. Bills with low yields move the schedule less far to the left, if at all, at low bond rates. Bills permit economy in money-holding, but in smaller degree at low than at high bond rates.

A relatively flat or elastic money-demand schedule is only a slight nuisance to the Policy and Banking Bureaus. It is a nuisance because, other things equal, an elastic money-demand schedule implies that comparatively large changes in the nominal stock of money are required to bring about a given change in the rate of interest; the bond market is relatively insensitive to monetary policy in the short run. The monetary system must take more aggressive action than would otherwise be necessary. This is not important for a governmental monetary system that is indifferent to its earnings. It could be an important consideration for a private banking system, as will be shown in Chapter VII. An elastic demand for money requires severe restraint on bank portfolios, for short-run monetary control, when the bond rate is high, and it requires comparatively large portfolios when the bond rate is low. Bills are more closely competitive with money as their yield rises, and they have an adverse effect on bank earnings by decreasing the demand for money just when banks could extract the highest returns from their earning assets.

In a special sense, public-debt management is a technique of monetary control. It is not a technique for regulating the nominal stock of money, but it is a technique that affects the demand for money. Hence it can be and is used to regulate excess supply and demand on the money market. Through changes that it induces in spending units' demand for money, a Treasury achieves the results that the monetary system achieves through changes in the stock of money. Competition by the Treasury in supplying spending units with bills, a financial asset relatively stable in price, affects the demand for money in any given context of static equilibrium and, as a result, affects the appropriate size of the monetary system.

We return now to the results of adjustment in maturity of primary debt when the debt is inside debt owed by spending units who are also holders of money. What is the chance that unfunding increases debtors' demand for money in the same degree that it reduces demand on the part of creditors, so that there is no net effect aggregatively?

Replacing bonds with bills seems to have two effects on debtors working in opposite directions. First, the hazards of being in debt on short term may increase debtors' demand for money. Second, the opportunity to borrow at short term may be a partial substitute for money balances. The net effect of unfunding on debtors' demand for money, therefore, seems to be ambiguous. Since the net effect of unfunding on creditors is to reduce their demand for money, unfunding is likely to permit economy in the aggregate demand for money, though this is by no means certain.

THE PURCHASING-POWER CLAUSE

Primary securities up to now have been gilt-edge promises to pay fixed nominal sums of money; they have been nominal-bonds or nominal-bills. The real value of nominal-bonds (perpetuities) in spending units' portfolios can be expressed as $\frac{(B\text{-}B_g)}{ip}$, where B is the number of outstanding bonds, each promising to pay \$1 per year, B_g is the number of such bonds held by the governmental monetary system, i is the rate of interest, and p is the price level of current output. Thus, $B\text{-}B_g$ is the number of bonds in spending units' portfolios.

Now we change the bond contract by inserting a purchasing-power clause. Bonds become real-bonds promising payment in fixed real sums of money, so that the real value of primary securities in spending units' portfolios is $\frac{p(B\text{-}B_g)}{ip}$, which is equal to $\frac{(B\text{-}B_g)}{i}$ at all levels of prices for goods. Whatever the price level, the real value of primary securities is constant. We assume to begin with that bonds are of the outside variety. The real stock of money remains $\frac{Ms}{p}$.

There are three main effects upon the demand for money and upon the equilibrium real stock of money when nominal-bonds are replaced by real-bonds. First, in the presence of uncertainty regarding the price level, insertion of the purchasing-power clause into bond contracts may alter the desired mix of money and bonds in financial-asset accumulations of given real size. Second, the effect may be to alter the desired real size of financial-asset accumulations and hence the size of the money component. Third, the impact of monetary policy on the real variables of the economy depends on the nature of the bond contract.

When spending units' portfolios are limited to money and nominal-bonds (as contrasted with real-bonds), the desired portfolio mix at the present rate of interest and price level is affected by any prospect of a change in the rate of interest—in the relative real values of money and nominal-bonds. It is not affected by a prospect of change in the price level, unless spending units assume that price instability will be accompanied by instability in the interest rate. The reason is, of course, that a rise or fall in the price level by itself has equiproportional effects on the real values of money and nominal-bonds. When, on the other hand, portfolios are divided between money and real-bonds, the desired portfolio mix is affected directly by any prospect of a change in either the rate of interest or the price level. Then a rise in the interest rate or a fall in the price level lowers the real value of bonds relative to money, and a fall in the interest rate or a rise in the price level raises the real value of bonds in comparison with money. In this case, the outlook for prices of both bonds and goods must be considered in the present choice between bonds and money.

In the presence of uncertainty regarding the price level, spending units may set one target for accumulation of money and nominal-bonds, and a different target for accumulation of money and real-bonds. The anticipated rate of return on real-bonds is not affected by possible instability of the price level, while the real return on nominal-bonds is lowered by inflation, raised by deflation. Consequently, a possible effect is that desired portfolios of financial assets will be larger when, given a prospect for inflation, real-bonds replace nominal-bonds, and that desired portfolios will be smaller when deflation is looming. Any change in the scale of portfolios ordinarily must be expected to change the demand for money in the same direction.

When spending units have access to both nominal-bonds

and real-bonds as well as to money, expected inflation diverts demand to real-bonds from both money and nominal-bonds while expected deflation diverts demand from real-bonds to both money and nominal-bonds. Money must compete, then, with nominal-bonds in satisfying demand for protection against a falling price level, and it is inferior to real-bonds in satisfying demand for protection against a rising price level. As a general rule, this sort of differentiation of primary securities tends to reduce the demand for money, though the effect of differentiation in stimulating saving and investment, lending and borrowing, and financial-asset accumulation is toward increasing desired money balances.

We have argued that the introduction of real-bonds modifies the demand for money both because it affects the choice between money and bonds in portfolios of a given scale and because it may affect the scale of asset-holding. Now we wish to make the point that the introduction of real-bonds adds to the potency of monetary policy in regulating output, income, and employment; it gives money a stronger grip on the real world.

Assume that money and real-bonds are the only financial assets and that money is exclusively inside money created through purchases of real-bonds, of the inside variety, by the Banking Bureau. Given an initial general equilibrium, let nominal money balances be doubled and suppose that the price level also rises to twice its original level, with the interest rate unchanged. The result is not a new general equilibrium at the same level of real output and employment. Instead, the real demand for money is lower so that, with the real stock of money unchanged, there is an excess money stock and an excess demand for bonds, goods, and labor. In a new general equilibrium, the interest rate is lower, the price level is higher but not in proportion to monetary expansion, and output is increased.

Money is not neutral in its effects on the real variables in this case because at a doubled price level and a doubled nominal amount of outstanding real-bonds, $\frac{p(B)}{i}$, the Banking Bureau more than doubles its nominal holdings of real-bonds, $\frac{p(B_g)}{i}$. Its nominal portfolio increases by virtue both of the open-market operation, which increases B_g, and of the ensuing price inflation, which raises p, so that the nominal gain cannot be nullified in real terms by the inflation. Since the Banking Bureau gains a larger share of real-bonds, there must remain a smaller share for spending units. There is a net transfer of real-bonds to the monetary system, raising the proportion of money to bonds in private portfolios and reducing the real value of these portfolios. Private spending units are both more liquid and less well-to-do as the result of the open-market operation. As they dispose of excess real money and set about to restore the real value of their portfolios, all real variables of the economic system will be affected. Monetary policy is not trivial in this case because the Policy Bureau is able to manage the real stock of money and the desired stock.

THE PRODUCTIVITY CLAUSE

Each of the primary securities we have considered so far calls for a fixed return—fixed in either nominal or real amount. Bonds have been either nominal-bonds, with a nominal return of B and a real return of $\frac{B}{p}$, or real-bonds, with a nominal return of pB and a real return of B. Now we consider another mutation in the bond contract, involving a productivity clause. This specifies that creditors receive payments equal to some stable proportion of business income.

The purchasing-power clause and the productivity clause are the principal features distinguishing "stocks" from "bonds."

In a general-equilibrium model free of market imperfections and uncertainty, rates of return would be identical on nominal-bonds, real-bonds, and real-bonds with a productivity clause. Nor would there be any differences in rates of return because of differences in maturity. Any distinction between issues depends on market imperfections that result in differences in trading costs between kinds of security and on uncertainty regarding the price level, the interest rate, and business profits. Trading costs aside, the basis for dealing in issues of various maturities is uncertainty regarding the interest rate. The basis for trading in a combination of nominal-bonds and real-bonds is uncertainty regarding the price level. The basis for trading in real-bonds with the productivity clause is uncertainty regarding real business profits.

Demand for money balances is peculiar to a world of frictions and uncertainty. Money is a defense against transactions costs of buying and selling primary securities, and it is a defense against the possibility of a rise in the interest rate or a fall in the price level. When an alternative to money-holding is real-bonds with the productivity clause, money can be a defense against shrinkage in business profits. On the other hand, money is at a disadvantage as trading in primary securities becomes less expensive and when there are prospects for a falling rate of interest, a rising price level, or rising business profits.

When there are real-bonds bearing the productivity clause, a wealth effect may stimulate the demand for money, if the increased variety of financial assets raises the scale of desired portfolios. A substitution effect may decrease the demand for money or increase it, depending on the expected course of business profits. Real-bonds with the productivity clause are one more possible alternative to money in financial-asset accumulations.

We have seen earlier that a high bill rate, usually characteristic of periods in which growth is accelerating or of cyclic booms, may induce economy in the demand for money just when the monetary authority is trying to reduce the stock of money relative to desired balances. If accelerated growth or cyclic boom makes "stocks" more attractive, because of the productivity clause, demand for money may be economized still more just when it is the purpose of monetary policy to create excess demand for money. Then there is frustration of monetary policy in the sense that a higher velocity of money offsets the impact on the interest rate of contraction in the stock of money.

GILT-EDGENESS AND MARKETABILITY

With modern standards of banking and banking regulation, money is a prime financial asset. Very few other types of security have such strong defenses against debtor default. Hence, the implicit deposit rate of money must be credited, at each rate of interest on primary securities, with default losses avoided by holding money rather than primary securities. This implies that the demand for money is higher at any rate of interest on non-gilt-edge securities than it would be at the same rate of interest on "blue chips."

Money is a highly marketable asset. Transactions costs in turning it over are nil or negligible. And the owner of money may dispose of it in any volume without price concession; he faces a perfectly elastic demand schedule. All primary securities trade on less perfectly competitive markets. Government securities may approximate money as a marketable asset, but there are numerous issues that are significantly illiquid both because transactions costs are high and because markets are thin in the sense that quick sales or sales in heavy volume will call for considerable concessions in price. Any change in the marketability of securities that are alternatives to money in financial-asset portfolios may affect the demand for money.

Financial development improves the marketability of primary securities, reducing transactions costs and increasing the elasticity of demand schedules facing individual sellers of securities. It brings about a secular decline in the premium charged by lenders on non-gilt-edge as compared with gilt-edge securities and opens up narrow, provincial markets to a more competitive flow of bids and offers. From the standpoint of monetary analysis, its effect is to diminish the relative importance of the monetary system as a financial intermediary, shifting demand from money to primary securities.

PORTFOLIO BALANCE

The growth process generates almost continuous accumulation of primary debt and financial assets. The accumulation of financial assets stimulates the demand for money by spending units whose motive, we suppose, is to maximize the expected rate of return on financial-asset portfolios, after allowances for risk. In a rational allocation of the portfolio or asset budget, the demand for money is pressed to the limit at which the marginal implicit deposit rate (*plus* the explicit deposit rate, if any) on money is judged to be barely adequate recompense for market rates of interest foregone by choosing money over primary securities.

Money is pre-eminently a sanctuary, a haven for resources that would otherwise go into more perilous uses. The return imputed to it is a measure of spending units' reservations and doubts about nonmonetary assets, specifically of their doubts that the market rate of interest accurately defines the realizable net yield from nonmonetary assets.

Given the stock of financial assets and its pattern of differentiation, the demand for money is subject to the principle of diminishing marginal utility; the marginal deposit rate declines with each additional dollar held in money balances. At a given level of income and wealth, the share of money in asset accumulation is increased, then, only as alternative assets become more expensive—as the market rate of interest declines and so compensates the investor less generously for the possible hazards of holding nonmonetary assets.

In general equilibrium, present prices of all financial assets fall into the design that leaves no investor an opportunity to increase the anticipated yield on his total portfolio by shifting from any one asset to any other. Money stands at its invariable price, and the other assets are arrayed at the various discounts of present price relative to maturity price that equalize their yields with the deposit rate of money. The amount of money demanded is not dependent only on the liquidity of money; it is dependent on the relative attractions of money, at its price, and of other assets, at their respective prices.

Asset Differentiation and Monetary Equilibrium

Differentiation of primary securities provides spending units with a variety of financial assets to hold in addition to the gilt-edge bond and money that were admitted to our second model in Chapter III. One result is that our analysis of money in that chapter must be extended in two ways. First, the stock of primary debt and financial assets is larger for each level of real wealth and real income, because mixed asset-debt positions are encouraged by differentiation and possibly also because propensities to incur budget deficits and surpluses are increased. Second, with diversified alternatives to money available, one should expect a reduction in real money demanded as a proportion of total financial assets. There are bonds to hold, as well as money, on the chance of price deflation; bills to hold, as well as money, on the chance of a rise in the bond rate; equities to hold, in preference to money, on the chance of price or profit inflation. Differentiation is expected to have both wealth (or scale) and substitution effects on the desired level of real money balances.

The second result of differentiation is the topic of this section. It may be put very simply, that money is likely to "matter" in greater degree for the real variables of an economic system when financial assets are more highly differentiated. Money was neutral in both the first and second models until we introduced a combination of inside and outside money; changes in nominal money had no effect in general equilibrium on the real stock of money, on real balances desired, or on the rate of interest. Now that we allow for differentiation of primary securities, changes in nominal money may result in new levels of real money in existence and desired as well as in related adjustments of the interest rate and output. Such real effects of variations in nominal money do not depend on any relaxation of neo-classical ground rules of monetary analysis.

In the first and second models, one with outside money only and the other with inside money only, spending units could neutralize changes in nominal money by equiproportional changes in the price level and, in the second model, in nominal (or the number of) bonds. Given a combination of inside and outside money, equiproportional changes in nominal money, the price level, and the number of bonds did not restore real conditions of an initial equilibrium. By buying inside bonds, the monetary authority could increase the equilibrium ratio of real money to real bonds in spending units' portfolios and also reduce the aggregate real value of these portfolios. It could bring downward pressure to bear upon the rate of interest through changes in both the composition and the scale of spending units' financial assets.

At an earlier point in the present chapter, we suggested that the composition and scale of spending units' portfolios are vulnerable to purchases and sales by the Banking Bureau of real-bonds. If nominal money is increased by open-market purchases of real-bonds, an equiproportional increase in the price level and in the nominal value of primary securities leaves spending units with an unchanged real stock of money and a reduced real stock of real-bonds. The monetary system, in effect, hoodwinks spending units into surrendering something (a real value in bonds) for nothing (a nominal value in money). The outcome is a fall in the rate of interest.

One can construct literally dozens of financial-asset combinations—with or without outside money and outside bonds, including government bonds—that provide the monetary authority with a lever for manipulating the real stock of money and the real stock desired. Imagine, for example, that spending units hold inside money, inside bills, and inside bonds. Let the monetary authority double nominal money by purchase of bonds, raising the proportion of bonds to bills in its own portfolio. Then the real conditions of an initial general equilibrium cannot be restored by a doubling of the price level, nominal bills, and nominal bonds. With all nominal quantities increased equiproportionally, the monetary system holds a larger proportion of bonds than before, a smaller proportion of bills, while spending units have a smaller proportion of outstanding bonds and a larger proportion of bills. Real money balances are the same at the doubled price level, but they are in excess supply because the substitution in spending units' portfolios of bills for bonds has reduced the desired level of real balances. By raising the average maturity of its own portfolio, the monetary authority has reduced the average maturity of spending units' portfolios and displaced demand for money. In this case, monetary management ultimately turns out to be debt management in the sense that it unfunds private holdings of primary securities. Its effect is to depress rates of interest.

If the monetary authority adds only bills to its portfolio, decreasing the average maturity of its own earning assets, the result is a real funding of primary securities in private portfolios. At a price level increased in proportion with nominal money, spending units are discontented with their initial real money balances and demand more, because their portfolios are more heavily weighted with bonds relative to bills and money. There is an excess demand for money. In this case, a bills-only policy raises rates of interest and restrains real growth.

Consider one more of many possible experiments in monetary management by the Banking Bureau. In an initial equilibrium, spending units hold inside money based on (inside) bills owned by the Bureau, and their portfolios also contain inside bills and bonds. We imagine that nominal money is doubled, not by security purchases of the Banking Bureau, but by money issues to finance governmental deficit spending. Now a doubling of the price level reduces by half the real value of bills in the Bureau's portfolio, and there is a corresponding gain in real value of bills held by spending units —after nominal bills and bonds have doubled with the price level. The gain in real value of bills changes the financial position of spending units in two ways: it is a capital gain, which tends to increase the real demand for money; and it raises the proportion of bills to money and bonds combined, which tends to decrease the real demand for money. Some net effect on the real demand for money is to be expected, along with appropriate changes in rates of interest and the price level.

Contrary to net-money doctrine and to traditional formulations of quantity theory, the volume and structure of inside debt and financial assets is relevant both to the demand function for real money balances and to the ability of the monetary authority to impose its influence on such real variables as the interest rate, income, employment, and wealth. Consolidation of inside claims and counterclaims distorts relationships between real and financial variables, concealing numerous possible cases of money's nonneutrality. An economy's structure of gross financial assets and gross debt is potentially a factor affecting output and wealth in any state of general equilibrium and the growth rates of output and wealth in any process of balanced development.

Historical Growth in Demand for Money

The proportion of real money balances to real national income increased in the United States throughout the nineteenth century, and then, after the early 1900's, fluctuated around a plateau. That is to say, the income velocity of money (demand deposits and currency) declined, then moved above and below an apparently rather stable norm. One explanation of the century-long rise in the money-income ratio is that the income elasticity of demand for money exceeds unity—that money qualifies as a luxury good.

This may be the right explanation, but there are others to be tested before it can qualify as a law of financial growth. Over the period during which the money-income ratio rose, the ratio of financial assets in spending units' portfolios to national income also rose. And roughly over the period of stability in the money-income ratio, the ratio of financial assets to income stabilized. If the growth of financial assets did have the effect we suggest on the demand for money, trends in the financial asset-income ratio could have accounted for the observed behavior of the money-income relationship and velocity. That is to say, the ratio of money to income may have risen before 1900 because the demand for money was stimulated by the accumulation of financial assets relative to income. And perhaps the money-income ratio has tended to stabilize in the past half century because financial assets have accumulated in rough proportion to income levels.

There are other factors to be considered, however. In recent decades, differentiation of primary securities has tended to reduce the demand for money relative to income. Government securities, both federal and other, have become a much larger component of financial assets, so that the stock of primary securities has become more gilt-edge. Gilt-edgeness has been enhanced, too, by governmental guarantees of private primary issues and by monetary policies that have mitigated short-period fluctuations in some security prices. Furthermore, secular deflation of the price level during the latter part of the nineteenth century has given way to secular inflation in the twentieth century. Commodity prices have risen at a rate of roughly 2¼ per cent annually since 1900. The effect of this should be a growing aversion to money in asset portfolios and a shift relatively of preference toward securities that are protected against loss of purchasing power by some version of the purchasing-power clause.

On the other side, the demand for money relative to income has tended to rise in the past several decades owing to a long-run fall in market rates of interest. A secular fall in interest rates, making bonds more expensive in terms of money, tends to shift investor preference from bonds to money. There are other factors that may well have contributed to the historic trend in income velocity of money including, as we shall suggest in Chapter VI, the development of nonmonetary financial intermediaries.

Policy Implications of Growth in Demand for Money

In the growth process the market for money balances is bombarded continuously by disturbances that affect both the demand side and the supply side of the market. The real stock of money is subject to change by reason of change in either nominal stocks of money or the price level. Real balances desired may tend to rise because of growth in population, real income, and real portfolios or because falling rates of interest raise the cost of other financial assets in terms of money. Real balances desired may tend to fall because of increasing efficiency in the payments mechanism or because progressive differentiation of financial assets lowers the marginal utility of money as a defensive asset. The money market is continuously thrown off balance in the growth process and must seek out new positions of equilibrium.

The essential problem of monetary policy is to determine whether the excess demand for money that is endemic in the growth process is to be resolved by expansion in nominal money, by price deflation, or by various adjustments in real phenomena that hold growth in the demand for money in check—by an increase in interest rates, a slackening of growth in output and employment, or restraint on growth in portfolios. In a growth context, should the Policy Bureau order expansion in nominal money, or should it rely on "natural forces" to increase real balances by deflation or to restrain money demand by retarded growth in goods, labor, and bonds?

THE QUANTITY-THEORY SOLUTION

There is a model of economic activity—the "quantity-theory" model—according to which nothing real is at stake in the Policy Bureau's decision. The decision just does not matter in terms of any real economic magnitude such as the rate of growth of output. Any excess demand for money precipitated by the growth process is a "purely monetary" phenomenon that may be worked out either by a falling price level or an increasing nominal stock of money, and the choice between the two is arbitrary and adventitious. No law of growth can be specified for nominal money and the nominal size of the monetary system.

In this model, the rate of growth in the real demand for money, and the manner in which that demand is satisfied, affect none of the conditions of growth on markets for labor, capital, and output. Hence, the accumulation of primary debt and financial assets is a purely financial phenomenon with no relevance to the rate of interest that equates saving and investment, to total output, or to any other real variable. Even if financial accumulation were to stimulate growth in the real demand for money, and so require more rapid growth in nominal money or more rapid decay of the price level, it would have no other real consequences. Count money net of inside balances or count it gross; introduce financial determinants into the money-demand function or leave them out; only the market for money is involved.

No one contends that this quantity-theory world is the real world and that monetary policy is trivial in that it affects only the price level. In the quantity-theory world, prices for goods and labor would be perfectly flexible, in the sense that they would adjust without lag to correct an excess demand for or stock of money, restoring monetary equilibrium as quickly as it could be restored by a change in nominal money. Any primary debt would be so adjustable that changes in the price level would have no more severe distributive effects, as between debtors and creditors, than would changes in nominal money. Spending units would understand the purposes of changes in the price level or interest rate and would not interpret any rise or fall as the first step in cumulative inflation or deflation; elasticity of price expectations would be unity on markets for goods, labor, and bonds. Spending units would not be deceived by money illusion, in the sense that it would be of no importance to behavior whether adjustments in real money balances were to come about by adjustment in nominal money or in the price level. No one sees the real world this way.

A MODIFIED QUANTITY-THEORY SOLUTION

The quantity-theory solution for equilibrium on the money market, in a growth context, is designed for a neo-classical world. But a little tinkering may appear to make it applicable to the real world. One may allow for inflexibility of price and wage levels in the short run; price levels do not really change as quickly as the monetary system can adjust nominal money. It may be conceded that a change in the price level has distributive effects, for a time, and that unstable expectations regarding the price level and interest rates can have destabilizing consequences for the money market. Perhaps there is a degree of money illusion, so that spending units do after all respond differently to an adjustment in the real money stock when it comes about by a change in nominal money than when it results from a change in the price level.

However, one might argue, these neurotic aspects of the real world—its deviation from the quantity-theory world—are remediable. Prices are flexible in the long run, and their sensitivity to an excess demand for money can be increased by destroying elements of monopoly in the price structure. Distributive effects are probably not important to aggregative activity, and their inequities can be corrected by the purchasing-power clause. Spending units can be taught to think in real terms. There are structural reforms that can move the real world so closely to the image of the quantity-theory world that a change in nominal money would not be significantly preferable to a change in the price level as a way of maintaining equilibrium on the money market.

However, until these reforms take place, monetary policy does have a contribution to make to real growth. Price deflation has undesirable short-period effects on markets other than the money market, so that an expansion in nominal money is the efficient solution for growth in the real demand for money. Expansion in nominal money side-steps the real costs of price inflexibility, of distribution effects from a change in the price level, of unstable price expectations, or of the presence of money illusion.

The right kind of monetary policy sets about to make the real world as much in the image of the quantity-theory world as it can, pending structural reform. It contributes to real growth by clearing the money market of excess demand so that this excess demand may not feed back to other markets and retard growth in output. As an "artificial" substitute for the "natural force" of price deflation, it does not permit growth in the demand for money to interrupt real development.

On this modified quantity-theory view, more is to be lost than gained by provoking inflation in the price level. Inflation may transfer income temporarily from consumers to investors or wealth from savers to firms, intensifying capital accumulation, but the investment based on forced saving is likely to be temporary and time will reverse the distribution effects. In the long run, growth in nominal money at a rate faster than the rate of growth in real demand for money will simply induce inflation without real effects, good or bad. Secular inflation, then, may have unfortunate immediate results, in terms of equity and efficiency, and will have neutral results over the long run. In a world not quite like the quantity-theory world, price stability would be the course of wisdom; price deflation could eventually be made a feasible alternative; and price inflation would have only illusory advantages. The worst of all policy alternatives is erratic intervention by the monetary authority. Such mischief on the money market precludes rational responses to relative prices and touches off such unpredictable variation in the absolute price level that optimal real growth, its fruits equitably distributed, is out of the question.

THE KEYNESIAN OR SECULAR-STAGNATION VIEW

In a secular-stagnation model, monetary policy may be as trivial as in the quantity-theory model, but for different reasons. A mature society is so heavily stocked with tangible wealth that marginal rent on new investment sufficient to maintain full employment is very low indeed. An equally low bond rate of interest cannot be realized through expansion of nominal money, except possibly in enormous amounts that imply a virtual monopoly of bond-holding by the monetary authority, because the risk of loss on bonds keeps the marginal implicit deposit rate above marginal rent. Nor can expansion in real money through price deflation bring about a full-employment level of investment. The reason here is either that prices are rigid or that deflation arouses expectations of further deflation and so raises the marginal implicit deposit rate still higher relative to marginal rent and the full-employment rate of interest.

According to this view, there is chronic excess demand for money at full employment, and no device of monetary policy alone can feasibly satisfy this excess demand. The excess demand can be dispelled by unemployment. It can be dispelled, too, by government investment or by special stimuli to private spending that counteract the drag upon growth caused by the low return to tangible wealth. And there is a substantial advantage over the long run in combining such inducements to real demands for goods and labor with enough expansion in nominal money to guarantee secular inflation. With inflation in prospect, the implicit deposit rate of money is reduced, the demand for money is economized, and there is less excess demand for money to be overcome by special programs to accelerate growth. Once the inflationary process is under way, its pace may be set by the "push" of imperfectly competitive prices and wage rates, and then it is the duty of the monetary authority to increase nominal money appropriately so that real money balances do not lag behind demand for them.

Money is trivial for secular stagnationists, but it is not trivial in the sense that it is neutral. Neutrality is not relevant because the price structure is shot through with rigidities, expectations regarding the price level and the interest rate are unstable, distribution effects of price changes may be significant for growth, and money illusion is commonplace. Money is trivial in the sense that monetary expansion alone cannot satisfy an excess demand for money at full employment in a mature society. If monetary policy tolerates price deflation, it is inimical to the public welfare, damping growth. Monetary policy congenial to some slow rate of inflation is not trivial, and is in the social interest, since it may induce private sectors to provide some of the growth in effective demand for output that would otherwise devolve upon government.

THE CASE FOR GROWTH IN NOMINAL MONEY

In any model of growth there tends to be endemic excess demand for money. The quantity-theory model resolves this excess demand, without lag or retardation in real growth, by either price deflation or expansion in nominal money, and there is no basis for choice in the model between these two alternatives. The modified quantity-theory model, applying to an economic system that is handicapped by rigidities and irrationalities, would have growth in the demand for money satisfied by growth in nominal money rather than by price deflation, because the latter may retard real development. The stagnation model has it that excess demand for money cannot be resolved consistently by either an expansion in nominal money or price deflation. The first and third of these models deny money a significant role in the growth process, while the second concedes that monetary policy has a contribution to make until structural reform can be imposed on the economy. No one of the three models is calculated to inflate the monetary authority's self-esteem.

Our own views on monetary policy in the growth process do not coincide with any one of these three models. We object to the basic premise of quantity theory that money is neutral, even with reference to an economy in which the neoclassical ground rules of analysis are appropriate. We object on the basis of our demonstration that—through manipulation of nominal money—the Policy Bureau can impose permanent capital gains or losses on spending units, can affect the mix or balance of spending units' portfolios, and hence can come to grips with real aspects of economic behavior. Acting as a financial intermediary, the monetary system can intervene in the flow of securities from borrowers to lenders, regulating in some degree the rate and pattern of private financial-asset accumulation, the real stock of money and real balances desired, and hence any demands for goods and labor that are sensitive to the real value of financial variables. Quantity theory underestimates the real impact of monetary policy in the long run.

Even if one grants the long-run neutrality of money, as we do not, it can still follow that price deflation is an ungainly and costly technique of adapting real money to demand for it. It seems axiomatic to us that no feasible structural reforms can transform the real world into the image of the quantity-theory world. This means that price deflation is subject to special handicaps, not applying to expansion in nominal money, in adjusting real balances to those desired—the handicaps of rigid prices, unstable expectations, distribution effects, and money illusion.

As real demand for money increases during the growth process, nominal money should increase with it. This is not a complete specification for an ideal monetary policy, because growth in the real demand for money at a relatively stable price level is itself subject to some degree of influence from the "credit policy" of the monetary system, that is, from the system's choice of primary securities for its own portfolio. It does make a difference to growth in the demand for real balances whether the monetary system intermediates in bills or bonds, nominal-bonds or real-bonds, inside securities or outside, open-market securities or those from the less competitive segments of the bond market. In determining the right rate of growth in nominal money, the ideal monetary system accepts the presumption in favor of a stable price level and, in addition, sets its real objectives for bringing influence to bear on the real demand for money through the composition of its own portfolio. Until more is known about the money-demand function, the monetary authority is probably wise, for the time being, to set its sights simply on price-level stability. But neither quantity theory nor secular-stagnation theory justifies our assuming that research into the money-demand function will not reveal opportunities for the monetary system to exert significant real effects in the long run on interest rates and the pace of growth in capital and output.

Summary

In the previous chapter we considered growth in the quantity and quality of primary securities in preparation for discussing in this chapter how such development in nonmonetary finance affects monetary growth. There is an approach to monetary theory, however, that would say that development of nonmonetary finance is irrelevant to real aggregative behavior and in particular to analysis of the money market. This is net-money doctrine. Our approach may be termed gross-money doctrine.

Net-money doctrine consolidates private domestic accounts so that private domestic debt cancels out against an equivalent amount of private domestic financial assets in both monetary and nonmonetary form. The only financial assets remaining in aggregative analysis are those held by the private sectors as net claims against the outside world—against, that is, government and the foreign sector. Thus, money, as part of these outside financial assets, is itself entirely of the outside variety. According to net-money doctrine, the quantity and quality of private domestic debt and its counterparts—inside debt and financial assets—are irrelevant to aggregative analysis and in particular to the demand for money and to the stock of money.

There are five objections to net-money doctrine. First, it consolidates and deconsolidates social accounts capriciously; it consolidates private domestic spending units to eliminate their claims and counterclaims, but then it deconsolidates them so that they may haggle over a price for these nonexistent securities—for the interest rate is a determinant of real demands. Second, net-money doctrine implies that the price level is indeterminate when the economy contains only inside money and securities; the falsity of this view was demonstrated in Chapter III. Third, the doctrine assumes that a change in nominal inside money cannot affect the real variables of the economy in the long run, within the neo-classical framework; this, too, is not true. Fourth, net-money doctrine implies that the quantity of inside debt and its counterparts in financial assets have no net effects on the aggregate real demand for money, but this overlooks the desire for diversified financial positions by both firms and consumers. Finally, the doctrine distinguishes too sharply between the behavior of private domestic sectors and that of outside sectors.

Stockpiling of financial assets is a defensive measure for spending units in a hostile economy, much as stockpiling of weapons is a defensive measure for nations in a hostile world. And in each case diversification of the stock usually pays off. Spending units' demand for money, as one financial asset among many, depends partly on the types of frictions and uncertainties associated with alternative financial assets.

When an alternative to money-holding is long-term bonds, money can be a defense against a rise in the bond rate. When an alternative is real-bonds, which promise payment in fixed real sums of money, money can be a means of exploiting a fall in the price level. When an alternative is real-bonds with a productivity clause, which specifies payments equal to some stable proportion of business income, money can be a defense against shrinkage of business profits. When an alternative is non-gilt-edge bonds, it can be a defense against default of payment. Finally, when an alternative is bonds with low marketability, it can be a defense against illiquidity in the form of high transactions costs and thin markets.

Within the neo-classical framework, money was neutral in its effects on the real variables in our rudimentary and second economies, until we introduced a combination of inside and outside money. Now that we allow for differentiation of primary securities, changes in nominal money may result in changes in the interest rate, output, and wealth, even when all money is of the inside variety. The reason is that the monetary system can alter the composition of spending units' portfolios by dealing in only one of the several types of primary securities outstanding. For example, if the monetary system, holding both bills and bonds, creates nominal money by purchasing only bonds, it can reduce the average maturity of spending units' portfolios and thus alter their demand for real money balances.

The essential problem of monetary policy is to determine whether the excess demand for money that develops during output growth is to be resolved by expansion in nominal money, by price deflation, or by an increase in the interest rate and a slackening of output growth. The quantity-theory model dissipates the excess demand for money by either price deflation or an increase in nominal money, and the choice between the two does not matter. The modified quantity-theory model, applying to an economy that is handicapped by rigidities and irrationalities, satisfies excess demand for money by growth in nominal money rather than price deflation because the latter would retard real development. In the secular-stagnation view, there is chronic excess demand for money at full employment, and no device of monetary policy alone can feasibly satisfy this excess demand. The first and third models deny money a significant role in the growth process, while the second concedes that monetary policy has a contribution to make until structural reform can be imposed on the economy.

CHAPTER VI

Nonmonetary Financial Intermediation

WE HAVE LOOKED THUS FAR at the financial aspects of economic activity with a minimum of financial institutions in the picture. Financial assets have consisted of primary securities and money, the former created by nonfinancial spending units and the latter by a governmental monetary system. This monetary system was the only financial institution in the analysis. It will be retained in this chapter so that we can delay considering those determinants of the money supply that reflect profit considerations of a private banking system and the network of controls employed by a central bank over its members; a monetary system of this type will be introduced in the next chapter. Our intention now is to consider the activities of those financial institutions that are commonly known as nonbank intermediaries. However, we shall refer to them as "nonmonetary" intermediaries, to indicate that even though some of them are called banks they do not create money.

The first section below discusses some of the elements of intermediation. The next two sections analyze the markets for nonmonetary indirect assets, including that of time deposits of the monetary system, the various ways in which the activities of nonmonetary intermediaries disturb equilibrium on the markets for money and primary securities, the effects of government financial activities on financial markets, and the favorable and unfavorable climates for the growth of nonmonetary intermediaries. We then examine, within the general-equilibrium framework, the conditions under which money is neutral when nonmonetary intermediaries are on the scene, and finally the effectiveness of monetary policy in the presence of these intermediaries.

Elements of Intermediation

Economists disagree concerning the role of financial institutions in economic activity. What part do these institutions play in the saving-investment process? How do nonmonetary intermediaries differ from commercial banks or the monetary system? In what sense do commercial banks act as intermediaries? In the following pages we address ourselves to these and similar questions.

FUNCTIONS AND TYPES OF INTERMEDIARIES

The principal function of financial intermediaries is to purchase primary securities from ultimate borrowers and to issue indirect debt for the portfolios of ultimate lenders. Although primary securities are their principal asset, financial intermediaries also hold the indirect debt of other intermediaries and own tangible assets as well.

Financial intermediaries may be divided into two main groups: the monetary system and nonmonetary intermediaries. The monetary system, in its intermediary role, purchases primary securities and creates money. In its role as administrator of the payments mechanism, the monetary system transfers deposit credits on its ledgers between spending units. Nonmonetary intermediaries, in contrast, perform only the intermediary role of purchasing primary securities and creating nonmonetary claims on themselves, which take the form of savings deposits, shares, equities, and other obligations. These claims are nonmonetary indirect debts or financial assets, depending on whether they are looked at from the standpoint of the issuer or the holder.

There are various criteria for classifying nonmonetary financial intermediaries. Some intermediaries are private, others governmental. Mutual savings banks, savings and loan associations, private life insurance companies, and credit unions, among others, are included in the former category. Federal land banks, the Postal Savings System, and government insurance and pension funds, among others, are in the latter. Some of the private intermediaries are incorporated for stockholders' profit, and some are mutuals or cooperatives. Most make purchases from a narrow band of primary securities—mortgages, or corporate equities, or government securities—while a few purchase a wide assortment. Many intermediaries issue only a few varieties of indirect debt, but others, such as life insurance companies, issue a bewildering array of debt. A few intermediaries, principally sales finance companies, rely heavily on other intermediaries as purchasers of their indirect debt.

The product of intermediation is the indirect financial asset coined from the underlying primary security and bearing its own bundle of utilities. The reward of intermediation arises from the difference between the rate of return on primary securities held by intermediaries and the interest or dividend rate they pay on their indirect debt. There are notable differences in the utilities provided by indirect financial assets. These utilities command a market price and yield a profit to intermediation. Money is a means of payment; claims on life insurance companies provide a defense against misfortune; shares in mutual funds offer opportunities for portfolio diversification and capital gains; shares in credit unions and deposits in mutual savings banks provide utilities of convenience and perhaps camaraderie; shares in savings and loan associations may give one future access to mortgage funds, and so on. Yet there are also notable similarities among indirect financial assets. For most of them there is a constant or determinable redemption value, investment costs are low, and contracts are divisible into convenient units from low to high denomination. In these and other respects, indirect financial assets are a class apart from the bulk of primary securities that are the raw material for the process of intermediation.

Financial intermediaries exploit economies of scale in lending and borrowing. On the lending side, the intermediary can invest and manage investments in primary securities at unit costs far below the experience of most individual lenders. The sheer size of its portfolio permits a significant reduction in risks through diversification. It can schedule maturities so that chances of liquidity crises are minimized. The mutual or cooperative is sometimes favored with tax benefits that are not available to the individual saver. On the borrowing side, the intermediary with a large number of depositors can normally rely on a predictable schedule of claims for repayment and so can get along with a portfolio that is relatively illiquid. The advantages of large-scale borrowing and lending with numerous creditors and debtors can be distributed to the intermediary's debtors in the form of favorable terms of lending, to its creditors in the form of interest payments and other benefits, and to its stockholders in the form of sufficient dividends to attract additional capital funds.

Because economies of scale are important, the assets and liabilities of intermediaries are highly specialized. On the asset side, savings and loan associations and to a lesser degree mutual savings banks specialize in mortgages, sales finance companies and credit unions in consumer loans, investment companies in corporate equities, and life insurance companies to a large extent in corporate and government bonds. On the liability side, many intermediaries sell only deposits at short-term. A few sell only shares, and some only pension equities. Given the environment of primary security issues, specialization by intermediaries tends to increase their chances for survival. But such specialization may work against them when the environment changes. A downturn in building activity abruptly dampens the growth rate of savings and loan associations. Sales finance companies languish when consumer durable purchases decline, and land banks when agriculture is depressed. More generally, since most nonmonetary intermediaries specialize in private rather than government primary securities, the virtual disappearance of private borrowing in wartime and the preponderance of government issues selling at high, pegged prices slows them down considerably.

There are also external economies associated with the growth of financial intermediaries. External economies are particularly evident and important in the case of the monetary system. An efficient monetary system is an essential condition for real growth in the community. But external economies are important, too, in the cases of social and private insurance or even of mortgage and consumer finance. Consequently, for this and other reasons, the community takes a special interest in intermediation, imposing on it an exceptional degree of regulation to insure, among other things, that potential external economies are realized.

INTERMEDIARIES IN THE SAVING-INVESTMENT PROCESS

Intermediating techniques tend to raise the levels of saving and investment and to allocate more efficiently scarce savings among alternative investment opportunities. Their role in the saving-investment process is very much like the role of other techniques that have been previously examined, and will be reviewed briefly.

An economy without financial assets would require each spending unit to invest in new tangible assets whatever part of its current income was not consumed, assuming that there is no trading in existing tangible assets. No unit could invest more than its saving because there would be no way to finance the excess expenditures. And no unit could invest less than its saving because there would be no financial assets in which to put the excess saving. Each spending unit would be forced into a balanced budget position, with saving equal to investment. This sort of arrangement would very likely lead to a relatively low level of investment and saving and, hence, to a relatively low growth rate of output.

The absence of financial assets, moreover, would bring about an inefficient allocation of resources. An ordering of investment opportunities by their expected rates of return almost always implies investment by some spending units that exceeds their saving (that is, deficits) and investment by others that falls short of their saving (that is, surpluses). But without financial assets this efficient ordering of investment cannot often be achieved. Relatively inferior investment projects are undertaken and many of the superior ones go by the boards simply because there is no efficient way to distribute investment projects among spending units in a manner that differs from the distribution of saving among them.

The presence of money balances would improve the situation, as we indicated in Chapter II, for these balances would permit some spending units with highly promising investment opportunities to make investment expenditures in excess of their saving, and would allow others, who do not have such opportunities, to save in excess of their real investment through the accumulation of money. By allowing some specialization among spending units in investment and saving, money opens up the possibility for a more efficient ordering of investment throughout the economy. Other financial techniques, such as the formation of partnerships, the holding of lotteries, and transfers of existing tangible assets, work in the same direction.

Further improvement is possible by the development of external financing through primary security issues—by the development of distributive and intermediating techniques. Distributive techniques get primary securities distributed efficiently from borrower to lender and from one lender to another, through such facilities as dealers and security exchanges. They tend to raise the level of investment and saving by increasing the marginal utility of the last dollar's worth of financial assets to the lender and reducing the marginal disutility of the last dollar's worth of debt to the borrower. At the same time, they tend to increase the efficiency of resource allocation by pitting more investment projects against one another for lenders to examine.

Intermediating techniques turn primary securities into indirect securities for the portfolios of ultimate lenders. They give lenders a wide variety of financial assets particularly suited to their needs, and they also make it less necessary for borrowers to issue these types of securities, which are ill-adapted to their own businesses. Financial intermediaries, too, are capable of improving the efficiency of distributive techniques in many ways. Their role in the saving-investment process is quite similar to that of distributive techniques, lotteries, or land sales. They enable spending units to escape the strait jacket of balanced budgets and to order their spendings more efficiently.

INTERMEDIARIES AND CREATION OF FINANCIAL ASSETS

All financial intermediaries create financial assets. The monetary system creates money when it purchases primary securities. Other intermediaries create various forms of nonmonetary indirect assets when they purchase money. Moreover, nonfinancial spending units can create primary securities by purchasing money. Each financial asset, quite obviously, is created by someone.

The difference between the monetary system and nonmonetary intermediaries in this respect, then, is not that one creates and the other does not, but rather that each creates its own unique form of debt. And the difference in this respect between nonfinancial spending units and financial intermediaries is that the former create primary securities and the latter create indirect securities. These are, of course, differences, but there is nothing in these processes of creation to suggest that we should stand in awe of one to the neglect of the other. In each case the financial asset is created by the purchase of another financial asset—or, in some cases, by the purchase of tangible assets.

The Banking Bureau of our governmental monetary system may purchase various types of primary securities. It may, therefore, create money in an amount that is a multiple of any one type of primary security it holds. If for some reason the Policy Bureau instructed the Banking Bureau to hold a certain type of primary security in an amount equal to some fraction of its monetary liabilities, the Banking Bureau would be able to create money by some multiple of these "legal reserves." Nonmonetary intermediaries initially purchase currency and demand deposits when creating nonmonetary indirect securities. In the same way, then, these intermediaries can create liabilities by some multiple of either their currency or their deposit balances. And since the intermediaries can then sell money for primary securities, they can create liabilities by some multiple of any one type of asset they hold. If intermediaries were subject to quantitative controls, they, too, would create liabilities by a multiple of their "legal reserves" —by a multiple of the one type of asset they were required to hold.

Money is unlike other financial assets, for it is the means of payment. Corporate stocks are unlike other financial assets, too, for they carry ownership rights in corporations. And policyholders' equities in insurance companies are different because they are linked to certain insurance attributes. The fact is that there is differentiation of financial assets throughout the economy.

THE PROCESS OF INTERMEDIATION: INDIRECT FINANCE

When the distribution of income among spending units is exactly the same as the distribution of spending among them, all units have balanced budgets on income and product account. In this case all expenditures for current output are internally financed. However, when income and spending distributions differ, some spending units have surpluses and others an equivalent amount of deficits, *ex-post*. Surplus units supply options on current output equal to their surpluses and in return acquire an equivalent amount of net financial assets—that is, financial assets less debts incurred and equities issued. Deficit units take up and exercise these options, paying for them by increasing their net debt and equity (other than earned surplus). These budget imbalances normally lead to net issues of primary securities, and net accumulations of financial assets.

There are three channels through which primary security issues may flow. First, as before, these issues may be sold directly to other nonfinancial spending units. Second, as before, they may be sold to the monetary system, in which case the ultimate lenders acquire money instead of primary securities. The third and new method is that primary securities may be sold to nonmonetary financial intermediaries, the ultimate lenders acquiring nonmonetary indirect assets instead of primary securities or money. The first case is direct finance; the last two are cases of intermediation, of indirect finance.

The role of nonmonetary intermediaries in this process can best be seen if we trace out the method of external financing in each of the three cases. Suppose, for simplification, that spending units with deficits issue primary securities in an amount equal to their deficits, and that surplus units acquire an equivalent amount of financial assets. When the external financing is direct, the deficit units sell primary securities to surplus units, receiving previously-created demand deposits in the monetary system. These deposits are then spent for current output by the deficit units—otherwise they would not be deficit units—and the deposits eventually return to surplus units. The latter now have additional financial assets—the same amount of money and more primary securities—which represent their surplus on income and product account.

When there is intermediation by the monetary system, the deficit units sell their primary securities to the monetary system and receive newly-created demand deposits. These deposits are then spent by the deficit units for current output. Surplus units eventually acquire the deposits, which represent the amount of options on current output they have released to deficit units. In these transactions, the deficit units have created primary securities, the monetary system has created money, and the surplus units have acquired financial assets as a reward for not spending on the market for current output. Unspent incomes have been transferred from surplus to deficit units through the intermediation of the monetary system.

Nonmonetary Financial Intermediation

Let us, finally, trace the process of indirect finance through nonmonetary intermediaries. Surplus units write checks on their demand deposits in the monetary system and present these checks to nonmonetary intermediaries. In return they receive claims on these intermediaries—that is, nonmonetary indirect assets. The intermediaries endorse the checks and send them to the monetary system, receiving the demand deposits given up by the surplus units. The intermediaries then use these deposits to purchase primary securities from deficit units.[1] The latter now have the demand deposits. These deposits are next spent by the deficit units for current output, and they are eventually received by the surplus units. The surplus units end up with the same amount of demand deposits that they started with but they now have more nonmonetary indirect assets, which represent the unspent income they have transferred to deficit units.

In these transactions, the deficit units have again created primary securities, nonmonetary intermediaries have created nonmonetary indirect assets, and the surplus units have acquired financial assets as a reward for not spending on the market for current output. The nominal size of the monetary system, measured by assets or liabilities, has not changed: the same amount of demand deposits remains outstanding throughout the transactions. The deposits are transferred from surplus units to nonmonetary intermediaries, then to deficit units, and finally back to the surplus units. There has been no intermediation by the monetary system; its role has been that of administering the payments mechanism, of transferring deposits on its ledgers.

The monetary system and nonmonetary intermediaries, therefore, are both capable of intermediating in the transfer

1 We are ignoring the small percentage of demand deposits usually retained by the intermediaries. This will be considered below.

of unspent incomes from surplus to deficit units. These financial institutions intermediate in the sense that they themselves do not have the imbalances on income and product account. These imbalances are possessed only by nonfinancial spending units.[2]

There are many similarities between the monetary system and nonmonetary intermediaries, and the similarities are more important than the differences. Both types of financial institution create financial claims; and both may engage in multiple creation of their particular liabilities in relation to any one class of asset that they hold. Both act as intermediaries in the transfer of unspent incomes from surplus to deficit units. Moreover, as we shall show later, both are capable of creating loanable funds, of bringing about an excess stock of money, and of producing an excess of *ex-ante* investment over *ex-ante* saving.

The Market for Nonmonetary Indirect Assets

In previous chapters the economic system was discussed in terms of four markets, those for labor services, current output, money, and primary securities. The economy is in general equilibrium when demand is equal to supply in each of these markets. Now that nonmonetary intermediaries are in the picture we have a fifth market to consider, that for nonmonetary indirect financial assets (excluding for the moment time deposits of the monetary system). This market, like the

[2] Actually, to a small extent, financial intermediaries do have transactions on income and product account, and so they may have a small amount of imbalances. To this extent, they are originators rather than intermediaries in unspent incomes.

others, is described by a demand function, a supply function, and a market-clearing equation. We shall proceed in that order.

THE DEMAND FOR NONMONETARY INDIRECT ASSETS

Spending units' real demand for nonmonetary indirect assets depends on the level of real income, real holdings of financial assets (in both quantity and quality), "the" rate of interest on primary securities, and the explicit deposit rates paid by the monetary system and by nonmonetary intermediaries on their indirect debts. These are also determinants of spending units' real demands for money and primary securities. Additional determinants are the real rental rate on capital goods and the ratio of spending units' primary debt to tangible assets, but we choose to neglect these in the analysis that follows.

A rise in real income, other things the same, has opposing effects on spending units' demand for nonmonetary indirect assets. In the first place, such a rise increases spending units' demand for money, and in attempting to get these additional balances they reduce their demands for other financial assets. Hence, a rise in real income tends to reduce the demand for nonmonetary indirect assets. In the second place, though, the demand for certain types of these assets, such as insurance reserves, pension equities, and so on, may be positively related, though only roughly, to levels of real income. We shall assume that on balance a rise in real income will reduce slightly spending units' real demand for nonmonetary indirect assets.

As financial-asset portfolios increase, there is an increase in spending units' demand for nonmonetary indirect assets. The extent of this incremental demand depends not only on the absolute growth of financial-asset portfolios but also on the composition of this growth—on the mix of primary security issues. If these issues compete actively with the indirect securities of intermediaries, the incremental demand for nonmonetary indirect assets will be depressed. If, on the other hand, the issues are generally repugnant to ultimate lenders, the incremental demand for claims on intermediaries will be stimulated.

A higher interest rate on primary securities reduces the demand for nonmonetary indirect assets, for this makes primary securities cheaper and so more attractive relative to both money and nonmonetary indirect assets, inducing a shift out of indirect assets and into primary securities. A higher explicit deposit rate paid by the monetary system means that money becomes more attractive relative to nonmonetary indirect assets and primary securities and so reduces demands for these assets. Finally, a higher explicit deposit rate paid by nonmonetary intermediaries increases the demand for claims on these intermediaries and draws demand away from money and primary securities.

The real demand for nonmonetary indirect assets is aggregative, applying to all nonfinancial spending units in the economy. Consequently, it is affected by the distribution of financial assets among these units, since some units—consumers, for example—hold a larger proportion of their assets in the form of nonmonetary indirect assets than others do. This factor affects not only the aggregate demand but also the demands for particular types of claims on nonmonetary intermediaries.

THE SUPPLY OF NONMONETARY INDIRECT ASSETS

The willingness of nonmonetary intermediaries to supply claims on themselves, in real terms, depends on the rate of interest on primary securities that they buy, on the deposit rate on nonmonetary indirect debt that they sell, on their variable expenses in managing assets and liabilities, and on the types of primary securities available to them. An increase in the rate of interest on primary securities increases their willingness to supply nonmonetary indirect assets. An increase in their deposit rate or in other variable expenses, on the other hand, reduces their willingness. They will also tend to supply less claims on themselves when the composition of primary securities is unfavorable to their activities. These things constant, their real supply of claims is constant at all price levels of current output.

In the short run, at a given interest rate, an increase in real demand for nonmonetary indirect assets will lower the equilibrium deposit rate because the supply of these assets is not perfectly elastic. In the long run, however, existing firms will expand and new firms will enter the industry, increasing supply sufficiently to restore the previous deposit rate. This assumes constant real returns to the industry in the long run, an assumption adopted here for convenience.

The supply function is aggregative, applying to the community of nonmonetary intermediaries. Since intermediaries specialize in types of primary securities, the interest rate does not move identically in the supply function for each class of intermediary. Hence changes in relative interest rates may produce relative shifts in profit capacity among intermediaries. And changes in relative efficiency in extracting net from gross revenues result in changes in the relative volumes of output that different intermediaries can afford to supply at each deposit rate. Among intermediaries, then, one may expect more or less frequent shifts in competitive advantage as the result of adjustments in the structure of interest rates and in operating efficiency.

It should be noted, too, that the aggregate supply function may include claims offered by governmental nonmonetary intermediaries. If so, allowance must be made for the possibility that the supply of these claims is influenced by factors other than those governing the supply of private indirect claims.

MARKET EQUILIBRIUM

In a competitive setting, the equilibrium level of the deposit rate paid by nonmonetary intermediaries is determined by the intersection of the demand and supply schedules, as shown in Chart VI, which measures the deposit rate on the vertical axis and real nonmonetary indirect assets on the horizontal one. The equilibrium deposit rate in the chart is d'_0. The short-run demand schedule slopes up from left to right because higher deposit rates on these assets make them more desirable compared to both money and primary securities. The short-run supply schedule slopes down from left to right because lower deposit rates increase the willingness of intermediaries to supply claims on themselves. It is assumed that the rate of interest, the monetary system's deposit rate, real financial asset holdings of spending units, and the level of real income, among other things, are given.

At a deposit rate lower than d'_0, the real demand for these assets falls short of the amount that intermediaries want to supply. Competition among intermediaries then tends to push the deposit rate up toward the equilibrium level. At a deposit rate higher than d'_0, demand exceeds supply, and so the deposit rate tends to fall.

An increase in spending units' real holdings of financial assets raises their real demands for money, primary securities, and nonmonetary indirect assets. Thus, the growth of financial-asset portfolios causes the demand schedule in Chart VI to shift to the right. Given the short-run supply schedule, the intermediaries' deposit rate tends to fall, for at the initial deposit rate demand now exceeds supply. In the long run, a growing demand for nonmonetary indirect assets entices more firms into the industry and this shifts the supply schedule to the right. The deposit rate then tends to rise back toward its initial level. The output of the industry is enlarged owing to

CHART VI

Equilibrium in the Market for Nonmonetary Indirect Assets

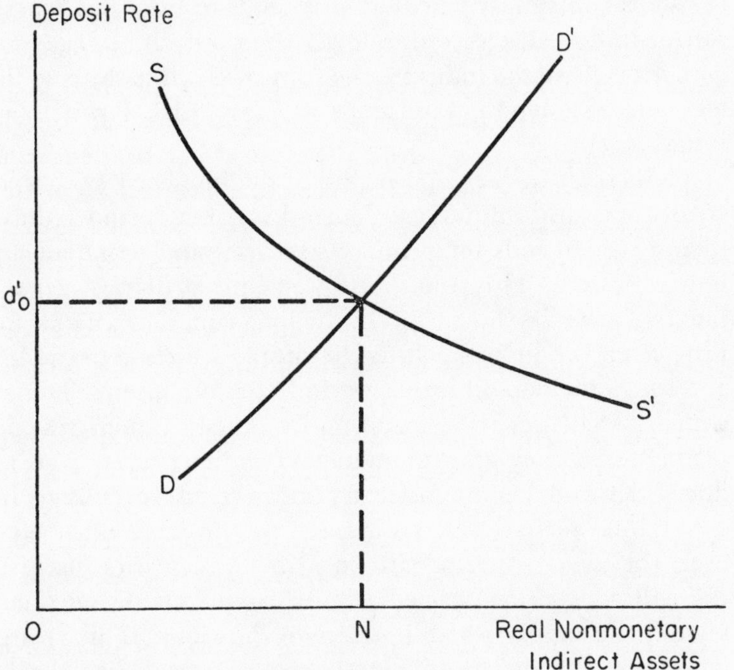

the expansion of existing firms and to the entrance of new ones.

If primary security issues compete actively with claims on intermediaries, the demand schedule shifts to the right by less than it otherwise would. If, at the same time, these issues are not well suited to the business of intermediation, the supply schedule shifts to the left. In the short run, the growth of intermediaries is held back for both reasons. Other compositions of primary issues have different repercussions on the two schedules and so on the growth rate of intermediaries.

A rise in the level of real output, with real holdings of financial assets constant, is assumed to reduce slightly spending units' real demand for nonmonetary indirect assets. Given the short-run supply schedule, this tends to raise the deposit rate of intermediaries and to lower their output. In the long run, firms leave the industry, the supply schedule shifts to the left, and the deposit rate tends to move back down to its initial level.

An increase in the deposit rate of the monetary system increases spending units' real demand for money and reduces their real demands for primary securities and nonmonetary indirect assets. This, too, causes the intermediaries' deposit rate to rise in the short run. In the long run, the exit of some firms from the industry shifts the supply schedule to the left and forces the deposit rate back down. If the interest rate on primary securities rises, spending units reduce their real demands for money and nonmonetary indirect assets; the reduced demand for nonmonetary indirect assets tends to increase intermediaries' deposit rate. At the same time, however, the higher interest rate on primary securities increases the willingness of intermediaries to supply claims on themselves: the supply schedule shifts to the right. This creates additional upward pressure on the deposit rate, which may be further reinforced in the long run by the entrance into the industry of new firms.

Finally, an increase in the price level accompanied by equiproportional changes in all other nominal variables, including nonmonetary indirect assets, leaves all real demands and real supplies the same in the long run. The real size of nonmonetary intermediaries and their deposit rate are unaffected by such nominal changes.

NONCOMPETITIVE ELEMENTS

In a highly competitive environment, nonmonetary intermediaries' deposit rate rises and falls quickly to eliminate an excess stock of and an excess demand for nonmonetary indirect assets. In a less competitive setting, the response of the deposit rate may be more sluggish. Intermediaries may at first attempt to eliminate an excess stock by stepping up their advertising efforts or by offering bonuses and prizes of various sorts to new depositors and shareholders. They may at first attempt to eliminate an excess demand by reducing advertising expenditures, by limiting the amount of money that any one spending unit can deposit, or simply by turning customers away. When the excess demands and stocks are large and persistent, however, the deposit rate eventually responds.

Time Deposits of the Monetary System

Up to now we have allowed the governmental monetary system to issue only money, composed of demand deposits and currency. Nonmonetary indirect assets are created by the other financial intermediaries. We shall now consider an in-between case, the creation of time deposits by the monetary system. Time deposits are not part of the stock of money because they are not means of payment. And they are obviously not primary securities issued by the nonfinancial sectors of the economy. They are properly classified as nonmonetary indirect assets, "nonmonetary" because they are not money, and "indirect" because they are issued by a financial intermediary.

We will first examine the elements of time deposit creation. An analysis of the market for time deposits follows.

THE ELEMENTS OF TIME DEPOSIT CREATION

Suppose that the Policy Bureau instructs the Banking Bureau to sell time deposits to spending units. These deposits bear a positive explicit deposit rate that is set by the Policy Bureau.

When spending units purchase time deposits from the Banking Bureau, they do so with money, usually with checks on their demand deposits. Imagine that $100 of time deposits are purchased in this way. The result is that the demand deposit liabilities of the monetary system are reduced by $100 and time deposit liabilities of the monetary system are increased by the same amount. There is no change in the monetary system's total liabilities or total assets. However, the nominal stock of money is reduced by $100. The same is true when time deposits are purchased with currency. In this case, time deposits rise by $100 and the currency liabilities of the monetary system fall by the same amount. Again, there is no change in the monetary system's total liabilities and total assets, and the nominal stock of money declines by $100.

It is instructive to compare the purchase of time deposits with the purchase of claims on nonmonetary intermediaries. When spending units purchase the latter, the nominal stock of money in the economy—in the portfolios of spending units and nonmonetary intermediaries—is unchanged, while nonmonetary indirect assets are higher. Hence, such purchases raise the total amount of indirect securities in the economy. The purchase of time deposits, on the other hand, increases one type of indirect security and decreases another, leaving the total amount of indirect securities the same. These are, of course, only the initial changes, before the Policy Bureau issues further instructions.

THE MARKET FOR TIME DEPOSITS

When time deposits are offered by the Banking Bureau, the real demands of spending units for money and (other) nonmonetary indirect assets depend not only on the factors already discussed but also on the explicit deposit rate paid by the Banking Bureau on its time deposits and on the amount of such deposits in financial-asset portfolios. The real demands for money and other nonmonetary indirect assets fall when this deposit rate is raised, other things the same.

In addition to the financial markets for money, primary securities, and nonmonetary indirect assets, there is now a market for time deposits. The real demand for time deposits depends on spending units' real holdings of financial assets (as to both quantity and quality), the level of real income, the rate of interest, and the three deposit rates—on demand deposits, nonmonetary indirect assets, and time deposits.

This real demand rises with spending units' real holdings of financial assets and with the deposit rate on time deposits. It falls when the rate of interest on primary securities and the other two deposit rates rise. Finally, we suppose that an increase in real income reduces somewhat the real demand for time deposits, as spending units shift from these to real money balances.

The nominal stock of time deposits is given by the Policy Bureau's instructions to the Banking Bureau. These instructions may authorize the Banking Bureau to supply time deposits in whatever amounts are demanded by spending units at the given deposit rate, as set by the Policy Bureau, or they may authorize something else. There is equilibrium on the market for time deposits when the demand for time deposits is equal to the stock of them.

Nonmonetary Intermediaries and the Demand for Money

It is now time to focus more closely on how the activities of nonmonetary intermediaries affect the demand for money, or, more generally, how they disturb the financial markets. We are not principally concerned here with the feed-in of these disturbances to real markets or the feed-back from real to financial markets. We begin first with a sketch of equilibrium on the money market.

EQUILIBRIUM ON THE MONEY MARKET

The market for money is in equilibrium when the real demand for money is equal to the real stock of money. We suppose that spending units' real demand for money depends on the quantity and quality of their real holdings of financial assets, the level of real income, the rate of interest, and the explicit deposit rates. We are neglecting two other determinants—the real rental rate on capital goods and the ratio of primary debt to capital goods. Spending units' holdings of financial assets may include money, primary securities, and nonmonetary indirect assets (other than time deposits, which will be considered later). The explicit deposit rate on money balances is set by the Policy Bureau.

The nominal stock of money comes from the Banking Bureau as a counterpart to its holdings of primary securities. Given the real demand for money and the price level aimed at by the Policy Bureau, there is only one nominal stock of money that fills the bill.

Equilibrium on the money market is illustrated in Chart VII. The rate of interest on primary securities (or, more accurately, an average of such rates) is measured on the vertical axis and real money balances are plotted on the horizontal one. The demand schedule for money, *DD′*, is drawn on the assumption of given levels of real financial assets, real

CHART VII

Equilibrium on the Money Market

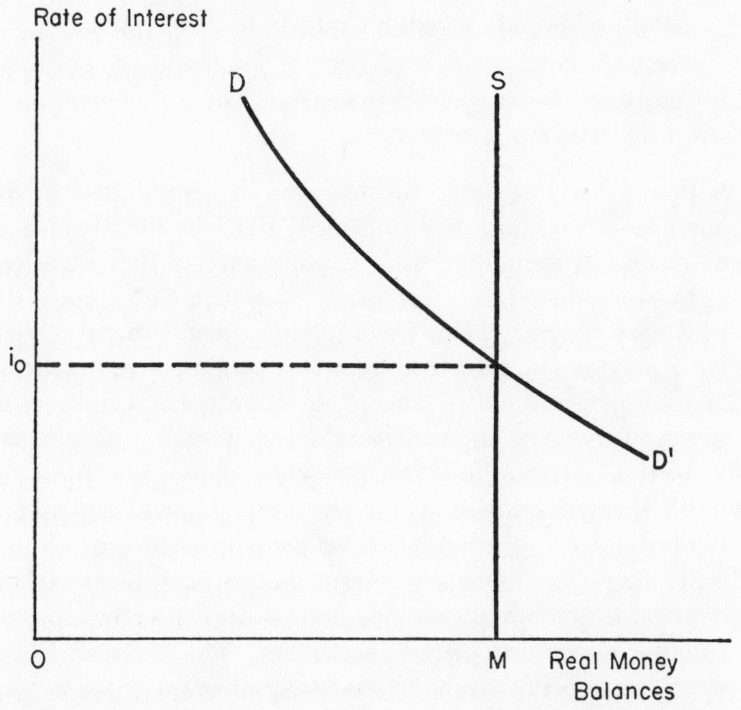

income and deposit rates. The schedule slopes downward to the right, indicating that at lower interest rates on primary securities spending units desire to hold more of their financial assets in money balances. An increase in spending units' financial assets shifts the schedule to the right, as does an increase in real income or a rise in the Banking Bureau's deposit rate. On the other hand, an increase in the deposit rate paid by nonmonetary intermediaries shifts the schedule to the left as nonmonetary indirect assets become relatively more attractive. The real stock of money is shown by the vertical line *MS*. Given the price level sought by the Policy Bureau, we can deduce the nominal stock of money. The equilibrium rate of interest is assumed to be i_0, where the demand and supply schedules intersect.

DISTURBANCE OF EQUILIBRIUM ON THE MONEY MARKET

Suppose that the above equilibrium was established in the absence of nonmonetary intermediaries—in the absence of a demand by spending units for nonmonetary indirect assets. Let us now introduce these assets, except time deposits of the monetary system. Their introduction means, in effect, that their deposit rate rises from zero to a positive level. This increases spending units' demand for nonmonetary indirect assets and reduces their demands for money and primary securities.[3] Given the nominal stock of money and the price level, the reduction in spending units' demand for money tends to lower the interest rate on primary securities. On the other hand, nonmonetary intermediaries may increase their demand for money as their assets grow, and this tends to raise the interest rate on primary securities. The outcome in the short run depends on the relative weights of these two factors.

It is worthwhile to consider an extreme case first, one in which spending units reduce their demand for money by the full amount of the increase in their demand for nonmonetary

[3] This assumes that there is no change in spending units' demand for current output.

indirect assets, and nonmonetary intermediaries have no incremental demand for money. Suppose that spending units want to reduce their money balances by $100 and increase their holdings of nonmonetary indirect assets by the same amount. They write checks on their demand deposits in the monetary system and pay the checks to nonmonetary intermediaries, receiving in return an equivalent amount of claims on these intermediaries. The intermediaries use the money to purchase $100 of primary securities. These securities must be purchased from spending units because the monetary system is assumed to hold on to its primary securities in order to keep the nominal stock of money constant throughout the transactions. At the current interest rate, however, spending units desire to reduce their money balances and not their holdings of primary securities. They want less money, the same amount of primary securities, and more nonmonetary indirect assets. In order to induce spending units to part with primary securities, therefore, the intermediaries bid up the prices of these securities, which means that the rate of interest falls until spending units are satisfied to hold the same amount of money that they started with, less primary securities, and more nonmonetary indirect assets. This, of course, is a short-run effect. There is upward pressure on commodity prices and money wage rates as a result, which in turn exerts upward pressure on the interest rate, given the nominal stock of money. In general, price levels will be higher and the interest rate lower after long-run adjustments.

The short-run outcome is shown in Chart VIII. The increase in nonmonetary intermediaries' deposit rate induces spending units to increase their demand for nonmonetary indirect assets and to reduce their demand for money by the same amount. Consequently, the demand schedule for money shifts to the left so that there is a reduction in demand for money of $M'M$, at interest rate i_o, equal to the purchases of nonmonetary indirect assets. With the nominal stock of money unchanged, and at a given price level, the rate of interest falls from i_0 *to* i_1.[4] It should be noted that the demand

CHART VIII

Disturbance of Equilibrium by Nonmonetary Intermediaries

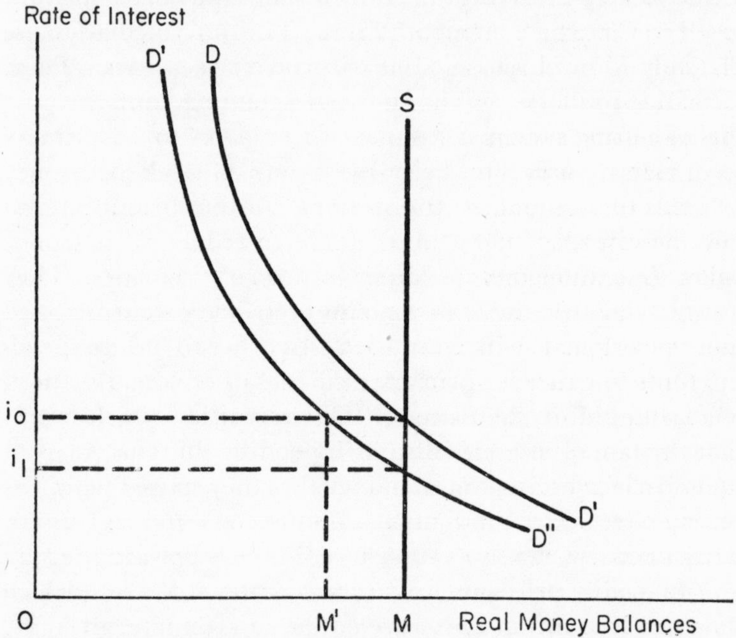

schedule still refers to spending units' demand for money and that the money-stock schedule is the real amount of money possessed by spending units. When nonmonetary intermediar-

[4] The fall in the rate of interest shifts the supply schedule of nonmonetary indirect assets to the left and the demand schedule for these assets to the right (as drawn in Chart VI). This lowers the deposit rate paid by nonmonetary intermediaries and may change their output, causing further repercussions on the money market, which we shall not follow through.

ies momentarily have the money deposited with them by spending units, the real stock of money in the hands of spending units is only *OM′*. But as intermediaries spend the money for purchases of primary securities the money-stock schedule shifts to the right, back to its original position, *OM*.[5]

It should also be noted that these transactions have an effect on the rate of interest similar to unfunding operations, discussed in Chapter V.[6] In both cases, spending units exchange relatively illiquid assets for liquid ones and so reduce their demand for money. Unfunding and intermediation are two ways of getting at the same thing.

We swing now to the other extreme by assuming that spending units do not reduce their demand for money at all when they increase their demand for nonmonetary indirect assets and that nonmonetary intermediaries raise their demand for money to the full extent of the increase in their assets. In this case, the original demand schedule in Chart VIII does not shift while the money-stock schedule (the stock of money held by spending units) shifts to the left by the increase in nonmonetary intermediaries' assets. Consequently, the interest rate on primary securities rises, given commodity prices. This comes about because spending units desire to give up, at the current interest rate on primary securities, only primary securities when they purchase nonmonetary indirect assets. However, to purchase these assets they must temporarily give up money. They then attempt to recoup this money by sell-

[5] Alternatively, the demand schedule could reflect demand for money by both spending units and nonmonetary intermediaries, and the money-stock schedule could reflect the amount of money possessed by both. From this viewpoint, when intermediaries momentarily have the money there would be no change in either schedule. As the money was spent by them for primary securities the demand schedule would shift to the left, ending finally in the *D′D″* position. From either viewpoint, of course, we get the same final result.

[6] Pp. 160-65.

ing primary securities, but these sales must be to each other, for nonmonetary intermediaries do not purchase any, holding money instead. Therefore, the yield on primary securities rises until spending units are content to hold smaller money balances, the same amount of primary securities, and more nonmonetary indirect assets.

These two extreme cases suggest the generalization. The interest rate on primary securities falls, given the nominal stock of money and the price level, if the growth of nonmonetary indirect assets induces spending units to reduce their demand for money by more than intermediaries increase theirs. This is most likely to occur when nonmonetary indirect assets are close substitutes for money in spending units' portfolios, since the very nature of intermediation requires only small money holdings by intermediaries. The interest rate rises in the opposite case. The growth of nonmonetary intermediaries has no effect on the interest rate when intermediaries increase their demand for money by precisely the amount spending units decrease theirs.

Assuming, then, that nonmonetary indirect assets are close substitutes for money, the growth of nonmonetary intermediaries is likely to cause the interest rate to fall in the short run at a given level of commodity prices. This increases spending units' real demand for current output, which tends to raise commodity prices and to pull the interest rate back toward its initial level. Through this process, the growth of nonmonetary intermediaries produces an excess stock of money and an excess of *ex-ante* investment over *ex-ante* saving.

DISTURBANCE OF EQUILIBRIUM ON THE MARKET FOR PRIMARY SECURITIES

We have shown that an increase in spending units' demand for nonmonetary indirect assets can create an excess stock of money or an excess demand for money at the current interest rate on primary securities. An excess stock of money shows up initially as an excess demand for primary securities, and an excess demand for money as an excess stock of primary securities. Hence, when nonmonetary intermediaries disturb equilibrium on the market for money they also disturb it on the market for primary securities.

It can be shown, from the standpoint of the market for primary securities, that nonmonetary intermediaries are capable of changing the supply of loanable funds—in particular, of increasing this supply—in the orthodox meaning of that term. Assuming that saving is done by one group of spending units and investment by another, the supply of loanable funds is:

$$\text{(1) Supply of loanable funds} = \begin{cases} \text{Planned saving of spending units} \\ + \\ \text{Increase in stock of money} \\ - \\ \text{Increase in economy's demand for} \\ \quad \text{money (hoarding).} \end{cases}$$

Planned saving by spending units is their increase in demand for primary securities, money, and nonmonetary indirect assets, assuming they do not repay debt. And the increase in the economy's demand for money less the increase in spending units' demand for money is the incremental demand for money by nonmonetary intermediaries. Using these definitions, Equation 1 may now be rewritten as follows:

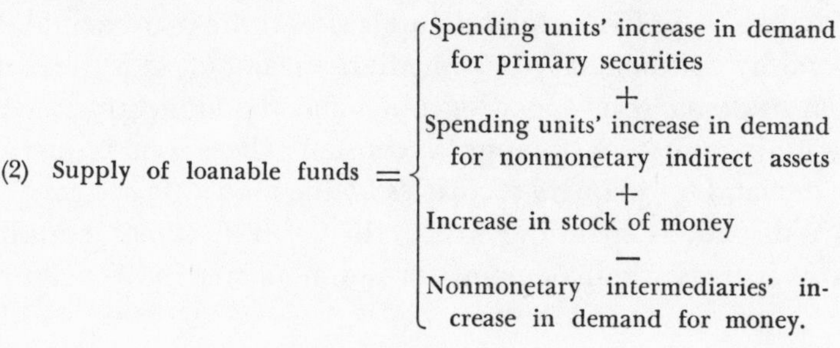

$$\text{(2) Supply of loanable funds} = \begin{cases} \text{Spending units' increase in demand} \\ \quad \text{for primary securities} \\ + \\ \text{Spending units' increase in demand} \\ \quad \text{for nonmonetary indirect assets} \\ + \\ \text{Increase in stock of money} \\ - \\ \text{Nonmonetary intermediaries' in-} \\ \quad \text{crease in demand for money.} \end{cases}$$

Finally, we note that spending units' increase in demand for nonmonetary indirect assets is equal to nonmonetary intermediaries' increase in demand for money and for primary securities; and the increase in the stock of money is equal to the monetary system's increase in demand for primary securities. This means that:

(3) Supply of loanable funds = {Spending units' increase in demand for primary securities
+
Nonmonetary intermediaries' increase in demand for primary securities
+
Monetary system's increase in demand for primary securities.}

The (incremental) demand for loanable funds is the increase in investors' stock of primary securities. Hence, starting from a position of equilibrium, the market for primary securities remains in equilibrium when:

(4) Increase in stock of primary securities = Increase in demand for primary securities by spending units, nonmonetary intermediaries, and the monetary system.

or when the (incremental) demand for loanable funds is equal to the supply of loanable funds.

Nonmonetary intermediaries, therefore, can increase the supply of loanable funds by demanding primary securities. The total supply of loanable funds rises if the incremental demand by nonmonetary intermediaries is not offset by a reduction in demand by spending units and the monetary system. Assuming the stock of money is constant, there is no reduction in demand for primary securities by the monetary system.

What about spending units? In general, when spending units increase their demand for nonmonetary indirect assets, the resulting increase in demand by intermediaries for primary securities is more likely to lead to a net increase in demand for these securities the greater is the accompanying decline in spending units' demand for money rather than for primary securities. This, of course, is just the other side of the coin that we have already looked at: if the growth of nonmonetary intermediaries leads to an excess stock of money, it also leads to an excess demand for primary securities—a net increase in the supply of loanable funds.

CREATING AND SWITCHING OPERATIONS

The creation of indirect financial assets by nonmonetary intermediaries, then, may bring about an excess stock of money and an excess demand for primary securities, at current levels of interest rate, commodity prices, and real income. These intermediaries can further affect spending units' demand for money by altering the composition of primary securities held by spending units. Suppose, for example, that nonmonetary intermediaries sell government securities to spending units and purchase mortgages from them. This "switching operation" removes from spending units' portfolios relatively illiquid securities and replaces them with highly liquid ones. Therefore, spending units can afford to hold less money balances and so reduce their demand for money. Given the stock of money, there is then an excess stock of money and an excess demand for primary securities. If nonmonetary intermediaries switch the other way, spending units become less liquid and so increase their demand for money.

Either way, by switching operations or by creating indirect debt, nonmonetary intermediaries are capable of reducing spending units' demand for money and thus of creating an excess stock of money. The monetary system by switching and creating can also bring about an excess stock of money, in the first case by reducing the demand for money and in the second by increasing the absolute stock of it. In fact, these switching and creating operations by financial intermediaries are dual methods of taking one type of security off the market and issuing another. In this respect, they stand on the same footing as debt management techniques of the government.

TIME DEPOSITS AND THE DEMAND FOR MONEY

We have seen that when spending units increase their holdings of time deposits the immediate consequence is an equivalent reduction in the stock of money. What happens to the demand for money? This depends on the financial assets that spending units wish to give up when they shift to time deposits. Suppose, to begin with, that they desire to give up $100 of money when they purchase this amount of time deposits. Then, assuming no action is taken by the Policy Bureau, the demand for and stock of money fall by the same amount, and equilibrium is maintained on the money market. The interest rate on primary securities is unaffected because there is no additional offer of these securities by spending units and no additional demand for them by the monetary system.

Alternatively, suppose that spending units wish to give up $100 of primary securities when they purchase this amount of time deposits. Then the demand for money is constant, while the stock of money falls by $100, again assuming no action by the Policy Bureau. There is now an excess demand for money, which has its counterpart in an excess stock of primary securities. At the prevailing interest rate, spending units want $100 more of time deposits, the same amount of money, and $100 less of primary securities. To reach this position, they attempt to sell $100 of primary securities to gain back the money given up when they purchased time deposits.

But, if the monetary system sits tight, there is no additional demand for these securities at the current interest rate; hence, the additional supply raises the interest rate, given the price level. The interest rate rises until spending units are satisfied to hold the smaller stock of money.

Assume, finally, that spending units wish to give up $100 of (other) nonmonetary indirect assets when they purchase time deposits. As a first step, they withdraw this amount from nonmonetary intermediaries, the latter giving up money balances and losing an equivalent amount of liabilities. Spending units now have $100 less of (other) nonmonetary indirect assets and $100 more of money. They then purchase time deposits with the money. At this point, at the current interest rate and price level, spending units are in their preferred position: they have more time deposits, the same amount of money and primary securities, and less nonmonetary indirect assets. But nonmonetary intermediaries are not necessarily in *their* preferred position: they have lost $100 of money and the same amount of nonmonetary indirect debt. If the intermediaries desire to hold a constant proportion of their assets in money, they now sell primary securities to acquire money. With no additional demands for these securities coming from the monetary system or from spending units, the interest rate rises, given the price level.

In summary, if the Policy Bureau takes no positive action, an increase in demand for time deposits leaves the interest rate unchanged if spending units reduce their demand for money by the full extent of the rise in time deposits. If spending units do not reduce their demand for money to this extent, there is necessarily a reduction in the aggregate demand for primary securities—either because spending units reduce their demand for these securities or because they reduce their demand for claims on nonmonetary intermediaries, forcing the latter to reduce their demand for primary securities. The reduction in demand for primary securities raises the interest rate in the short run.

Suppose, on the other hand, that the Policy Bureau issues instructions to the Banking Bureau to hold the stock of money constant. Then an increase in demand for time deposits does not reduce the stock of money. Hence, any reduction in demand for money lowers the interest rate. This may come about in two ways. First, spending units may reduce their demand for money when they purchase time deposits. Second, spending units, by reducing their demand for other nonmonetary indirect assets, may cause intermediaries to reduce their demand for money as their total assets decline.

Government Financial Activities and Financial Markets

The government, through its financial activities, can affect spending units' real demands for money and other financial assets in several ways. The financial activities that we shall consider are: (1) issues of government securities; (2) insurance of indirect securities; (3) insurance or guaranty of primary securities; and (4) establishment of governmental nonmonetary intermediaries.

ISSUES OF GOVERNMENT SECURITIES

When government securities become a larger proportion of a given total of primary securities, spending units tend to increase their real demand for primary securities generally and to reduce their real demands for indirect securities. The reason is that government securities, especially savings bonds and short-term marketable issues, compete more actively with many types of indirect securities than does the bulk of private primary securities. In particular, growth in the relative importance of government securities tends to reduce spending units' real demand for claims on the monetary system. Given the nominal size of the monetary system, this creates an excess real stock of money at current commodity prices, and thus tends to lower the interest rate on primary securities. Upward pressure then develops on the price level, which reduces the real size of the monetary system.[7] The monetary system's real size is also reduced if the nominal stock of money is decreased to prevent price inflation. In either case, government securities are a close competitor of the monetary system.

Growth in the relative importance of government securities also tends to reduce spending units' real demand for private nonmonetary indirect assets. At the same time, because these intermediaries are specialists for the most part in various types of private primary securities, the relative decline in these securities reduces the willingness of intermediaries to supply claims on themselves. Both the real demand for and real stock of these claims decline, and hence the real size of nonmonetary intermediaries is reduced.

INSURANCE OF INDIRECT SECURITIES

The government may insure some or all of the indirect securities of financial intermediaries and, by so doing, make them more attractive to spending units relative to other financial assets. Indeed, though we have not mentioned it before, the

[7] This occurs whether spending units reduce their real demand for money or for time deposits. In the first case, the demand for money falls while the stock of money is constant. In the second case, the demand for money is constant while the money stock rises—because spending units reduce their time deposits and increase their money balances in order to purchase primary securities.

demand and time deposits of the governmental monetary system must be assumed to be insured by the government. This in itself raises spending units' real demand for these assets above what it would be if the deposits were uninsured and were liabilities of a private banking system. Thus, given the nominal size of the monetary system and the price level, the insurance of demand and time deposits tends to raise the interest rate. This exerts downward pressure on the price level and so serves to increase the real size of the monetary system. At the same time, the real size of nonmonetary intermediaries tends to decline, as the demand for their liabilities is reduced by the insurance program.

If the government insures all indirect securities, there is an increase in spending units' real demand for these securities at the expense of their demand for primary securities. Such a program tends to increase the real size of the monetary system. Since there is an increase in spending units' real demand for private nonmonetary indirect assets, and since the intermediaries may be willing to offer more of these assets at each interest rate in view of the reduced chance of "runs" on them, the insurance program also tends to increase their real size as well.

INSURANCE OF PRIMARY SECURITIES

The government may insure or guaranty certain types of private primary securities. This program may increase spending units' real demand for primary securities and reduce their real demands for indirect securities generally. Thus, both the monetary system and private nonmonetary intermediaries tend to be smaller in real size at a higher price level. However, an offsetting factor is that private intermediaries may now be willing to supply more indirect assets, due to the insurance of primary securities that they buy. Moreover, spending units may raise their demand for the indirect securities that are backed by insured primary securities. Hence, the real size of these intermediaries may not change much on balance as a result of this program.

If the government limits the ownership of insured primary securities to financial intermediaries, not allowing spending units to own them, there may be an increase in spending units' real demand for the indirect securities that are backed by insured primary securities. Also, private intermediaries may still increase their willingness to supply claims on themselves at each interest rate. For these reasons, then, the real size of financial intermediaries tends to grow.

ESTABLISHMENT OF GOVERNMENTAL NONMONETARY INTERMEDIARIES

The government may establish nonmonetary intermediaries of its own—usually called federal lending agencies—other than the time deposit department of the governmental monetary system. These institutions may be established for either of two purposes. First, they may be designed to purchase certain types of private primary securities that are not easily marketable in the private areas of the economy. Second, they may be designed to issue to spending units certain types of indirect securities that are not supplied by others.

Some governmental nonmonetary intermediaries may purchase primary securities and obtain funds for this purpose by selling various types of indirect securities, such as savings deposits, bonds, debentures, and so on, to spending units. These issues may be fully guaranteed as to interest and principal by the government. Others may obtain funds by selling their own indirect securities to the government, which in turn sells government securities to spending units. Thus, the intermediaries may purchase private primary securities and replace them in the portfolios of spending units with either their own indirect securities, perhaps guaranteed, or government securities.

One effect of this is to reduce spending units' real demand for claims on the monetary system and on private nonmonetary intermediaries, which tends to reduce the real sizes of these intermediaries at a higher price level. If, concurrently, governmental intermediaries skim off some of the cream from primary security issues, private intermediaries suffer from having narrower choices among these issues. They, therefore, reduce their willingness to supply indirect assets, which further tends to reduce their real size.

Growth of Nonmonetary Intermediaries

Nonmonetary intermediaries are competitors of the governmental monetary system. That is to say, the growth of nonmonetary intermediaries generally reduces growth in spending units' demand for money, and this, within the context of a given set of policy aims, lowers the appropriate expansion of the monetary system. If the monetary system has time deposits, the growth of these claims generally reduces the required growth of the money stock.

A favorable climate for the growth of nonmonetary intermediaries is one in which there is an expansion of national output based predominantly on private expenditures (including local government expenditures) that are financed to a great degree by external means—by primary security issues. In such a climate the distribution of income among spending units is markedly different from the distribution of spending among them, so that budget deficits and surpluses are large relative to national output. Also the location of these budget imbalances in private sectors gives the maximum stimulus to financial intermediation. Then ultimate borrowers' primary security issues are not only large but are highly suitable to the specialized functions of the intermediaries, while ultimate lenders not only have large accumulations of financial assets but are disposed to accumulate indirect rather than primary securities.

Private nonmonetary intermediaries are further aided if the monetary system's deposit rates are set at low levels and if monetary policy is generally restrictive. For then, assuming nonneutrality of money, rising interest rates on primary securities induce the private intermediaries to raise their own deposit rates for the purpose of attracting additional demand for their products. The growth of these intermediaries is also favored by governmental insurance of their indirect debts, by such insurance of at least some of the primary securities they purchase, and by the absence of competition from governmental lending institutions.

Many of these factors are likely to be present during an upswing in private economic activity when aggregate demand for current output threatens to be excessive at prevailing price levels and when the Policy Bureau attempts to protect these price levels. However, private nonmonetary intermediaries may not have time in a short upswing to take full advantage of the favorable circumstances. Longer growth periods offer more opportunities to the intermediaries to expand in a congenial climate. There are several reasons for this. First, the intermediaries' deposit rate may rise in response to increases in the rate of interest only after a considerable lag, though other types of sales efforts may be subject to shorter delays, and this tends to hold back their growth over short periods. Further, only over longer periods do the intermediaries have time to introduce new types of indirect financial assets, to modernize existing offices and open new branches, and to obtain more liberal regulations on what they buy and sell.

Moreover, when favorable conditions persist, there is time and incentive for new firms to enter the industry, some of them similar to existing firms and others representing radical departures. And there is time and incentive for the intermediaries to elicit from borrowers the primary securities that meet the intermediaries' particular requirements as to maturities, terms of repayment, and so on. The tailoring of primary securities to the advantage of intermediaries enables them to pass on the benefits through lower interest rates to borrowers, higher deposit rates to lenders, or larger dividends to owners. Also, though of lesser importance, private nonmonetary intermediaries may gain at the expense of governmental lending institutions over long growth periods, a development that may fail to show up to any significant extent in short upswings.

It is not necessary to discuss in detail the unfavorable climates for growth of nonmonetary intermediaries, for the conditions are generally the opposite of those already mentioned. Two examples of uncongenial climates, however, may be noted—those existing during war periods and during fairly sharp setbacks in output growth. During war periods, intermediaries are favored by large differences between distributions of spending and income among spending units, which lead to heavy issues of primary securities and accumulations of financial assets. More important, however, are the possibilities that an overwhelming proportion of primary security issues may consist of government securities and that interest rates on these securities may be held at low levels by the monetary system. The first factor tends to depress spending units' incremental demands for indirect securities, while the second tends to increase them. But both factors, for reasons already discussed, tend to reduce intermediaries' willingness to supply claims on themselves, so that on balance their growth is retarded. During extended periods of depressed economic activity, spending units move toward balanced budget positions, slowing down primary security issues and accumulations of financial assets, including claims on intermediaries. If the small amount of primary issues is weighted heavily toward government securities, and if there is monetary ease, the growth of nonmonetary intermediaries tends to be further depressed.

Nonmonetary Intermediaries and the Neutrality of Money

How do nonmonetary intermediaries fit into the general equilibrium framework of our second model? In that model, it will be recalled, there were three sectors: consumers, nonfinancial business firms, and government. In equilibrium, consumers had either balanced or surplus budgets; in the latter case, they accumulated financial assets—money and homogeneous business bonds. Business firms had either balanced or deficit budgets. They issued bonds to finance their deficits and their acquisitions of money balances. Government had no income and no spending on income and product account. Instead, it operated the monetary system, which was composed of a Policy Bureau and a Banking Bureau, the latter purchasing bonds and creating money, on orders of the former.

Chapters III and V showed that, within a neo-classical framework, money is neutral on the real variables of the economy if all money is of the inside variety—if money is based entirely on domestic private debt, in this case domestic business bonds.[8] That is, if the Banking Bureau purchases business bonds to increase the nominal stock of money, the total nominal amount of bonds increases in the same proportion, as do commodity prices and money wage rates. The real variables of the system, including the rate of interest, are unaffected in the long run by this nominal monetary expansion. Consumers end up with the same real holdings of primary securities and money; firms have the same real indebtedness and money balances; and the share of real bonds held by the monetary system is unaffected.

We also saw that money is not neutral, within a neo-classical framework, when there is a combination of inside and outside money—where outside money is defined as money not based on domestic private debt, but based on, say, gold or 'foreign" securities (including government securities). Suppose, for example, that the monetary system holds both gold and business bonds behind its monetary liabilities. Then an increase in the nominal stock of money through purchases of business bonds by the monetary system leaves spending units —after prices, money wage rates, and nominal bonds have increased equiproportionally—with relatively larger real holdings of money and relatively smaller real holdings of bonds. The monetary system has a larger share of real bonds. Hence, the equilibrium interest rate is lower, and money has non-neutral effects on the real variables of the system.

TIME DEPOSITS: STATIONARY EQUILIBRIUM

Suppose now that time deposits are introduced into this picture. These deposits, we assume, are held only by consumers and are liabilities of the governmental monetary system. Con-

[8] Pp. 75-82, 144, 174.

sumers hold primary securities, money, and time deposits, while business firms have outstanding debt and hold money balances. Assume, further, that there is stationary equilibrium, so that each sector has a balanced budget, and each is satisfied with its real holdings of financial assets and debt. From this position of equilibrium, suppose that the Banking Bureau purchases sufficient business bonds (say) to double the nominal stock of money. This, however, does not represent a doubling of the monetary system's nominal liabilities, for it is also indebted on time deposits. Suppose that in the initial situation time deposits are equal to the system's demand deposits and currency, so that the above bond purchases mean a 50 per cent rise in the system's nominal liabilities. Equiproportional increases in commodity prices, money wage rates, and nominal bonds leave spending units in the same real position as before, provided the monetary system permits time deposits to rise in the same proportion—that is, allows spending units to exchange money balances for time deposits. If it does, money is neutral on the real variables of the system.

When time deposits are outstanding, money is not neutral if any of the monetary system's liabilities is backed by gold or "foreign" securities—when either demand deposits, currency, or time deposits is of the outside variety. For example, suppose that the stock of money is wholly inside money, while time deposits are partly of the outside variety (assuming that the monetary system's assets can be segregated in this way). Then money is no longer neutral, for purchases of business bonds by the monetary system for the purpose of increasing its liabilities leave it—at equiproportional increases in prices and nominal bonds—with a higher share of real bonds. The interest rate, therefore, is lower, and this affects other real variables of the system.

PRIVATE NONMONETARY INTERMEDIARIES: STATIONARY EQUILIBRIUM

Let us now drop time deposits and replace them with claims on private nonmonetary intermediaries. These intermediaries hold money and business bonds; consumers hold primary securities, money, and nonmonetary indirect assets; and firms have outstanding debt and hold money.

Start once again from a position of stationary equilibrium, and assume that both money and nonmonetary indirect assets are of the inside variety. Suppose now that the nominal stock of money is doubled by purchases of business bonds by the monetary system. This leads to a doubling of prices and nominal bonds. It also leads to a doubling of consumers' nominal demand for nonmonetary indirect assets. Since the intermediaries willingly supply these additional assets, by doubling their nominal holdings of money and bonds, the neutrality of money is preserved. For then spending units have the same real holdings of bonds, money, nonmonetary indirect assets, and debt as before. The group of financial intermediaries—the monetary system and nonmonetary intermediaries—maintains its share of real bonds.

Money is not neutral when money is partly of the outside variety, because an increase in the nominal stock of money—at equiproportional increases in prices and nominal bonds—now leaves the group of financial intermediaries with a larger share of real bonds. Spending units have relatively larger real holdings of indirect securities and relatively smaller holdings of primary securities; this lowers the equilibrium rate of interest.

Money also ceases to be neutral, within the same framework, if nonmonetary indirect assets are at least partly of the outside variety, even though all money is inside money. In this case, nonmonetary intermediaries hold not only money and business bonds but also some gold or "foreign" securities behind their liabilities. A doubling of the nominal stock of money again leads to a doubling of the nominal amount of nonmonetary indirect assets. But, because nonmonetary intermediaries hold outside securities, a doubling of nonmonetary indirect assets means more than a doubling of nominal holdings of business bonds by these intermediaries. Hence, the group of intermediaries ends up with a larger share of real business bonds at the doubled price level; spending units have relatively larger real holdings of indirect securities and relatively smaller real holdings of primary securities. This is true even if we assume that the willingness of nonmonetary intermediaries to supply real indirect debt is not affected by the composition of their bond portfolios between business and outside securities.

In summary, money is not neutral, within a neo-classical framework, if there are any outside indirect securities in the economy—if any of the financial intermediaries, including the monetary system, holds gold or "foreign" securities behind its liabilities. And, of course, as shown in Chapter III,[9] money is not neutral if any of the neo-classical rules is violated.

NONMONETARY INTERMEDIARIES: BALANCED GROWTH

Finally, consider the case of balanced growth, within the neoclassical framework. All indirect securities are of the inside variety. Real and nominal values of business bonds and financial assets of spending units grow at the same constant rate, n, as labor services, real income, and the capital stock.

During each period, business firms issue bonds and consumers and firms acquire financial assets. At the given bond

[9] Pp. 86-88.

rate of interest, however, spending units normally reject a portion of the bond issues in favor of money, time deposits, and other nonmonetary indirect assets. The price level is stable if the monetary system purchases sufficient business bonds to provide the money and time deposits demanded by spending units at this price level, and if private nonmonetary intermediaries purchase sufficient money and business bonds to provide the indirect assets demanded by spending units at this price level. During balanced growth at stable prices, each of the asset components of financial intermediaries grows at the constant rate, n. It is assumed that in the long run private intermediaries are willing to supply additional claims on themselves at a constant deposit rate; and the deposit rates of the monetary system are held constant, too.

Under these circumstances, if the bonds held by the monetary system grow at a rate higher than n, commodity prices and money wage rates rise. If the monetary system's bond holdings grow at a rate lower than n, the opposite occurs. In either case, money has neutral effects on the real variables of the economy. More generally, indirect finance through financial intermediaries has neutral effects.

If, on the other hand, indirect securities have both inside and outside components, then both components must grow at the balanced growth rate of n to insure neutrality of financial intermediation. For if financial intermediaries meet the growing demands for indirect securities by purchasing only business bonds—when their real holdings of outside securities are constant—they steadily increase their share of real bonds, leaving spending units with relatively smaller real holdings of bonds at the current bond rate. This lowers the bond rate, and other real variables in the economy are affected.

Monetary Policy and Nonmonetary Intermediaries

The Policy Bureau issues instructions to the Banking Bureau regarding its purchases and sales of primary securities, its creation and destruction of money and time deposits, and the levels of its deposit rates. The Policy Bureau, therefore, has complete control over the size and activities of the monetary system. It has no direct control, on the other hand, over the size and activities of private nonmonetary intermediaries. To achieve any set of policy aims, it may use the monetary system as a counterweight to offset any unwanted effects of nonmonetary intermediation.

MONETARY CONTROL OF NONMONETARY INTERMEDIARIES AND THE PRICE LEVEL

When money is neutral on the real variables of the economy, any change in the nominal stock of money changes commodity prices and money wage rates in the same proportion without affecting the interest rate on primary securities. Under these circumstances, as we have shown, the presence of private nonmonetary intermediaries has no effect on the final outcome, in real terms. An increase in the nominal stock of money, for example, increases equiproportionally the nominal size of these intermediaries, prices, money wage rates, and nominal bonds. Deposit rates paid by intermediaries, the interest rate, and other real variables are unchanged in the new equilibrium position.

There is a determinate price level in the economy, given the nominal stock of money, even when all financial assets, including nonmonetary indirect financial assets, are of the inside variety. Hence, by setting the nominal stock of money at the right level, the Policy Bureau can achieve any price level that it desires.

The Policy Bureau could, however, achieve exactly the same thing by directly controlling the nominal amount of nonmonetary indirect assets and the deposit rate on these assets, while allowing the Banking Bureau free rein to maximize profits as a competitive banking system. In this case, too, there is only one price level associated with each nominal amount of nonmonetary indirect assets, within a given real context. At this price level, and at the equilibrium deposit and interest rates, the nominal stock of money that banks desire to supply would be equal to spending units' demand for money.

To show the existence of a determinate price level, when the nominal amount of nonmonetary indirect financial assets, rather than nominal money, is controlled, suppose that the price level is arbitrarily raised from a level that is compatible with general equilibrium. Even with equiproportional increases in nominal money, nominal bonds, and money wage rates, spending units will be in disequilibrium, since the higher price level reduces the real value of a given nominal amount of nonmonetary indirect assets. Spending units will have relatively larger real holdings of bonds, relatively smaller real holdings of indirect assets, and a lower real value of total financial assets. This situation exerts upward pressure on the interest rate and downward pressure on the price level. The economy will eventually grope its way back to the original equilibrium position, with the same interest rate, price levels, and nominal amounts of financial assets.

In this milieu, the Policy Bureau can raise the price level by ordering an increase in nominal nonmonetary indirect assets, through an increase in the deposit rate on these assets. This raises spending units' real demand for nonmonetary indirect assets at the expense, we assume for convenience, of their real demand for money. Nonmonetary intermediaries may be supposed to increase their demand for primary securities by the full amount of the rise in their liabilities, and the result of the Policy Bureau's intervention is an excess stock of money at the initial price level, interest rate, and bank deposit rate. With money neutral, there ensues an inflation in prices, proportional to the excess stock of money, and nominal bonds rise in the same proportion. After appropriate adjustment in the nominal value of claims on nonmonetary intermediaries, the outcome in real terms reflects a real reduction in money balances, a real increase in claims on nonmonetary intermediaries, and a rise in the deposit rate on claims against nonmonetary intermediaries relative to an unchanged bond rate of interest and bank deposit rate. This assumes that the real unit costs of banking are constant to scale.

Conversely, if the Policy Bureau orders a decrease in the deposit rate paid by nonmonetary intermediaries, it can induce excess demand for money and deflation in prices on the markets for goods and labor. The Policy Bureau, therefore, is able to achieve a desired price level by controlling either the banking system or nonmonetary intermediaries.

MONETARY POLICY AND THE RATE OF INTEREST

Suppose now that the Policy Bureau once again has control of the Banking Bureau, and that money is not neutral because part of the money stock is of the outside variety. Then any change in the nominal stock of money through dealings by the Banking Bureau in private domestic securities affects the real variables of the economy, including the rate of interest. In this event, the absence of direct controls over private nonmonetary intermediaries is likely to reduce the effectiveness of monetary policy, in the sense that a given change in the nominal stock of money has less effect on the rate of interest than it otherwise would have. Alternatively, the activities of uncontrolled intermediaries make it necessary for the Policy Bureau to increase or decrease the money stock by more than would otherwise be required to achieve a given change in the interest rate.

We can see how this comes about by assuming that the Banking Bureau is instructed to sell private domestic securities for the purpose of reducing the money stock and raising the interest rate. At the higher interest rate, spending units have lower real demands for money and nonmonetary indirect assets; the aggregate real size of intermediaries is reduced. At the same time, however, the uncontrolled intermediaries are now willing to supply more claims on themselves at their prevailing deposit rate. Given this deposit rate and the deposit rates of the monetary system, a higher interest rate and a lower price level can be reached at which spending units are temporarily satisfied with their real holdings of financial assets. This higher interest rate would "stick" if nonmonetary intermediaries were prevented from taking further action. But at their present deposit rate there is now an excess supply of nonmonetary indirect assets. This leads to a rise in their deposit rate, which increases spending units' real demand for nonmonetary indirect assets and reduces their real demands for money and primary securities. The short-run effect is to lower the interest rate below what it otherwise would be and to raise the price level. In this way the effectiveness of monetary policy is watered down by the activities of uncontrolled intermediaries.

By an analogous process the uncontrolled intermediaries can partially frustrate a policy of monetary ease. Suppose that the Banking Bureau increases the nominal stock of money and lowers the interest rate. The lower interest rate increases spending units' real demands for money and nonmonetary indirect assets, and reduces the willingness of the uncontrolled intermediaries to supply nonmonetary indirect assets. This creates an excess demand for nonmonetary indirect assets at the current deposit rate paid by the uncontrolled intermediaries, which is worked off by a fall in the deposit rate. But this increases spending units' real demand for money and so raises the interest rate above what it otherwise would be. And the price level is pushed down from its higher, temporary level.

The Policy Bureau can offset the effects of the perverse actions of the uncontrolled intermediaries. If, for example, during output growth, these intermediaries expand rapidly, the Policy Bureau need only restrict the growth of the monetary system by more than it otherwise would have to do to achieve any set of policy aims. Thus the growth of private nonmonetary intermediaries may induce the Policy Bureau to tighten the reins on growth of nominal money. If intermediary growth is somewhat erratic, the Policy Bureau may have to contend also with additional problems of timing. Finally, it should be noted that the Policy Bureau can engage in offsetting actions by varying its deposit rates and in this way change the real demand for money.

MONETARY POLICY AND RESOURCE ALLOCATION

If each ultimate borrower could sell primary securities just as easily to one intermediary as to another, and was indifferent in this choice, it would not matter to him which intermediary's growth was restrained as compensation for uncontrolled growth elsewhere. At any interest rate, the composition of the group of ultimate borrowers would be the same whether the Policy Bureau restrained intermediary growth here or there. To the extent that these conditions do not prevail, however, restraining one part of financial intermediation to compensate for uncontrolled intermediary growth elsewhere will most likely change the composition of borrowers. Some will find it more difficult or more inconvenient to raise funds; others will be unaffected. Hence, the allocation of resources depends in part on the particular area of financial intermediation that the Policy Bureau controls.

MONETARY POLICY AND THE CONTROLLED AREA

A governmental monetary system may be reduced or increased in size, shoved this way or that, and controlled tightly in all respects, without any deleterious effects on its performance. Our Banking Bureau, in fact, did exactly what it was told to do, regardless of whether such actions were "good for it." When, however, the monetary system contains private commercial banks that are in business for profit, a system of controls over their activities may in time create problems for the monetary authorities. Such controls may weaken the profit and capital positions of the banking system and sap its vitality in other ways, especially if it is subject to severe competition from uncontrolled intermediaries, making it less than fully responsive to the wishes of the monetary authorities. In the next chapter we shall be concerned with this and other problems connected with the conversion of our Policy and Banking Bureaus into a central bank and its profit-seeking members.

Summary

Up to now the only financial institution in our models has been the governmental monetary system, with its Policy and Banking Bureaus. This chapter introduces a second type of financial institution—nonmonetary financial intermediaries. These intermediaries purchase primary securities from ultimate borrowers and issue nonmonetary claims on themselves—nonmonetary indirect assets—for the portfolios of ultimate lenders.

The principal function of these institutions is to intermediate in the transfer of unspent incomes from surplus to deficit units. In carrying out this function, they tend to raise levels of saving and investment and to allocate scarce saving optimally among investment alternatives. The governmental monetary system also performs the function of intermediary in the transfer of unspent incomes. There are other similarities, too, between the two types of institution. Both create indirect securities by purchases of primary securities. Both are capable of creating an excess supply of loanable funds; both can create an excess stock of money and an excess of *ex-ante* investment over saving. The monetary system, however, is unique in being the administrator of the payments mechanism.

Spending units' real demand for nonmonetary indirect assets depends on their real holdings of financial assets, the level of real income, the interest rate, and the explicit deposit rates paid by the monetary system and by nonmonetary intermediaries. The willingness of nonmonetary intermediaries to supply these indirect assets, in real terms, depends on the interest rate and on their deposit rate, among other things. Time deposits of the monetary system are also nonmonetary indirect assets. Real demand for them depends on the factors listed above. Their nominal stock is determined by the Policy Bureau's instructions.

From a position of equilibrium, spending units may increase their demand for claims on nonmonetary intermediaries as a result of a change in taste or deposit rate. The interest rate on primary securities initially falls if the growth of nonmonetary indirect assets induces spending units to reduce their demand for money by more than intermediaries increase theirs as they expand. This is likely to happen when nonmonetary indirect assets are close substitutes for money in spending units' portfolios. The interest rate initially rises if the growth of nonmonetary indirect assets results in a net increase in the demand for money. If the Policy Bureau allows the nominal stock of money to decline when there is an increase in demand for time deposits of the monetary system, the interest rate on primary securities rises, unless spending units reduce their demand for money by the full amount of the rise in time deposits. If the Banking Bureau, on the other hand, is instructed to hold nominal money constant, an increase in demand for time deposits does not reduce the money stock. Hence, any reduction in spending units' demand for money owing to the shift will tend to lower the interest rate.

The growth of nonmonetary intermediaries is stimulated most when output growth is based predominantly on private expenditures that are financed to a great extent by external means. Intermediary growth is also stimulated when the monetary system's deposit rates are set at low levels, when monetary policy is generally restrictive, when nonmonetary indirect assets are insured by the government, when at least some of the primary securities purchased by intermediaries are so insured, and when there is little competition from governmental lending institutions.

Monetary policy is neutral in its effect on the real variables of the economy, within the neo-classical framework, if the monetary system and nonmonetary intermediaries hold only private domestic debt (and money) behind their issues of money and nonmonetary indirect debt. Then an increase in nominal money by open-market purchases of private domestic debt by the monetary system leaves spending units in the same real position after prices and money wage rates have risen in the same proportion. If, however, any monetary or nonmonetary liabilities of the financial institutions are backed by "outside" securities, monetary policy is not neutral on real variables in the same circumstances. Not only does a combination of inside and outside money break the neutrality of money, but a combination of inside and outside nonmonetary indirect assets does the same.

The price level is determinate, given the nominal stock of money, even when all financial assets, including nonmonetary indirect assets, are of the inside variety. The Policy Bureau can achieve a desired price level by directly controlling the nominal stock of money. It can, however, do the same thing by directly controlling the nominal amount of nonmonetary indirect assets (and the deposit rate), leaving commercial banks free to seek an output that maximizes profits.

The expansion of nonmonetary intermediaries during output growth may reduce the effectiveness of monetary policy in the sense that a given change in nominal money has less effect on the interest rate and on the price level than it otherwise would have. During business declines, the effectiveness of monetary policy may also be reduced by the activities of uncontrolled intermediaries. The Policy Bureau can counter these actions by increasing or decreasing nominal money in larger amounts than would otherwise be necessary.

The Policy Bureau regulates the size of the group of financial intermediaries by imposing controls on one segment—the monetary system—allowing the uncontrolled segment to expand and contract freely. Monetary controls, therefore, may produce a different allocation of resources than would prevail if the impact of controls were elsewhere on the intermediary group or if the impact were distributed evenly among the intermediaries. Monetary controls, however, do not affect the efficiency of performance of the governmental monetary system, for the Banking Bureau does whatever it is told to do. But when the monetary system comprises private commercial banks seeking profits, a system of controls over their activities, especially when banks are subject to rigorous competition from uncontrolled intermediaries, may in time create problems for the monetary authority.

CHAPTER VII

Basic Elements of Monetary Control

THE NOMINAL STOCK of money was determined in earlier chapters very simply—by mandate of the Policy Bureau to the Banking Bureau. The Policy Bureau ordered issues of money for the purchase of current output or primary securities or for transfer payments, and the Banking Bureau complied. Once the nominal stock of money appropriate to the demand for it and to policy objectives was ascertained, there were no economic problems of money creation.

Modern monetary systems are not this simple. Some part of the money stock—primarily coin and paper currency—is governmental issue, but the larger part is the product of commercial banks. These private corporations, organized to make profits, can and do create money and even nonmonetary claims, such as time deposits, under a complex of incentives and inhibitions that did not apply to the Banking Bureau. When there is commercial banking, the Policy Bureau or Central Bank has to solve its problem of monetary equilibrium in a context of private economic choice on both the demand side and the supply side of the market for money. And it must concern itself with the economic viability of the private banking institutions in order to maintain the efficiency of the banking system as a financial intermediary and as an administrator of the payments mechanism.

One objective of this chapter is to explain the restrictions that must be put on a private-enterprise banking system if it is chosen, in preference to other financial institutions, as the vehicle for regulating the price level and if the Central Bank is not permitted to rule the banks, as it ruled the Banking Bureau, by simple decree. What is the necessity for the limitation of bank reserves, for reserve requirements, for fixing the explicit deposit rate, for capital requirements and bank examination and other elements of the modern technique of monetary control?

A second objective of this chapter is to work out the consequences for bank profits and bank capital of monetary control by the Central Bank. As Chapter VI has indicated, commercial banking need not be the medium for price-level policy if some other financial institution is put under adequate control. Since commercial banks have been chosen as the focal point for financial controls, what is their destiny in terms of stockholders' real investment and profits? And what effect do trends in bank profits and capital have on the efficiency of monetary policy?

The Deposit Rate in Preceding Models

We assumed that the explicit deposit rate was set at zero by the Policy Bureau in our rudimentary economy and its successor. It will be helpful now, for the analysis to follow, to return briefly to these economies to see how changes in the deposit rate would affect their equilibrium positions.

THE RUDIMENTARY ECONOMY

Aside from the market for labor services, which is assumed to be in equilibrium at all times, our rudimentary economy contains two markets—for current output and for money. If one of these markets is in equilibrium, the other is too. Consider the money market. In equilibrium the real stock of money is equal to spending units' desired level of real balances. Neglecting real wealth and the real rental rate on wealth, spending units' desired real money balances depend positively on their existing balances $\left(\frac{M}{p}\right)$, real income (Y), and the explicit deposit rate (d) paid by the Banking Bureau on its monetary liabilities. The economy is in general equilibrium when:

$$\frac{M}{p} = L\left(\frac{M}{p}, Y, d\right). \tag{1}$$

If the Policy Bureau specifies the level of nominal money (M) and the deposit rate, the price level of current output is determined, given real income. There is only one price level that preserves the equality of Equation 1. Any higher price level reduces existing real balances in greater degree than it reduces desired real balances so that there is excess (incremental) demand on the market for money and excess supply on the market for goods. Any lower price level generates an excess stock of money and an excess demand for goods.

Suppose now that the Policy Bureau raises the deposit rate. The effect is to increase the desired stock of real balances relative to the existing stock, to induce (incremental) demand for money, and to lower real demand for current output. Equilibrium is restored by a decline in prices and money wage rates, since deflation increases real money balances by more than it increases real balances desired. Given nominal money, the fall in prices creates more real money to satisfy (incremental) demand for it. Demand for current output is restored, and the economy achieves a new equilibrium at the deflated price level. Conversely, a reduction of the deposit rate is associated with a higher price level in the new equilibrium. As the Policy Bureau manipulates the deposit rate, spending units adapt their desired real stock of money and, by adjustments in price level, the existing real stock; in Equation 1 changes in p counterbalance changes in d.

Within any real context, and given nominal money, there is a unique price level for each deposit rate; the Policy Bureau must specify the deposit rate to achieve its desired price level. Changes in the deposit rate can be used by the Policy Bureau, in place of changes in nominal money, to reach its price-level goal.

THE SECOND ECONOMY

In our second economy, aside from the market for labor services, there are three markets—for current output, money, and business bonds (perpetuities). Business firms issue bonds to finance deficits and to accumulate money balances; consumers "invest" their budget surpluses in money and business bonds; and the Banking Bureau purchases bonds and creates money. The government sector has no transactions on income and product account. Though all financial assets are of the inside variety, the price level is determinate provided that the Policy Bureau specifies nominal money and the deposit rate. Neo-classical ground rules of analysis are in force.

Neglecting the real rental rate and firms' real debt burden, the real demand of spending units for current output depends positively on existing real portfolios of bonds and money and real income, negatively on the bond rate of interest (i) and on the deposit rate. Desired real stocks of money depend positively on existing real portfolios of bonds and money, on real income and deposit rate, but negatively on the bond rate of interest. Desired real stocks of bonds rise with existing real portfolios of bonds and money, with real income and the bond rate of interest, but they are reduced as the deposit rate is raised.

The economy is in general equilibrium when equilibrium prevails in the markets for current output and money—for then the bond market is also in equilibrium. Equilibrium in the market for current output (Y) can be described as follows:

$$Y = E\left(\frac{M}{p}, \frac{B\text{-}B^g}{ip}, Y, i, d\right). \tag{2}$$

The notation $\frac{B\text{-}B^g}{ip}$ represents spending units' real holdings of bonds, where B is the outstanding number of bonds, each paying \$1 per annum, and B^g is the number of such bonds held by the Banking Bureau. There is equilibrium in the money market when:

$$\frac{M}{p} = L\left(\frac{M}{p}, \frac{B\text{-}B^g}{ip}, Y, i, d\right). \tag{3}$$

The real holdings of bonds by the Banking Bureau $\left(\frac{B^g}{ip}\right)$ are equal to its real monetary liabilities $\left(\frac{M}{p}\right)$. Business firms, in a neo-classical world, adjust the number of bonds outstanding to the price level, keeping $\frac{B}{p}$ constant within any real context. Given nominal money, deposit rate, and real income, the economy determines the price level, outstanding nominal bonds, and the bond rate of interest.

Suppose now that the Policy Bureau disturbs an initial position of general equilibrium by raising the deposit rate. This increases spending units' desired real money balances, induces incremental demand for money by raising desired balances relative to existing balances, and reduces real demands for bonds and current output. We assume that (incremental) demand for money is at the expense of both goods and bonds and is neutral with regard to demand for goods *vis â vis* bonds. In this case, excess demand for money that results from an increase in the deposit rate is resolved by a fall in the price level, money wage rate, and outstanding nominal bonds—all in the same proportion—without long-run effects on the rate of interest, real wealth, and real income.

In the new equilibrium, spending units have larger real money balances and smaller real bond portfolios. Their real money balances have increased because nominal money is constant at a lower price level. Their real holdings of bonds have decreased because outstanding real bonds are constant and the Banking Bureau has increased its real bond holdings—its nominal bonds are constant at a lower price level. Conversely, under the same conditions, a reduction in the deposit rate by the Policy Bureau would raise the price level, money wage rate, and outstanding nominal bonds without affecting the rate of interest in the long run. However, if incremental demand for money is not neutral with regard to preferences between goods and bonds, the interest rate and other real variables are affected when the deposit rate is altered.

Laissez-Faire in Banking

Economics tells us that consumers and firms in a competitive setting are guided by relative prices to use scarce resources efficiently. Does this rule apply to the industry that produces money and to the consumers of its product? Can monetary control be left to the market place and to the unseen hand of cost-price relationships that presumably directs a private-enterprise economy?

Suppose that our governmental monetary system is eliminated. The Policy Bureau is shut down and is not replaced by any such automatic device as the gold standard. There is no Policy Bureau to specify the nominal amount of money or the explicit deposit rate. The Banking Bureau also disappears. Private banking firms take its place and are permitted to purchase and sell business bonds and to create and destroy money as their self-interest dictates. This self-interest also leads them to seek out the "best" deposit rate: the deposit rate is the price that the banking industry pays for its borrowings, by money-issues, from spending units, and the industry tends toward the rate at which the marginal cost of borrowing is equal to anticipated marginal revenues from investing loanable funds in business bonds. Assume that, in their quest for profit, banking firms think in real terms; they are free of money illusion. The banks are subject to just one rule, that their debt shall be continuously acceptable as money to the community. Otherwise, we work within the context of the basic version of our second model, with all neoclassical rules operating.

In the absence of controls over other financial sectors, such a banking system implies, as we shall show, an aimless drift of nominal money, nominal bonds, and the price level. In successive steps below, we introduce the controls that tie down nominal variables and money prices to determinate levels.

BANK PROFITS AND THE REAL STOCK OF MONEY

This economy with a *laissez-faire* banking system is in general equilibrium, just as before, when equilibrium prevails in the markets for current output and money. Now, however, nominal money and the deposit rate are no longer set by a monetary authority. Instead, commercial banks decide on the real amount of money they would like to supply and on the deposit rate they would like to set, in pursuit of maximum real profits.

The commercial banks' desired real stock of money outstanding depends at least on the bond rate of interest, the deposit rate, and the real wage rate $\left(\frac{w}{p}\right)$. Monetary expansion is encouraged by a rise in the bond rate and by a fall in the deposit rate or real wage rate. The real wage rate is equal to labor's marginal product and is determined in the market for labor services. The commercial banks' desired real stock of money outstanding may depend, too, on estimated risks of banking and on the stock of bank net worth as a buffer against risk. The money-supply function becomes:

$$(4) \qquad \frac{M}{p} = S\left(\frac{B^g}{ip}, i, d, \frac{w}{p}\right).$$

The money market is in equilibrium at some real stock of money when the real balances desired by spending units are equal to real balances that banks desire to provide.

This economy, with its private banking system free of money illusion and seeking maximum real profits, determines all real variables such as real stocks of money and bonds along with the deposit rate and the bond rate, but it does not determine such nominal variables as nominal money and number of bonds or the price level and money wage rate. There is, in particular, a unique level of real money balances determined by equality of real balances desired as an asset by spending units with real balances desired as debt by banks. But this real stock can be fashioned from numerous combinations of nominal money and the price level. *Laissez-faire* banking fails to pin down the nominal quantities.

The real equilibrium stock of money is associated with a unique level of real bank profits. These profits represent the community's reward to banking for its services in intermediation and in administering the payments mechanism. They vary positively with the real amount of bonds in the banking system, the bond rate of interest, and the banks' technological efficiency in employment of labor services. They vary negatively with real money owed by the banking system, the explicit deposit rate, and the real wage rate. Measured as a return on net worth, they are in balance with returns on alternative uses of stockholder funds. It is not important now to inquire whether real unit profits in banking (that is, profits per dollar of money) are constant to scale, increasing or decreasing.

Assume that commercial banks are in real profit equilibrium and that all real variables in the economy are at equilibrium levels. Now suppose that commercial banks, for whatever reason, purchase additional nominal bonds and create additional nominal money. Growth in nominal money raises prices of current output, money wage rate, and nominal bonds equiproportionally. Since money is assumed to be neutral, the bond rate of interest and other real variables are unchanged by this nominal expansion. It follows that the banks' nominal revenues, expenses, and profits rise in the same proportion as nominal money, leaving real profits as they were. Bank expansion has affected no real variable, including real money desired by spending units and the real reward from spending units to banks for financial services. The nominal size of commercial banks is adventitious.

This means that nominal money and the price level are indeterminate. It matters to no one, including the banks, whether some index of nominal money and the price level is 1 or 100 or 1,000. Nominal money is subject to no rational rule and is free of guidance by any hand, visible or invisible. The price level is whatever it needs to be for fashioning nominal money to the desired real stock of money.

COMPETITION AND MONOPOLY IN BANKING

We shall have more to say later about the individual bank in the system. For the present, we suppose that the individual bank is not permitted to run up an indefinite amount of clearinghouse debt to its competitors; its deposits must remain exchangeable at par with deposits elsewhere. The real size of the individual bank is given by the real demand for its issues on the part of spending units. Deposit rates are the same for all competitors, so that any differences in size among banks tend to reflect advantages in location and technical skill of management in applying labor to the production of money in real terms.

Evidently, if nominal money and the price level are indeterminate with a *laissez-faire* banking system, they remain indeterminate when a competitive banking system is supplanted by a monopoly. The monopoly maximizes its real profits at some real stock of money and deposit rate, but this real stock may be the arithmetic product of innumerable combinations of nominal money and price level. As we have designed our model, the banking monopolist is indifferent to the nominal value of its assets and debt.

Fundamentals of Monetary Control

Since *laissez-faire* banking cannot produce a determinate price level, we restore the Policy Bureau in the guise of a Central Bank. And we inquire into the minimum powers that the Central Bank must have if it is to enforce a price-level policy. We experiment with a case in which the Central Bank has the power to create nominal reserve balances, in the form of deposit claims on itself. The commercial banks desire real reserves both for resolving balances at the clearinghouse and as a protection against capital loss on primary securities. The Central Bank decides the nominal stock of member reserves, adding to the stock by buying primary securities and reducing it by selling primary securities. In the first experiment below, the yield on these reserves to commercial banks—the "reserve-balance" rate—is determined by competitive bidding among the banks. In the second experiment, the yield is specified by the Central Bank. In neither experiment is there a reserve requirement: liquidity preference is a matter of choice, not of compulsion, for commercial banks.

MARKETS FOR RESERVES AND MONEY

In addition to markets for current output, bonds, and money, there is now a market for reserves. The nominal stock of reserves (R) is set by the Central Bank and is equal to its nominal holdings of bonds. The real stock of reserves, of course, is the nominal stock deflated to purchasing-power terms $\left(\frac{R}{p}\right)$.

Commercial banks demand real reserves for portfolio diversification just as spending units demand real money. Their desired real stock of reserves varies positively with the real stock of money owed by the banks and hence with the banks' total real assets in cash and bonds. It varies positively, too, with the reserve-balance rate earned by the banks on their balances with the Central Bank. It varies negatively with yields expected on real earning assets, and these yields depend on the bond rate of interest and real-wage costs of portfolio administration. Since a rise in the deposit rate paid to spending units reduces the banks' desired levels of real money debt and real assets, it tends to reduce desired stocks of reserves. Incremental demand for real reserves is inversely related to real reserves already in the banks' possession.

This market is in equilibrium when the real stock of reserves outstanding is equal to the real stock that commercial banks desire to hold, that is, when:

$$\text{(5)} \qquad \frac{R}{p} = R\left(\frac{\overset{g}{Bc}}{ip}, \frac{\overset{g}{Ba}}{ip}, i, d, d', \frac{w}{p}\right),$$

where $\frac{\overset{g}{Bc}}{ip}$ represents bonds held by the Central Bank, which are equal to members' reserves; $\frac{\overset{g}{Ba}}{ip}$ is members' own bond portfolio; and d' is the reserve-balance rate. With nominal reserves fixed by the Central Bank, this market in isolation tends to eliminate excess demand for reserves by a reduction in d' even to negative levels that imply payment by commercial banks to the Central Bank of interest charges on their reserve holdings.

Now that there is a market for reserves, the banks' money-supply function (Equation 4 above) must be modified. It may be written:

$$(6) \qquad \frac{M}{p} = S\left(\frac{B_c^g}{ip}, \frac{B_a^g}{ip}, i, d, d', \frac{w}{p}\right).$$

An increase in real reserves and in the reserve-balance rate raises the banks' real stock of desired money debt, while an increase in the real value of bonds held may have the opposite effect, given net worth, in view of risk considerations. As before, the real money stock desired by banks is positively related to the bond rate of interest, negatively related to the deposit rate and real wage rate.

MARKET DETERMINATION OF RESERVE-BALANCE RATE

In our first two economies, the monetary authority enforced its price-level policy by stipulating nominal money and the deposit rate. When an authority with these prerogatives is eliminated and then replaced by *laissez-faire* banking, nominal money and the price level wander aimlessly about. To anchor the price level once more, is it sufficient to restore to the monetary authority the power only to stipulate nominal reserves of the commercial banks, deposit rate on these reserves being determined by competitive bidding among the banks?

Imagine that there is an initial equilibrium extending through all the markets including the market for reserves. Both spending units and commercial banks are content with their real aggregate portfolios and with diversification of their portfolios between cash assets and primary securities. Assume that commercial banks, for any reason, disturb the peace of equilibrium by purchasing additional primary securities from spending units, thereby creating additional nominal money for spending units to hold. With money neutral, the price level rises and nominal bonds increase proportionally with nominal money. Spending units are returned to their initial real position, but real balance sheets of the commercial banks and the Central Bank are not the same as before. There is a net real transfer of bonds from the Central Bank to its members: in Equations 5 and 6, $B\overset{g}{c}$ is held constant while $B\overset{g}{a}$ and p increase. Members gain real bonds and revenues, but the real reserves of members are reduced proportionally with shrinkage in the purchasing power of money. While the Central Bank regulates nominal reserves, the commercial banks may do as they like with real reserves.

At the initial reserve-balance rate, the higher price level and the reduced real volume of reserves imply a shortage of reserves, from the commercial banks' standpoint, and hence excess demand for reserves on their part. If the banks were content with their portfolio balance before equilibrium was disturbed, they must now be uneasy over the decline in their reserve ratio. Should one expect this excess demand for reserves at the higher price level to put the price level back in its initial position? No. For one thing, the commercial banks are compensated for their reduced liquidity by their windfall in real bonds and real interest income. This compensation is at the expense of the Central Bank. For each dollar of real reserves lost, one real dollar in bonds is gained to yield revenue at the bond rate of interest. There is a second effect of price inflation on bank earnings because the banks are receiving interest from or paying interest to the Central Bank, at the initial reserve-balance rate, on a reduced total of real reserves. If the net balance of these two changes in revenues precisely compensates the commercial banks for their loss of liquidity, general equilibrium is restored at the higher price level with no change in the reserve-balance rate. Then neither commercial banks nor spending units will have any incentive to restore the initial price level; the price level is clearly indeterminate.

If the change in bank revenues is more or less than necessary to compensate for illiquidity of banks at the reduced real stock of reserves, general equilibrium can be restored at the higher price level with a rise or fall respectively in the reserve-balance rate that the Central Bank pays. Because the reserve-balance rate is freely determined in the present model, commercial banks can bid the rate up or down as they choose to the level that makes them content with their portfolio mixtures of cash and bonds. There seems to be no reason why the banks should regret their adventure in expanding nominal money and retreat to the initial nominal stock of money and the initial price level. The conclusion follows that nominal money, nominal bonds, and the price level are indeterminate when the Central Bank regulates only the nominal stock of reserves, imposes no reserve requirement or deposit rate and pays a competitively determined reserve-balance rate. A Central Bank armed, or rather disarmed, in this fashion cannot impose its price-level policy on the community.

REGULATION OF NOMINAL RESERVES AND OF RESERVE-BALANCE RATE

In our second experiment, the Central Bank stipulates not only the nominal reserves of commercial banks but the reserve-balance rate as well. It may already be evident, from the discussion above, that the Central Bank now is able to regulate creation of nominal money and the price level. Nominal money, nominal bonds, and money prices of goods and labor are now determinate.

Assume once more an initial equilibrium and then imagine that it is disrupted by purchases of primary securities and monetary expansion on the part of the commercial banks, with quantity-theory effects upon nominal bonds and the price level. With nominal reserves given, real reserves of commercial banks are reduced and real bond-holdings of the commercial banks gain at the expense of the Central Bank's portfolio. Since there has been no change in the real stock of money or in the bond rate, the commercial banks may sense a shortage of real reserves at the reserve-balance rate decreed by the Central Bank. But now this excess demand for reserves cannot be resolved by market adjustment of the reserve-balance rate. The commercial banks discover, to their regret, that they can restore the desired balance of their portfolios between real cash and real bonds only by contracting nominal money. They must drive the price level back to its initial position and, in the process, restore the real value of the Central Bank's portfolio. With its control over both nominal reserves and the reserve-balance rate, the Central Bank can compel its members to prefer one price level over all others, in any real context; only one price level is compatible with portfolio balance in the commercial banking system.

The Central Bank with these two prerogatives of stipulating nominal reserves and reserve-balance rate is still a less powerful monetary authority than the Policy Bureau of earlier chapters. In the first place, its control over nominal money is indirect. With nominal reserves and the reserve-balance rate given, the commercial banks may change their notions of the right balance of cash and bonds in their portfolios and adjust the existing balance by expansion or contraction in nominal money. The Central Bank can prevent such adjustments, of course, and can frustrate its members' use of the price level as a means of increasing or decreasing their real reserves, by appropriate changes in nominal reserves and the reserve-balance rate. If members desire less liquidity, the Central Bank may contract nominal reserves, raise the reserve-balance rate, or do both. If members desire more liquidity, the Central Bank may expand nominal reserves, lower the reserve-balance rate, or do both. But this way of regulating nominal money is a roundabout way in comparison with the direct technique of the Policy Bureau.

The Policy Bureau also had authority, as our present Central Bank does not have, to specify the deposit rate allowed to spending units on their nominal money balances. In our current model, the deposit rate is a market price determined competitively by spending units and commercial banks. Any fall in the rate that reflects an effort of the banks to maximize profits by reducing the scale of their real assets and real debt must reduce the real stock of money desired by spending units and generate price inflation. Any rise in the rate that reflects an effort of the banks to maximize profits by increasing real assets and real debt must increase the real stock of money desired by spending units and generate price deflation. The Central Bank is competent to prevent these disturbances in the price level by countermeasures—by changes in nominal reserves and the reserve-balance rate—bearing on the liquidity of the banks. By reducing nominal reserves and raising the reserve-balance rate, it can prevent a reduction in the deposit rate which, through inflation, would intensify the shortage of real bank reserves. By raising nominal reserves and lowering the reserve-balance rate, it can prevent an increase in the deposit rate which, through deflation, would aggravate an excess of real reserves. The Central Bank does have these countermeasures at its disposal, but the Policy Bureau of earlier chapters was in the stronger position of regulating the deposit rate directly.

We know now the minimal elements of monetary control over a private-enterprise banking system, assuming that the deposit rate of commercial banks is set by the market. The nominal stock of bank reserves must be regulated by the Central Bank. And the Central Bank must decide the price of these reserves in the form of the reserve-balance rate. With these techniques at its command, the Central Bank can impose its price-level policy. In particular, it can thwart any attempt on the part of its members to inflate or deflate nominal money and the price level for the purpose of adjusting their real stock of reserves. Control over the commercial banks' own deposit rate is a convenient, though dispensable, instrument of control for the Central Bank. By regulation of the deposit rate, the Central Bank can forestall any attempt on the part of its members to change the real stock of money desired by spending units and, through subsequent inflation or deflation of the price level, the members' own size in terms of real assets and real money-debt.

The Technical Apparatus of Monetary Control

Private enterprise is not competent to do with nominal money what private enterprise does with steel or cotton or real-bonds—that is, to construct a market, confront an amount demanded with an amount supplied, and derive a value per unit that is anchored to the real variables of marginal utility in consumption and marginal cost in production. In a neo-classical world, shifting the decimal point in a figure that measures the nominal stock of money affects no one's real income and no one's real costs in a way that any consumer or firm can detect. If the value of the money unit is to be anchored in a closed society, public enterprise must take over the responsibility.

There are numerous techniques for determining nominal money and price level. We have looked at two general approaches to the problem: a Policy Bureau and a Central Bank regulating an array of private commercial banks. The second approach employs various possible techniques of regulation that enable the Central Bank to work its will on the nominal stock of bank reserves, reserve-balance rate, and the deposit rate of commercial banks. The present chapter is not the place for examining off-beat techniques of stipulating the determinants of nominal money. The discussion that follows is confined, in the main, to conventional instruments of control.

THE OPEN-MARKET OPERATION

The common method of supplying nominal reserves is for the Central Bank to sell them in the form of deposit claims against itself, taking government securities in payment. Anything else in the economy could be taken as payment—goods, labor, private bonds, or commercial banks' deposits—if the Central Bank were equipped to deal in it and either use it or store it. But the government bond is the typical *quid pro quo* on the market for reserves.

A common problem in supplying the right amount of nominal reserves is that the Central Bank may be required, on someone else's initiative, to pay out or retire deposit claims on itself in exchange against such things as gold or foreign bills, coin and currency or float. Through nominal reserves, the Central Bank signals to its members the instruction to expand or contract nominal money. But reserves may not be the ideal medium for communication because they pick up a confusion of signals. A gold flow, for example, rings the same bell as an open-market operation. Unless the Central Bank is alert to the need for countermanding all signals but its own, by offsetting operations, nominal money may expand or contract in ways inappropriate to the Central Bank's price-level policy.

Reserves may not be an ideal medium of communication for another reason. The signal of a change in reserve balances is not given to all commercial banks simultaneously, even assuming that all banks are members of the system. The first bank hearing it passes it on to others by adjustments in its own portfolio and money-debt that affect clearing balances. Ultimately each bank gets a fraction of the change in reserves that is determined by spending units' demand for its deposits in preference to deposits owed by other commercial banks. Reserves are a multi-party line carrying a confusion of signals, and they pass a message from the Central Bank to commercial banks not simultaneously but in some time-consuming sequence.

THE MEMBER-BANK RESERVE REQUIREMENT

A minimum ratio of reserves to commercial banks' assets or deposits, specified by law or regulation, is not a necessary part of the technique for determining and manipulating the nominal stock of money and the price level. Nominal money and the price level are determined when the Central Bank sets nominal reserves and the reserve-balance rate, given a reserve-demand function (liquidity-preference function) that defines the optimal portfolio balance for banks between reserves and primary securities at alternative combinations of bond rate, reserve-balance rate, deposit rate, and real stock of money. A minimum-reserve ratio puts a constraint on shifts in bank preference against reserves, say as the bond rate rises relative to the deposit rate and the reserve-balance rate. It is not accepted practice to stipulate a maximum-reserve ratio that imposes a comparable restraint on shifts in bank preference in favor of reserves, perhaps because of sentiment against compelling private enterprise to take risks against its will.

Chart IX illustrates equilibrium in the market for money at the bond rate of i_0 and real money balances of *OM,* and may be helpful in demonstrating why the reserve requirement is not an essential technique of monetary control. Given a nominal stock of reserves, the reserve-balance rate, and the deposit rate, banks are willing to supply more real money balances at higher bond rates, as suggested by the supply curve *SS′*. Spending units' real demand for money tends to increase as the bond rate falls, as indicated by the demand curve *DD′*. At the equilibrium level of real money balances *OM,* there is a determinate nominal stock of money supplied by banks and a determinate price level. The reason is that, of all the combinations of nominal money and price level that would be acceptable to spending units who desire *OM* in real money, only one combination provides the ratio of real reserves to real money, when nominal reserves are given, that will induce banks to supply *OM* in real money at bond rate i_0.

Suppose that the liquidity preference of banks diminishes, that they wish to reduce real reserves and increase their portfolios of real bonds at the initial bond rate, reserve-balance rate, and price level. The way for them to proceed is to create additional nominal money, that is, additional real money at the initial price level as indicated by the new supply curve *S′S″*. Then there is excess real money for spending units to hold; the price level rises, reducing real reserves and returning the supply curve to its original position; and equilibrium is restored at the real stock of money, *OM,* with real reserves making up a smaller fraction of bank assets. When the adjustment is finished, the real financial position of spending units is unchanged, but banks have decreased their real

CHART IX

Equilibrium in the Money Market

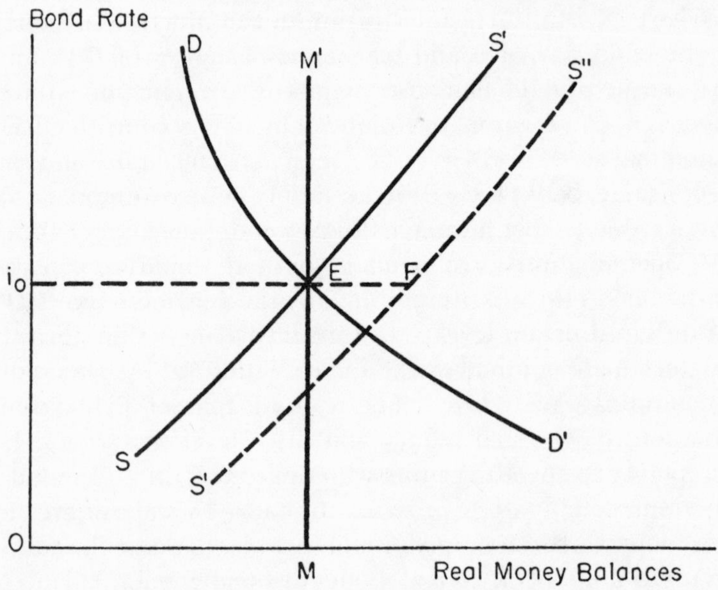

liquidity and increased both their real bonds and their real earnings at the expense of the Central Bank's price-level policy.

At a given reserve-balance rate, the Central Bank could meet this shift in bank preference by reducing the nominal stock of reserves through open-market sales of primary securities; it could relieve the banks of excess liquidity by reducing nominal reserves at a given price level instead of permitting the banks to reduce real liquidity by price inflation. This tactic would hold the money-supply curve of Chart IX firmly in its original position SS'. Alternatively, at a given volume of nominal reserves, the Central Bank could raise its reserve-balance rate, so that the commercial banks would lose their incentive to dispose of reserves in favor of bonds. This, too, would prevent any shift of SS' rightward.

The minimum-reserve requirement is a substitute for these two tactical responses by the Central Bank, reduction in nominal reserves and increase in the reserve-balance rate. By compelling commercial banks to maintain a proportion of reserves to primary securities that is not in accord with their desired portfolio balance, it becomes a "direct" control over bank operations. The reserve ratio, set by law or regulation, maintains the right nominal stock of money by compelling the commercial banks to get along with an unbalanced portfolio—with portfolio disequilibrium—and relieves the Central Bank of responsibility for countervailing action against its members' shifts in demand for real liquidity. By reason of the reserve requirement, banking is a "disequilibrium system" part of the time.

Thus, in Chart IX, the Central Bank could meet the rightward shift in the supply schedule of banks by imposing a reserve requirement that, given nominal reserves and the price level, prevents banks from producing real money balances in excess of OM. This maximum stock of money is shown by the vertical line MM'. The banks would like to produce real money that exceeds demand for it by EF. They are placed in a disequilibrium position by the reserve requirement.

It may be argued that the minimum-reserve requirement saves work for the Central Bank in simulating a free market for reserves. It may be argued, too, that a Central Bank would have an insufficient share of total real earnings in the monetary system if there were not a reserve requirement on commercial banks. The reason presumably is that commercial banks would desire so small a volume of reserves, at the nominal stock of money stipulated by the Central Bank, that primary securities available to the Central Bank would not yield enough income to cover its necessary costs. From this standpoint, the reserve requirement is a device for allocating total real bonds and total real profits in the monetary system between the Central Bank and its members. However, shares of the Central Bank and its members in total profits could be regulated by the reserve-balance rate. The Central Bank is a pure monopolist in the supply of reserves and can adjust supply and price, at a given nominal stock of money and price level, in such a way as to maximize profits. Whether such profits are sufficient matters very little in view of the Central Bank's status as a government agency.

A case might be made for the minimum-reserve requirement in an imperfect market for primary securities. At a given nominal stock of money and price level, members might discriminate against one class of primary securities and its issuers. The discrimination could be broken by forcing members to hold reserves in excess of the amount they desire, the reserves being provided by the Central Bank's purchases of the securities discriminated against. In this case, the reserve requirement is the instrument chosen to neutralize price-level effects of Central Bank operations bearing on the quality rather than the quantity of credit. But again an increase in reserves need not be neutralized by forcing banks into a disequilibrium position. Instead it can be neutralized by an increase in the reserve-balance rate.

It has been alleged frequently that banks would maintain voluntarily such low proportions of reserves to primary securities or deposits that any small change in reserves would have relatively explosive effects on the nominal stock of money: the "multiple of expansion" would be too high for reasonable stability in nominal money and the price level. But if banks' liquidity preference at the margin is so low that any small increase in reserves tends to be accompanied by a very large increase in members' portfolios to restore portfolio balance, any possible hazards can be overcome either by more nimble manipulation of reserves by the Central Bank or by an increase in reserve-balance rate that intensifies banks' liquidity preference.

We conclude that the minimum-reserve requirement is a dispensable element of the mechanism for monetary control. It is a substitute for a synthetic market in reserve balances, supplied and priced by the Central Bank, that could be so manipulated as to bring banks within the system of general equilibrium. It makes commercial banks a disequilibrium sector set apart from other sectors of the economy that are guided by the pricing mechanism rather than by direct controls.

REDISCOUNTING AND REDISCOUNT RATE

Borrowing by commercial banks from the Central Bank at a rediscount rate that is raised when the Central Bank wishes to intensify banks' liquidity preference and lowered when the Central Bank wishes to ease their liquidity preference is a step toward an equilibrium system of monetary control. In combination with open-market selling as banks rediscount and with open-market buying as banks repay rediscounts, the rediscount technique imposes a varying marginal charge on commercial banks for a more or less constant total of reserves. The mixture of operations, open-market selling (or buying) on the initiative of the Central Bank and rediscounting (or repayment of rediscounts) on the initiative of commercial banks, is a rather awkward way of bringing a varying negative reserve-balance rate to bear at the margin on banks' reserve balances. The same result could be achieved if the Central Bank held bank reserves constant, without the by-play of rediscounts and open-market operations, and applied a negative reserve-balance rate on a part of total reserves.

The minimum-reserve requirement on commercial banks may be regarded as a "sharing ratio" that specifies the Central Bank's share in the primary securities held by the monetary system. Rediscounting amounts to a violation of the sharing ratio, with commercial banks acquiring a larger portion of primary securities than the reserve requirement specifies. The violation is accepted practice, but it is subject to the restraint of the rediscount rate, the rediscount prejudice (the preference of banks for liquidity as against debt to the Central Bank), rules of eligibility, and moral suasion. In a control technique utilizing the reserve-balance rate, without a minimum-reserve requirement, no question would arise concerning "shares" in primary securities and earnings or concerning "rights" and "privileges" of rediscount. The Central Bank would simply decide upon a nominal amount of reserves and play upon commercial banks' preference for reserves relative to primary securities by varying the reserve-balance rate. Any single bank with a lower marginal liquidity preference than its competitors would borrow reserves not from the Central Bank but from competitors, through the market for reserves (federal funds).

COIN AND CURRENCY

If private banking corporations are granted a charter to create deposit money, then why are they not granted a charter to create coin and currency, especially if spending units' demand for deposit money is large in comparison with their demand for pocket money? It may be argued that assets underlying coin and currency are a source of earnings that should be reserved for the monetary authority. In American experience, however, earnings from issue of coin and currency and from the reserve requirement on commercial banks' deposits have produced earnings for the monetary authority far in excess of its requirements for efficient operation.

A second justification for locating coin and currency issue in the monetary authority is that the "currency drain" in inflationary times draws on the reserves of commercial banks, forcing them to rediscount and hence into payment of an increasing rediscount rate on an increasing share of reserve balances. This justification is not a persuasive one, since a Central Bank privileged to vary the reserve-balance rate could shift bank demand away from primary securities to reserves without waiting for the public's demand for pocket money to bring commercial banks to the rediscount window.

A third reason is somewhat more substantial. The economy, it may be argued, cannot do without a reliable means of payment, always acceptable at par and exchangeable through an efficient payments mechanism. Pressure can be brought to bear upon private banking corporations to maintain the moneyness of their deposits if they are required to maintain continuous interchangeability at par with coin and currency issues of government itself. This device is a strong protection against excessive service charges, collection charges, or other means to which the banks might resort as a way of increasing real profits at the expense of the money-using public. It subjects the banks to the discipline of competition in supplying the market for money and restrains their freedom in degrading the quality of their product or raising charges for using it. This is an instance in which "good money" threatens to drive "bad money" out of production. And it is an interesting example of the way in which discipline of the market place can be exploited by the monetary authority.

PRINCIPLE VS. TECHNIQUE

Throughout this chapter we have assumed that the Central Bank does not achieve a determinate price level by restraining the nominal amount of some nonmonetary financial asset —whether claims on nonmonetary intermediaries, government debt or private primary securities—but rather by controlling the nominal amount of money. We have assumed, too, that the monetary system is composed partly of private banking firms. On these assumptions, minimum specifications can be listed for measures to make nominal money and price level determinate. These specifications, however, can be satisfied by a variety of control techniques; some are right for economies with mature security markets and others are better for economies less advanced; some link the domestic economy to the world outside and others fit a closed economy; some are best adapted to an independent Central Bank and others are preferable when the Central Bank and Treasury are linked by the common objective of stable financial growth.

The first general specification, of course, is that the monetary authority must take any measures necessary to preserve the moneyness of members' indirect debt. Such measures may include capital requirements, deposit guaranty, bank examinations, and issue of coin and currency by the Central Bank itself. Granted that commercial banks are qualified by these or other measures as money-issuers, the Central Bank may regulate nominal money directly, as in our earlier models, or by indirect techniques discussed in this chapter. Of three indirect techniques—fixing nominal reserves, setting the reserve-balance rate, and setting members' own deposit rate—the Central Bank can get along with any two in regulating all nominal variables in the economic system.

Money and Government Debt

Throughout this volume little has been said about "public debt," that is interest-bearing nonmonetary issues of the Treasury. We have been concerned primarily with private securities. This is a serious omission. The common assumption is right that a large government debt has important consequences not only for the Treasury but also for the Central Bank, its member banks, and spending units. It may affect goals of monetary policy, control techniques, the responses of commercial banks to various techniques, and the real profits of the monetary system. We call attention in this section to some effects of public debt on the demand for reserves by commercial banks and on the demand for money by spending units. The conclusions we come to are illustrated by a hypothetical merger of monetary control and public-debt management. A financial authority competent to manage both nominal money and public debt has a grip upon interest rates, in the short run, and upon the price level as well as upon real variables, in the long run, that the traditional Central Bank cannot achieve.

GOVERNMENT DEBT AS SECONDARY RESERVE

If there is no very close substitute for reserves in satisfying commercial banks' demand for liquidity, the banks' preferred ratio of reserves to primary securities may fluctuate widely when the bond rate of interest varies relative to the deposit rate and to the reserve-balance rate. At a relatively high bond rate, the preferred ratio may be very low; at a relatively low bond rate, it may be significantly higher. If there is a reserve requirement, the preferred balance between reserves and primary securities cannot be attained when the bond rate is high, but the banks may react to a low bond rate by maintaining reserves in excess of the legal minimum.

When, on the other hand, there is a close substitute for reserves in satisfying the banks' preference for portfolio balance, the desired reserve ratio fluctuates over a narrower range as rates of interest on primary securities vary relative to the deposit and reserve-balance rates. As the bond rate of interest falls, the demand for reserves may be diverted to short-term government securities or perhaps to brokers' loans or to bills on a foreign market. That is, banks may maintain portfolio balance by shifting less to reserve balances at the Central Bank and more to competitive assets. As the bond rate of interest rises, banks may reduce the liquidity of their portfolios not by trying so much to dispense with reserves as by selling the liquidity substitute—the Treasury bill, broker's loan, or foreign draft. By appropriate purchases and sales of these substitutes for reserves, banks can keep their desired reserve ratio in line with the required ratio. A tidal flow of the substitute asset into bank portfolios as the bond rate falls and a tidal ebb as the bond rate rises take the place of fluctuations in the preferred reserve ratio.

The secondary-reserve asset must go to some nonbank buyer as banks sell and come from some nonbank seller as banks buy. In a closed economy, the trading counterpart of banks may be spending units, the Central Bank, or the Treasury. Sales to spending units as the bond rate rises—that is, "switching" operations by the banks—substitute the banks' secondary-reserve asset for money in spending units' portfolios, supplying them with a close alternative to money and limiting the short-run rise in the bond rate that is associated with any rise in nominal national income. This is to say that the availability of an asset that satisfies the banks' demand for liquidity when interest rates are low, and enables them to dispense with excess reserves, also satisfies spending units' demand for liquidity when interest rates are rising, and enables them to dispense with money. The consequences of these switching operations for monetary policy have been considered in Chapter VI.[1]

Banks may also dispose of secondary reserves to the Central Bank. Outright sale is inflationary and is to be expected when short-run monetary policy is on a deflationary tack. Hence, the Central Bank's strategy is to accept government securities from member banks on a rediscount basis and to balance rediscounting with open-market sales from its own portfolio, keeping total reserves more or less constant. The increase in negative free reserves is penalized by a rise in the rediscount rate that, as we have seen, amounts to a rise in the marginal reserve-balance rate. The ebb of secondary-reserve assets from bank portfolios, then, tends to inhibit the demand for money when the assets are sold to spending units, but it can be seized upon as an opportunity to increase the banks' demand for reserves relative to primary securities, *via* rediscount techniques, when the assets are unloaded on the Central Bank. The first of these effects softens the impact of short-run restrictive policy by the Central Bank, but the second effect plays into the Central Bank's hand.

The third buyer of secondary-reserve assets from the commercial banks is the Treasury. If the Treasury takes up bills from the banks and simultaneously funds them with bonds

[1] Pp. 221-22.

sold to spending units, the effect is to intensify the latter's demand for money and strengthen the grip of restrictive monetary policy. If the Treasury takes up bills from the banks and applies a budget surplus to their retirement, the effect again is deflationary and presumably in accord with monetary policy since spending units lose net financial assets in liquid form. In this case, as in the second, the ebb of secondary-reserve assets from the banks can be the occasion for contra-cyclical financial policy. The return flow to the banks obviously may be exploited by the Central Bank or Treasury for contra-cyclical financial policy to stimulate demands on the markets for goods and labor.

It appears that a secondary-reserve asset of substantial amount is an advantage to most sectors in the economy. Commercial banks gain from it because it displaces excess reserves when the bond rate is low and is a convenient instrument for rediscount when the bond rate is high. In the form of Treasury bills, a secondary-reserve asset is advantageous to the Treasury because the average interest cost of this form of debt is low over the business cycle. Private spending units, in their turn, may balance their portfolios more economically with a secondary-reserve asset than with money alone. From the standpoint of the Central Bank, of course, a secondary reserve asset may complicate monetary control, but the Central Bank does have means of dealing with this situation.

CONSOLIDATION OF MONETARY AND GOVERNMENT-DEBT MANAGEMENT

These considerations suggest a hypothetical experiment in consolidating monetary and government-debt management. The price level can be determined by Central Bank control over nominal reserves and the reserve-balance rate or over nominal government debt and its yield, but regulation combining both is the most powerful and immediate in its effects on markets for reserves and money.

Imagine that responsibility for government-debt management is transferred to the Central Bank with interest and transaction costs underwritten by the Treasury. Treasury borrowing is done directly with the Central Bank. The latter then becomes a debtor on types of debt ranging from commercial banks' reserve balances through bills, certificates, notes, and bonds. The Congress and the Treasury would retain responsibility for changes in the quantity of debt assumed by the Central Bank—that is, for "fiscal policy"—as distinct from changes in the structure of the debt or "debt management." Imagine, further, that the Central Bank is instructed to change the mix of its debt, from reserves through long-term bonds, in such a fashion as to maintain a stable price level. Another instruction would be necessary, regarding the distribution of the costs and revenues of financial policy between the Treasury and the commercial banks.

Let an initial equilibrium throughout the economy be disturbed by an increase in real wealth and real income. The immediate result is an increase in spending units' real demand for financial assets generally and, in particular, for short-term assets including money. To avoid the eventual price deflation that would satisfy real demand for money, as well as short-run perturbations in interest rates and income, the Central Bank has a choice among control techniques. First, it may reduce the reserve-balance rate, inducing banks to buy primary securities and create nominal money. Second, the Central Bank itself may buy primary securities, increasing members' reserve balances at a given reserve-balance rate. Third, the Central Bank may lower the deposit rate paid by banks, thereby reducing spending units' demand for money. Finally, it may unfund public debt, selling bills and retiring bonds into its own portfolio and providing banks with bills that will induce them, in view of their enhanced liquidity, to expand nominal money, or providing spending units with bills as a money-substitute. The choice among these alternatives depends primarily on considerations regarding real costs in interest to the Treasury and real profits of the banking system.

In principle, government debt can be added to reserve balances owed by the Central Bank as a vehicle for maintaining equilibrium on the market for money at the price level elected by the monetary authority. Reserve balances at the Central Bank may be counted as a form of government debt, and they may be linked to the direct debt of the Treasury to make a versatile instrument of financial control. Government debt, bank reserves, and money are so important a segment of total financial assets that control over this segment is an extremely powerful lever for regulating the growth rate of total financial assets at their nominal value. Government debt, on the one hand, and debts of the monetary system on the other, are each so important a segment of total financial assets that management of them by different authorities working for dissimilar goals must be expensive in real interest costs to the Treasury, in monetary stability, or in real earnings of the banking system.

Bank Profits and Capital

The costs and revenues of money production did not concern us when our monetary system was composed of a Policy and a Banking Bureau. The Policy Bureau simply handed down instructions to the Banking Bureau on the amount of primary securities to be purchased and the nominal amount of money to be created. The Banking Bureau obeyed the instructions to the letter, regardless of the costs and revenues involved. In our present discussion, the "instructions" are issued by the Central Bank through changes in nominal reserves, the reserve-balance rate, and the deposit rate—and, in American experience, through rediscount rate and the minimum-reserve requirement. A private banking system is supposed to respond by producing the nominal stock of money that is appropriate, given real money desired by spending units and the Central Bank's policy objective.

Bank revenues and costs make a difference for monetary control, on a number of counts. First, the banking system will not produce any real volume of money that implies operating losses in the long run. By one means or another, including either overt or indirect changes in the deposit rate, it can be depended upon to modify spending units' demand for money and so to adjust the real stock of money, in any given context, to a level that is consistent with some positive level of profits. Briefly, bank revenues and costs have a bearing on the real stock of money and hence on the nominal stock that is right for the Central Bank's price-level goal.

Second, revenues and costs affect the banks' response to the Central Bank's prodding for monetary expansion. If it appears that an increase in the real stock of money will reduce profits or increase losses in real terms, the banks can be expected to disregard the signal for expansion of nominal money. Third, the banks' choice between types of primary securities when they expand or contract money is dictated by profit considerations. In the short run and on imperfect security markets, this "discrimination" may add side effects to monetary policy that are objectionable. Fourth, the profit experience of private banks affects their ability to accumulate net worth either by stock issue or by retention of earnings. An unfavorable record has the result of weakening bank solvency and of so compromising the moneyness of bank deposits that closer surveillance of bank operations is required and even public subvention may be necessary.

Fifth, profit experience in banking has a great deal to do with the structure of the industry and with the competitiveness of its behavior on the markets for bonds and money. Adverse profit experience for the industry as a whole puts a premium on noncompetitive banking practices. Sixth, profit experience of private banks affects incentives and resources to undertake technological development in the industry for long-run improvement in the efficiency of the payments mechanism. Risks of heavy outlay on capital assets in banking are not acceptable to the industry when the profit outlook is discouraging. Seventh, where banks may elect between competing jurisdictions of government, the jurisdiction most favorable for profits is preferred whether the result is conducive to effective monetary policy or not.

INGREDIENTS OF BANK PROFITS

Commercial banks obtain their earnings predominantly from interest on portfolios of primary securities. Their expenses consist largely of wages and salaries to employees and interest payments to depositors. The gross profits of banks are the difference between earnings and expenses, after allowance for capital gains or losses on security portfolios. Their net profits are gross profits less income taxes. These magnitudes may be measured in nominal or real terms. In what follows, we are concerned with their real values because, as we have pointed out previously, purely nominal changes in deposits, bank assets, and bank revenues and costs are of no concern to rational management in a neo-classical world.

The fundamental determinant of gross profits of commercial banks is the size of the stock of money. Given the money stock, bank earnings depend on the bond rate of interest; they vary directly with the bond rate. To earnings in the form of interest or dividends on primary securities one adds such auxiliary revenues as banks may earn on, say, their trust activities. And one deducts, of course, any losses from default or market depreciation.

For any stock of money and bond rate of interest, bank earnings depend on the proportion of assets in the form of reserves and on the reserve-balance rate paid or charged by the Central Bank. Obviously, as the required or desired ratio of reserves to total assets is raised and the reserve-balance rate reduced, bank earnings suffer. In holding reserves, commercial banks relinquish an equal amount of primary securities to the Central Bank, and their net loss of earnings depends on the share of the Central Bank's income that it returns to them.

From total earnings one deducts, in calculating banks' gross profits, the cost of administering bank security portfolios. These costs are subject to economies of scale for the individual bank and for the system, in selecting assets, supervising them and collecting upon them. As is the case with any financial intermediary, commercial banks can attract spending units' demand to indirect securities and away from primary securities essentially because of the advantages that they can exploit in diversifying portfolios cheaply and in applying methods of quantity production to portfolio management. The small-scale bank can succeed mainly by taking a noncompetitive profit from local imperfections in the markets for primary securities and deposits.

From total earnings one also deducts the cost of maintaining deposit accounts and administering the payments mechanism. Costs for clearing, collection, and record-keeping are also economized by routine operations on a large scale; hence, given the relative sizes of individual banking firms, these costs should decline on a per-unit basis as the real stock of money grows. If payment of a deposit rate is permitted by the monetary authority, its effect on banks' gross profits depends on the use that is made of the rate as an instrument for diverting spending units' demand from other financial assets to money, and on the elasticity of spending units' demand for money with respect to the rate.

This listing covers the principal items involved in the measurement of banks' gross profits. From these one deducts income taxes to arrive at net profits. These profits will be considered as a percentage return on total assets and as a percentage return on the net worth of banks.

MONETARY POLICY AND BANK PROFITS

A Central Bank, or monetary authority, can determine the price level by controlling the nominal stock of any financial asset—money, business bonds, savings and loan shares, consumer debt, or government securities. It can lower the price level by reducing the nominal stock of the controlled financial asset; it can raise the price level by increasing it. Under most circumstances, the issuer of the financial asset that is selected as the instrument of price level policy is placed at a relative disadvantage with respect to profits. The segment of the financial system almost always chosen for the key role in determining and stabilizing the price level is a private banking system, which thereby may be placed in an unfavorable profit position.

There are several reasons for this. First, given other nominal financial assets and the price and interest rate levels desired by the monetary authority, the nominal assets and liabilities of a controlled banking system are generally smaller than they otherwise would be. Commercial banks are placed in a disequilibrium position, wishing to produce more money output than they are permitted to produce, except when the bond rate of interest is very low. Banks are prevented from balancing real marginal revenue and marginal cost and thus from achieving maximum profits.

Second, the control mechanism may specify the holding by banks of reserve balances with the Central Bank at a low or zero reserve-balance rate. If so, banks' profits are reduced not only because of the smaller size of their assets but also because some profits are transferred from them to the Central Bank through the reserve requirement specification.

Third, primary security portfolios of banks are accumulated mainly at relatively low bond rates of interest. Monetary policy inhibits the expansion of commercial banks, in the short run, for the purpose of raising interest rates and it stimulates bank expansion, in the short run, for the purpose of lowering interest rates. Consequently, it is inherent in a monetary policy aimed at contra-cyclical objectives that banks should not add significantly to primary securities at high interest rates and should increase their holdings of primary securities generously at low interest rates. Portfolio turnover does give commercial banks some opportunity to benefit from tight money, but there is a lag in turnover as interest rates rise which retards improvement in the yield on bank assets and net worth.

Commercial banks are in the same position with regard to profits as a Treasury is with regard to interest cost when it actively uses government-debt management for contra-cyclical policy bearing on nominal national income and the price level. In pursuing this policy, a Treasury sells long-term securities to force interest rates higher in a cyclical boom, and pays the higher interest rates. It sells short-term securities to retire bonds at high market prices in recession. Thus it sells long-term debt cheaply and buys it dearly, and the losses on its bonds are not made good by capital gains on its bills.

Fourth, the costs to banks of short-run monetary policy are inflated by the response of issuers of other financial assets, including nonmonetary intermediaries, to tight-money policy in the boom. A rise in the bond rate initiated by monetary restraints creates incentives and opportunities for other issuers to divert demand away from money and toward competing financial assets. For example, nonmonetary intermediaries, as explained in Chapter VI, may raise their deposit rates and divert demand from money precisely when policy calls for growth in the demand for money relative to the stock of it. To maintain the rise in the bond rate, it is necessary for the monetary authority to offset the effects of nonmonetary intermediation on demand for money by further constraint on supply and so on bank additions to their portfolios at high bond rates. If tight money encourages innovations in nonmonetary finance, the resulting shift in demand from money to other financial assets at such times may be lost to the banks more or less permanently. Needless to say, banks fare better if there is a second string to their bow, such as a time-deposit department, that permits them to engage in nonmonetary intermediation.

Suppose that the special restraint on bank assets and on yield per dollar of bank assets causes banks to become less sensitive to the Central Bank's techniques of control. Are matters more difficult then for the Central Bank in applying monetary policy, assuming that the control mechanism does not cut deeply enough to endanger banks' solvency and the efficiency of the payments mechanism? The banks may come to respond more sluggishly to increases in their reserves as marginal returns decline on primary securities. But if the banks prefer reserves over primary securities, the Central Bank has only to take the primary securities into its own portfolio, supply the reserves that banks prefer, and simultaneously provide the nominal money that spending units demand at a given price level. Or the banks' preference for cash reserves may be overcome if attractive secondary-reserve assets, such as Treasury bills, are made available.

If the rate of growth in real money balances falls below the rate of growth in finance generally, does the efficiency of monetary policy suffer? Apparently not. In principle, the real stock of money may actually decline in the midst of general growth, falling to some very small positive amount, and still the price level can be determined and regulated by changes in nominal money. Any positive nominal stock of money gives the leverage that is necessary for determining real money and the price level.

THE THEORY OF BANK CAPITAL

As private corporations, commercial banks solicit capital funds by stock issue, and they build up capital by retaining net profits from dividends. They compete with other issuers of primary securities, through stock issues, for the savings of spending units, and ultimately retained profits are subject to the same tests of relative yield as new stock issues are.

Growth in bank capital is to be expected only in an amount sufficient to equate the expected yield of bank net profits on capital with yields on other financial investments of comparable risk. Bank capital can grow at the same rate as bank assets only if the percentage yield of net profits on bank assets bears a constant proportion to the market yield on nonbanking uses of stockholder funds. If the percentage yield on assets rises relative to the opportunity cost of investment in banking net worth, the yield on bank stocks increases relative to yields on competitive securities at a given market price of bank stocks. Then market bidding drives up prices on bank stocks, and banks strive to build up capital accounts by increasing stock issues and by paying out dividends less generously.

If, on the other hand, the percentage yield on bank assets declines relative to the opportunity cost of investment in banking, the capital-asset ratio also declines so that the return to bank capital may rise into line with returns to investment elsewhere. The capital-asset ratio may be brought down by partial withdrawal of stockholder capital, by surrender of charters, or by failure. The ratio, however, is more likely to be reduced as the result of decreases in bank stock issues and increases in dividends relative to net profit in periods when assets and deposits are rising. Assets and deposits are simply permitted to outgrow stockholder investment and to outgrow it the more as assets and deposits gain at a relatively rapid rate.

Historically in the United States, net profits of commercial banks relative to their assets have declined secularly. As one would expect, therefore, the secular trend of the capital-asset ratio has also been downward. The decline of the capital-asset ratio has enabled the banks' net profit-capital ratio to maintain a roughly stable relationship with major indexes of corporate bond rates. The earning capacity of banks per dollar of assets has fallen over the years and, as a result, so has their capacity to attract stockholder investment per dollar of assets.

REMEDIES FOR A DECLINING CAPITAL-ASSET RATIO

The selection of a private banking system as the focal point of financial control may weaken banks' profit position, especially if nonmonetary finance is highly active, which in turn leads to decay in their capital-asset ratio. A secular decline in the net profit-asset and capital-asset ratios is likely to make banks more vulnerable to potential adversity, endangering the parity of bank deposits and the efficiency of the payments mechanism. It may also cause banks to become more conservative in their purchases of primary securities, to respond more sluggishly to increases in reserves, and to innovate less vigorously.

The monetary authority can attempt to offset possible undesirable effects of secular declines in the ratios by a series of *ad hoc* measures. There may be government investment in bank stocks. Bank deposits may be insured, and tighter restrictions may be imposed on bank portfolios, with examination procedures made more exacting. Treasury securities may be adapted to bank taste. The payment of an explicit deposit rate may be forbidden or limited, and entry into banking restricted. By such means, the monetary authority can attempt to make the actual capital-asset ratios adequate ones. Under these circumstances, it should be noted, if the cause and effect relationship runs from declining capital-asset ratios to the corrective measures, it would be misleading to say that because of such measures banks *need* less capital.

There are many other solutions in the long run for the decline in banks' net profit-asset and capital-asset ratios, aside from the measures just mentioned. The earning capacity of the banking system and its capacity to draw stockholder investment could be increased by reducing reserve requirements. Then a smaller share of the monetary system's net profits would accrue to the Central Bank, a larger share to commercial banks. The same effect could be realized, perhaps with a higher level of technical efficiency in monetary control, by a positive and flexible reserve-balance rate on commercial banks' balances with the Central Bank. Moreover, if the banking system comprises many small and inefficient banking firms, and if these firms can realize economies of scale up to some relatively large size, new entries into the industry can be prohibited and existing firms can be merged. Banking could be recognized as a public utility and a fair return assured on a reasonable investment, with precautions taken against monopoly practices. The real stock of money could be defined as social capital on the order of facilities for water and power, and the industry producing nominal money could be ranked, as public utilities are, as a compromise between public and private enterprise.

An alternative solution is 100 per cent reserves—commercial banking without primary securities. This solution turns all primary securities underlying money-issue over to a public institution, the Central Bank, and limits private banking institutions to the job of administering the payments mechanism. In this case, the community acknowledges that primary securities in the monetary system's portfolio must be bought and sold, as government securities are bought and sold in a program of government-debt management, at times and at prices that are not completely rational in terms of private enterprise for profit. The community recognizes that there are real costs involved in determining nominal money and the price level, and it accepts these costs as social costs.

The same considerations suggest a more radical solution—nationalization of the banking system. Since private enterprise, driven by the profit incentive, cannot determine nominal money and the price level through ordinary market processes, and since private enterprise that is controlled for the purpose of regulating money and prices is under a special handicap in earning capacity, the responsibility and burden of maintaining a money stock and preserving its value could rest on the community at large. If there is a secular decline in rates of return on bank assets, accompanied by a secular decline in the capital-asset ratio, a question could eventually be raised of whether private investment in banking is sufficient, relative to assets and to the money stock, to justify private ownership and management.

There are still other alternatives, however, for the banking system is not the only possible instrument for defining a price level. The above considerations could mean that controls over the banking system should be eased and that government debt should become the means of price-level determination. In principle, fiscal policy and debt management are competent to take the place of monetary management. Further, it is possible to spread the mantle of control over private nonmonetary finance, so that the burden of control is distributed more evenly among issuers of financial assets. For example, controls could be extended to nonmonetary financial intermediaries. They may also be extended to nonfinancial spending units, the issuers of primary securities, as illustrated by consumer credit regulations or by private capital issues restrictions.

The relative feasibility of the various solutions depends on the given political, social, and economic context and on the extent to which profit and capital positions of the controlled financial area are weakened. Under most conditions, however, it is probable that the optimal solution is not the adoption of *ad hoc* measures that are designed to support the financial area chosen as the focal point of financial control.

The Single Banking Firm

There is little to say about the single banking firm that is not equally true of the industry. Except in short periods, when the firm may borrow from the Central Bank or other commercial banks, it is true for the firm as for the industry that size in terms of real assets depends on the ability to borrow from depositors, that is, on spending units' real demand for the firm's deposit obligations. Over the long run, in a competitive quantity-theory world, the size of the individual bank would be determined by the total real stock of money and by the share of the total stock that the individual firm could produce at a competitive return on capital.

Given its cost and revenue functions, the single bank tends to grow in step with the system of banks, attracting incremental demand for deposits at the same rate as the system. Given reserve requirements or individual bank preferences for liquidity ratios, the single bank tends to gain primary securities relative to reserves at the same rate as the system. The growth of the single bank is a small-scale replica of growth for the industry, in the general equilibrium model.

MULTIPLE EXPANSION

Banking theory has paid a great deal of attention to the relative growth rates, in nominal terms, of the single bank and the system during a dynamic adjustment from one aggregate of reserves in the system to a different aggregate. With the banks initially adjusted to the reserve requirement, an increment in reserves implies excess liquidity in banking and touches off an expansion in primary-security portfolios to the limit at which portfolio balance is restored. The analysis takes as constant the equilibrium share of each bank in total reserves, primary securities, and deposits, and assumes that the increment in reserves is initially distributed among banks in a random fashion; it demonstrates that no one bank may acquire and retain a part of the increment in reserves, primary securities, and deposits larger than its given share of total reserves, primary securities, and deposits. This is not a revealing conclusion, since it amounts to saying that a stable average share implies a marginal share equal to the average.

This exercise in multiples of expansion usually is couched

in terms of a convergent process in which the banking system returns to portfolio balance, as specified by the reserve requirement, through expansion in primary securities and deposits of individual banks. At the end of the process, the system of banks has created deposits by a multiple of the increment in reserves that it retains. And the same, of course, is true for each individual bank: the single bank has created deposits by a multiple of its terminal share in the increment of reserves. The single bank is a miniature replica of the system of banks.

As partial analysis to explain money-creation and the processes of clearing and collection, the exercise has its pedagogical uses. But its shortcomings as a way of explaining how the markets for reserves and money are cleared of excess supply—by bank spending of reserves and the public's spending of money—raise the question of whether it has had perhaps too central a role in banking analysis. It is comparable to a mechanical exercise in nominal terms with the investment multiplier. The difference is that preoccupation with the arithmetic of the multiplier has not distracted attention from the real consumption function to the degree that preoccupation with the multiple of expansion has distracted attention from the demand function for money and the general conditions of monetary equilibrium.

It seems to us that the description of multiple expansion might profitably be rephrased in terms that are less mechanical and more behavioral. Furthermore, the analysis is more meaningful if it is viewed as a dynamic adjustment in all markets to an initial shock on the market for reserves. The remainder of this section will illustrate this general equilibrium approach.

Let an initial stable relationship between nominal reserves of commercial banks, the banks' portfolios of primary securities, and nominal money be disturbed by an increase in reserves. The increase in reserves is a signal to commercial banks that the Central Bank has taken up its share of a proposed increase in the total portfolio of the monetary system and expects the commercial banks to follow. The excess stock of reserves at first affects few commercial banks. Given marginal rates of substitution—perhaps as dictated in a reserve requirement—between reserves, bond-holdings, and money-debt, these few banks reduce their excess reserves by adding to their bond portfolios and their money-debt. This increase in their money-debt exceeds incremental demand for it on the part of spending units so that reserves equal to a substantial portion of their money-creation are lost to other banks. Demand for reserves throughout the banking system approaches the increased stock of reserves as more and more banks are caught up in the process of exorcising excess reserves by expanding their portfolios and money-debt. There is a new equilibrium on the market for reserves when every bank has adapted its bond portfolio and its money-debt to its reserve position and when the distribution among banks of reserves, bonds, and money reflects spending units' desired apportionment of their money balances between banks.

After an initial disturbance on the market for reserves, equilibrium is restored at a larger stock of reserves and a correspondingly higher level of demand for them, concurrently with equilibrium on all other markets. Unless money-creation by the banks provides spending units with excess money balances that increase their demand for bonds, goods, and labor, there can be no convergent process of multiple expansion by the banking system. Partial disequilibrium on the market for reserves is not dissipated by multiple expansion unless it induces general disequilibrium—excess stocks of reserves and money which are the same as excess demands for bonds, goods, and labor.

The undesired increment in bank reserves provokes money-creation that adds undesired increments to money balances of spending units. Spending units with excess money balances increase their rates of spending on markets for bonds, goods, and labor. These same spending units realize a relatively small share of the resulting increase in income for all spending units together, and hence they incur budget deficits that draw off the lion's share of their excess money balances. The banks that initiate expansion experience a "leakage" of reserves, and the spending units that initiate a rising level of nominal national income experience a "leakage" of money. Demand for money throughout the community of spending units approaches the stock of money that banks desire to owe as more and more spending units are involved in the process of exorcising excess money by bidding up nominal national income and nominal stocks of nonmonetary financial assets.

A new equilibrium is attained simultaneously on all markets—for reserves, money, bonds, goods, and labor—when the stock of reserves desired by all banks is equal to existing reserves and when the stock of money desired by all spending units is equal to the stock of balances provided by the banking system. Assuming a uniform reserve requirement, each bank has added to its earning assets and to its deposits, in the new equilibrium, by multiples—relative to the increment in reserves—that are identical for all individual banks and the system of banks. Assuming a uniform money-demand function, each spending unit has added to its financial assets and to its income and spending by multiples, relative to its increment in money, that are the same for all spending units.

There are advantages in translating the convergent process of multiple monetary expansion into an exercise with multimarket adjustment to excess reserves. For one thing, the time lags of adjustment to a change in reserves are easier to identify. The convergent process within the banking system decays, and the time lags of adjustment are indefinitely long, either if the banks are insensitive to increments of reserves or if disequilibrium on the market for reserves does not branch out to other markets. The time lags are short, if both banks and spending units react promptly to excess stocks of liquidity by intensifying demand on markets for bonds, goods, and labor. One looks for an explanation of time lags in factors affecting speed of response on the part of banks to excess reserves and on the part of spending units to excess stocks of money and excess demands for bonds, goods, and labor.

Another advantage in substituting general analysis for partial analysis of monetary expansion is that general analysis explains, as partial analysis does not, the apportionment of growth in money between banks. The sequence in which banks share expansion and the ultimate division of expansion among them are not the mysteries they appear to be in the conventional model. Instead they are determined by spending units' path of adjustment to excess money and by spending units' relative demands for the deposit debt of individual commercial banks. Expansion is propelled by both banks and spending units, not by banks alone, and the pattern of a new equilibrium is inexplicable without reference to the demand side of the money market.

Finally, general analysis has the advantage of dispelling some of the aura of "uniqueness" that is attributed to banks and their expansion. The process of expansion embraces all markets and spending units as well as banks. It begins with excess supply on the market for reserves, and the banks' part of the process is to restore by multiple growth of deposits and bond portfolios an equality between existing and desired stocks of reserves. It extends to excess supply on the market for money, and spending units' part of the process is to restore equality between existing and desired stocks of money by multiple growth in spending on goods and labor as well as in existing and desired stocks of primary securities. The "uniqueness" of banks is that they buy and sell reserves whereas spending units do not, that they supply money whereas spending units demand it. There is nothing unique about the multiple expansion of bank debt relative to bank liquidity, since spending units achieve a multiple expansion in income and primary debt relative to their liquidity in money form.

INCREASING RETURNS AND MERGERS

The principal issue of theoretical interest in the case of the single bank has to do with the bank's relative size in the industry and with the bank's market behavior as a perfect or imperfect competitor. One starts with the truism that the real size of the firm, in terms of assets and money debt, depends on the real amount of its money product desired by spending units at the terms of the bank's deposit contract. It seems to be a fair hypothesis that the terms on which the banking firm could offer deposits, consistent with a given rate of return per dollar of assets, could be more generous to depositors as the bank gains in size; the banking industry appears to be subject to increasing returns up to some scale of operation above the average in American banking. Alternatively, with the number of competitors restricted, the rate of return on assets could be increased at given terms to depositors.

The banking firm may realize increasing returns, or decreasing unit costs, in administration both of its deposit debt and of its assets. Services provided by banks to depositors are subject to mechanization. And banks with large aggregates of deposits, divided among numerous accounts, can predict deposit behavior with such accuracy that low-yield reserves of liquid assets can be minimized in bank portfolios. Many phases of asset administration—from credit analysis to record-keeping to collection—are routine operations, most cheaply performed on a large scale. Loan contracts in large numbers, with homogeneous terms, are subject to probabilistic estimates with regard to expenses and losses that permit gains in efficiency as the size of the banking firm rises. Banking has enough in common with insurance to guarantee important economies of scale.

One expects, then, to find a falling unit cost curve in banking. At the same time, the markets on which banks buy and sell—markets for money, bonds, and labor—may have adequate defenses against exploitation by the large banking firm. The relatively high degree of substitutability between bank deposits and loans, on the one hand, and financial assets and credit provided to spending units by nonbank sources, on the other hand, means that banking cannot easily take monopolistic advantage of its markets. Intensive supervision of banking is additional insurance against exploitation of either depositors or borrowers.

Assuming decreasing costs in banking, relatively elastic demand functions on markets for banking services, and close regulation by government agencies, there may be a rational basis for merger in the banking industry. Before antitrust discipline is brought to bear on banking, it is important to determine whether a merger movement will advance the public welfare both by economizing costs of bank operation and by increasing the responsiveness of banks to monetary controls.

Summary

In Chapters II-VI, nominal money was created by a governmental Banking Bureau. Its quantity and its explicit deposit rate were decreed by a Policy Bureau. In this chapter, the Banking Bureau is supplanted by a private commercial banking system, the Policy Bureau by a Central Bank. The Central Bank stipulates not the nominal amount of money but the nominal amount of reserves, the reserve-balance rate, and, optionally, the deposit rate. The Central Bank does not have to impose a minimum-reserve requirement on commercial banks for the purpose of achieving a determinate price level and nominal stock of money.

The Central Bank, working its will on nominal money through the agency of private banking enterprise, is involved in the problem that private enterprise is imperfectly adapted to the role of money-creation. In such a role, banks are called upon to buy and sell assets, to borrow and lend, at times and on terms that are not completely rational from the standpoint of profit incentive. The social utility of its activities—anchoring the price level, administering the payments mechanism, and serving as a financial intermediary—may not pay off handsomely in earnings. As a result its capital position tends to deteriorate, and deterioration is hastened by development of nonmonetary finance outside the orbit of control. There are numerous solutions for a capital shortage in banking, among them a greater reliance on government-debt management for financial control or extension of controls to the nominal debt issues of nonmonetary intermediaries and spending units.

Mathematical Appendix

A Neo-classical Model of Money, Debt, and Economic Growth

BY ALAIN C. ENTHOVEN

I. *Introduction*

DURING THE PAST twenty years, there has been much formal discussion of the process of economic growth in the Keynesian tradition, based on assumptions of fixed prices and input-output coefficients.[1] In general, these analyses, following Sir Roy Harrod, have focused attention on the growth of income from the demand side. Harrod's model is based on the assumption of a fixed marginal capital-output ratio and a fixed savings ratio. Under these conditions, if saving is to be equal to investment at all times, income must grow at a constant relative (that is, exponential) rate. But this equilibrium growth path is unstable in two senses. First, if the rate of growth of income deviates momentarily from its equilibrium path, forces will be set up which will

[1] See *inter alia* Roy F. Harrod, *Towards a Dynamic Economics* (1948) and "An Essay in Dynamic Theory," *Economic Journal,* LIX, (March 1939), pp. 14-33, reprinted in *Readings in Business Cycles and National Income,* A. H. Hansen and R. V. Clemence, eds. (1953), pp. 200-19; Evsey D. Domar, "Expansion and Employment," *American Economic Review,* XXXVII (March 1947), pp. 34-55; D. Hamberg, *Economic Growth and Instability* (1956); William Fellner, "The Capital-Output Ratio in Dynamic Economics," *Money, Trade and Economic Growth* (1951).

cause it to deviate even further in the same direction.[2] Second, there is no force driving the rates of growth of capital and income on the one hand and labor on the other into equality. If the rates are different, because of the fixed marginal capital-output ratio, one or the other factor becomes redundant.

Recently, some significant advances in the theory of economic growth have been made along neo-classical lines. The work of James Tobin and Robert M. Solow has pointed the way to a fuller analysis of the process of economic growth in an economy in which the factors of production are substitutable and in which decision-making units have asset preferences.[3] The neo-classical approach is based upon the general hypothesis that the price mechanism works, that the factors of production are substitutable, subject to diminishing marginal returns, and that markets are stable. Hence, for example, if the capital stock starts to grow more rapidly than the supply of labor, the marginal product of capital will fall, and the rate of investment will be reduced. The economy moves on a stable path; it is not balanced on a knife edge.

Neo-classical monetary theory has recently received an extensive treatment at the hands of Don Patinkin.[4] Assuming the existence of a demand for real cash balances, a real cash balance effect on the demand for commodities, flexible prices, the absence of money illusion, and static expectations regarding the price level and interest rate, Patinkin attempted to demonstrate the neo-

[2] For example, if the rate of growth slows momentarily, the flow of savings-investment will generate capital at a rate greater than that required to sustain the current rate of output. Capital becomes redundant. Presumably this dampens investment if investment decisions are made separately from savings decisions. See Harrod, "An Essay in Dynamic Theory," *op. cit.*

[3] James Tobin, "A Dynamic Aggregative Model," *Journal of Political Economy,* LXIII (April 1955), pp. 103-15; Robert Solow, "A Contribution to the Theory of Economic Growth," *Quarterly Journal of Economics,* LXX (February 1956), pp. 65-94. For another analysis of economic growth along similar lines, see Richard R. Nelson, "A Theory of the Low-Level Equilibrium Trap in Underdeveloped Countries," *American Economic Review,* XLVI (December 1956), pp. 894-908.

[4] Don Patinkin, *Money, Interest and Prices* (1956).

classical propositions about the neutrality of money (for example, a doubling of the money stock will double the equilibrium money price level and leave all relative prices unchanged). However, the Patinkin model does not include a monetary system or a central bank that holds privately issued securities.[5] In the absence of government debt, the central bank is assumed to be unable to deal in debt at all. As a consequence, changes in the money stock have no effect on the interest rate except in the special case in which government debt is introduced. The Patinkin discussion suggests that it is the introduction of government securities which destroys the neturality of money. But this comes about only because, in the Patinkin analysis, the introduction of government bonds is implicitly connected with the ability of the central bank to deal in any bonds. In fact, if the central bank has purchased any bonds, of government or private issue, changes in the money stock will not be neutral in their effects except under very special circumstances. Thus, the Patinkin model is inadequate for analysis of the ability of the central bank or the monetary system to influence the allocation of resources.

Moreover, the Patinkin system is static and timeless. The capital stock and the supply curve of labor are parameters held constant throughout the analysis. There is positive net investment but no capital accumulation. Presumably, the speed of adjustment of monetary variables is sufficiently great relative to changes in the capital stock that the feedback from changes in the latter to the monetary variables can be neglected. Of course, this was the assumption made by Keynes in *The General Theory.* But this does mean that the lack of influence of monetary variables on economic growth is an assumption and not a conclusion in Patinkin's system. Thus, the model is not suitable for the analysis of the impact of monetary developments on economic growth in a neo-classical economy.

The purpose of this analysis is to present a neo-classical model of a growing monetary economy. Like Harrod's model, income and the capital stock in this model can grow, in equilibrium, at

[5] *Ibid.,* Chap. XII.

a constant relative rate. But unlike Harrod's model, factor proportions are variable and the equilibrium growth path is not necessarily unstable. Like Patinkin's model, in this model prices are flexible, households and firms have asset preferences but no money illusion, and financial asset holdings influence the demand for commodities. But unlike Patinkin's model, the economy is capable of balanced growth, changes in the rate of interest influence the size of the capital stock via investment, and there is either a central bank or a regulated monetary system, or both.

The model is examined first in a stationary state in which all net expenditure flows between sectors must be equal to zero. The labor supply is taken as constant. The money stock and the bond holdings of the monetary system are taken as parameters and some fundamental comparative statics propositions for a neo-classical economy with a central bank or a regulated monetary system are demonstrated.

Then the labor supply, the money stock, and the bond holdings of the monetary system are assumed to grow at a constant relative rate, and the behavior of the model in a state of balanced growth is studied. Partial analyses are used to show the stability of factor proportions and of the ratio of debt to income. In the growing economy, the various sectors can run persistent deficits or surpluses on income and product account. These deficits and surpluses are reflected in corresponding flows of financial assets. Now, changes in the flow of new money, whether issued for the purchase of goods or bonds, or for the purpose of making transfer payments, will have an impact on the size of output and its allocation. In a growing economy, changes in the flow of new money reinforce the effects of the corresponding changes in the stock of money in a stationary economy.

As a by-product, the analysis contains an attempt to broaden the formal analytical framework of neo-classical monetary theory to include positive equilibrium flows of loanable funds, asset accumulation and economic growth.

II. The Model

Let the economy be divided into three sectors: business firms, households, and a consolidated monetary system and government sector. The two private sectors can be thought of as engaged in a process of production, and accumulation of assets and indebtedness. Their behavior during the process will be influenced by their incomes, their asset portfolios and the prices they face. Given a constant set of external parameters, the accumulation policy of each sector should lead its portfolio to converge onto a desired equilibrium position.

Business firms employ the capital stock, which they own, and labor, which is supplied by the households, to produce all of current output. They save part of their incomes and they borrow from households.

Households receive income from supplying labor, from interest on bonds, from dividends, and from transfers from the government sector. They consume a part of current output and they accumulate bonds and cash balances.

The consolidated monetary system and government sector, henceforth referred to as the government sector, buys and sells bonds, buys goods, makes transfer payments and issues money.

A. THE BUSINESS SECTOR

Real output, Y, a homogeneous good used both as capital and as a consumer good, is produced with capital, K, and labor, L, by competitive firms under conditions of constant returns to scale and diminishing marginal returns to each factor as its employment increases, with the other factor held constant. The factors of production are substitutable for each other continuously and without limit. The aggregate production function can be written

$$Y = F(K, L). \tag{2.1}$$

The marginal products of both factors are never negative, and they are decreasing functions of their respective inputs (diminishing marginal returns), that is,

$$\frac{\partial F}{\partial K} = F_K \geqq 0,$$

$$\frac{\partial F_K}{\partial K} = F_{KK} < 0,$$

and similarly for labor. The assumption of constant returns to scale rules out the existence of any scarce input in fixed supply, such as land. It simplifies the analysis a great deal, although it is not a necessary condition for many of the basic conclusions of this analysis.

The factor markets are assumed always to be in competitive equilibrium, and each factor is paid the value of its marginal product, in real terms. Thus, the real wage, w, is always equal to the marginal product of labor; the real rent on capital, r, is always equal to the marginal product of capital, that is,

$$w = F_L(K, L) \tag{2.2}$$

$$r = F_K(K, L). \tag{2.3}$$

By Euler's theorem, constant returns to scale imply

$$Y = wL + rK. \tag{2.4}$$

Gross business receipts, in real terms, are equal to sales, Y, plus the proceeds from the issue of new bonds. Each bond is a perpetuity paying a dollar each period.[6] Letting B denote the number of nominal bonds outstanding, we may write the real receipts from the issue of new bonds (i.e., new bond issues deflated by the price of goods) per period $\frac{\dot{B}}{ip}$, where the dot over B denotes the first derivative of B with respect to time; i is the

[6] The firm issuing a bond can redeem it at its market price.

interest rate on bonds, and p, the money price level of goods. Gross business receipts are divided between wage payments, wL, interest payments, $\frac{B}{p}$, capital accumulation, $\dot{K}$, and dividends. Business firms remit to the households, as dividends, all of net business income, $rK-\frac{B}{p}$, except that part which is saved. (However, there is no market in equities.) For the sake of simplicity, it is assumed that business firms do not accumulate money balances. Letting S denote business saving, the budget identity for the business sector can thus be written

$$(2.5) \qquad Y+\frac{\dot{B}}{ip}\equiv wL+\frac{B}{p}+\dot{K}+\left(rK-\frac{B}{p}-S\right).$$

With the help of (2.4), we may deduce the supply function for new bonds,[7]

$$(2.6) \qquad \frac{\dot{B}}{ip}\equiv\dot{K}-S.$$

The business sector will determine $\dot{K}$, $\frac{\dot{B}}{ip}$, and S within the constraints that bond issues must be equal to investment minus saving and that saving, or retained earnings, must not exceed net business income. The decision will be a simultaneous multimarginal choice depending upon the sector's asset position, the prices it faces, and its income. The size of the capital stock itself, *ceteris paribus*, will act as a deterrent to further investment, as will the amount of business debt outstanding. A problem of

[7] This is, of course, based on the assumption that business firms do not accumulate cash balances. If firms were to accumulate money, (2.6) would have to be re-written as $\frac{\dot{B}}{ip}\equiv\dot{K}+D-S$, where D represents the incremental demand on the part of business firms for cash balances. Also, D would have to be added to the demand side of the money market. However, the assumption that firms do not accumulate cash balances greatly simplifies the analysis without affecting its content.

measurement arises in connection with the stock of debt. Its market value is, of course, $\frac{B}{ip}$. However, market value in this sense is not likely to be directly relevant for business behavior. For example, an increase in the market rate of interest is equivalent to a reduction in the market value of the debt. But it does not mean a reduction in the burden of the debt in the sense of reducing the flow of interest payments to which the sector is committed. It would seem more appropriate to use the real value of the flow of interest payments, $\frac{B}{p}$, as an index of the "burden of the debt."

The rate of capital accumulation is an increasing function of r, the rate of return on capital, and a decreasing function of i. In a riskless, perfectly competitive world, the equilibrium relationship between r and i would be one of equality. That is, when r exceeds i, it would pay firms to increase their rate of borrowing and investing; when r is less than i, the opposite, each until r and i are brought into equality. The presence of risk, uncertainty, and asset preferences, on the other hand, may make the equilibrium relationship between the two rates different from one of equality. Finally, investment will be an increasing function of net business income. Letting subscripts denote partial differentiation with respect to the indicated argument, these hypotheses can be summarized as follows:

$$\dot{K}=I\left(K, \frac{B}{p}, r, i, rK-\frac{B}{p}\right) \tag{2.7}$$

$$I_1<0, I_2<0, I_3>0, I_4<0, I_5>0.$$

Business saving is likely to be affected negatively by the size of the capital stock, *ceteris paribus*. On the other hand, business debt is likely to provide an incentive to greater saving, and it will be assumed that the relationship is positive. Increases in the profit rate and in net business income make saving easier, while increases in the interest rate provide a greater incentive for internal finance. Thus.

$$S = S\left(K, \frac{B}{p}, r, i, rK - \frac{B}{p}\right) \tag{2.8}$$

$$S_1 < 0,\ S_2 > 0,\ S_3 > 0,\ S_4 > 0,\ S_5 > 0.$$

If the supply of labor is held constant, the total effect on investment and saving of an increase in K will be the sum of the negative asset effects, the negative effect of the increased capital-labor ratio on r, and the income effect. The latter will be positive if the elasticity of substitution between K and L is high enough.[8] I shall assume that the investment and saving functions are of such form that the total effects of increases in K are negative. The total effect of an increase in bonds outstanding on savings is the sum of a positive debt-burden effect and a negative income effect. I shall assume that the debt-burden effect always dominates.[9] The foregoing hypotheses are summarized by the following:

[8] The total return to capital is rK. Its first partial derivative with respect to K is $KF_{KK}+F_K$ whose sign is ambiguous. A sufficient, though not necessary, condition for it to be positive is that the elasticity of substitution, σ, between K and L be at least unity. If F is homogeneous of degree one, $\sigma = -\frac{F_K F_L}{Y\frac{K}{L}F_{KK}}$. Let $S_L = \frac{LF_L}{Y}$ be the share of labor in total output. Then $\sigma = -S_L\frac{F_K}{KF_{KK}}$ whence $KF_{KK}+F_K \gtreqless 0$ as $\sigma \gtreqless S_L$. Of course, $0<S_L<1$, whence $\sigma \geqq 1$ is sufficient, though not necessary. For example: (1) $Y=\beta K^{\alpha}L^{1-\alpha}$, $(0<\alpha<1)$, (Cobb-Douglas), for which $\sigma=1$; (2) $Y=A[\alpha K^{-\beta}+(1-\alpha)L^{-\beta}]^{-\frac{1}{\beta}}$, $(0<\alpha<1)$, $(-1\leqq\beta)$, $\sigma=\frac{1}{1+\beta}$. (I owe this example to an unpublished paper of K. J. Arrow. It is the family of all constant σ production functions.) In this case, σ can be less than 1 for admissable values of β. $KF_{KK}+F_K>0$ if and only if $\left(\frac{\alpha}{1-\alpha}\right)\left(\frac{L}{K}\right)^{\beta}>\beta$.

[9] This does lead to a paradoxical situation with respect to the effect of price level changes on the distribution of real income. On the one hand,

$$(2.9)\qquad \begin{aligned} I_K &= I_1 + I_3F_{KK} + I_5(KF_{KK} + F_K) < 0 \\ I_B &= (I_2 - I_5)\frac{1}{p} < 0 \\ I_p &= (I_2 - I_5)\left(-\frac{B}{p^2}\right) > 0 \\ I_i &= I_4 < 0 \end{aligned}$$

$$(2.10)\qquad \begin{aligned} S_K &= S_1 + S_3F_{KK} + S_5(KF_{KK} + F_K) < 0 \\ S_B &= (S_2 - S_5)\frac{1}{p} > 0 \\ S_p &= (S_2 - S_5)\left(-\frac{B}{p^2}\right) < 0 \\ S_i &= S_4 > 0. \end{aligned}$$

Given the price level, the interest rate and the labor supply, the business sector is in full portfolio equilibrium when

$$(2.11a)\qquad I\left(K, \frac{B}{p}, r, i, rK - \frac{B}{p}\right) = 0$$

$$(2.11b)\qquad S\left(K, \frac{B}{p}, r, i, rK - \frac{B}{p}\right) = 0.$$

These equations define equilibrium values of K and B, say K^e and B^e.

---

since business firms are debtors and households are creditors on bond account, one would expect that, *ceteris paribus*, an increase in the price level would reduce the real value of the interest payments from the business sector to the household sector, thus shifting the distribution of real income in favor of the business sector. On the other hand, it will be shown that, given the assumptions of the model, household income is equal to national income, Y, plus transfers from the government, less business savings, whence if $S_B > 0$, implying $S_p < 0$, an increase in the price level, *ceteris paribus*, increases real household income by reducing business savings. However, the adoption of the alternative hypothesis would complicate the analysis later on, and lead to worse paradoxes.

Differentiating totally with respect to i, we find

(2.12a) $$\frac{dB^e}{di}=\frac{I_iS_K-I_KS_i}{I_KS_B-I_BS_K}<0$$

(2.12b) $$\frac{dK^e}{di}=\frac{I_BS_i-I_iS_B}{I_KS_B-I_BS_K}.$$

The sign of $\frac{dB^e}{di}$ is implied by (2.9) and (2.10). The sign of $\frac{dK^e}{di}$ is not determined by the assumptions that I have made so far. The reason for this is that the reduction in K^e brought about directly by an increase in i may be offset by the increase in investment brought about indirectly by the decrease in indebtedness caused by an increase in i.[10] However, ordinarily one would expect $\frac{dK^e}{di}$ to be negative. Given the earlier assumptions, it will be negative if (and only if) the numerator of (2.12b) is positive, that is, if

(2.13) $$I_BS_i-I_iS_B>0.$$

What does this inequality imply about business behavior? In order for it to be satisfied, the second term, which is positive when taken with its sign, must be greater in absolute value than the first, which is negative. This will be the case if the interest rate is relatively more important in the determination of the rate of investment, while the stock of accumulated debt is relatively more important in the decision whether to finance the investment internally or externally, in the sense $\frac{I_i}{I_B}>\frac{S_i}{S_B}$. For example, (2.13)

[10] Differentiating (2.11 a) totally with respect to i, one obtains $\frac{dK^e}{di}=-\frac{I_i}{I_K}-\frac{I_B}{I_K}\frac{dB^e}{di}$. The first component, which is negative under our assumptions, might be called the direct effect of i on K^e. The second, which might be called the indirect effect via B^e, is positive if $\frac{dB^e}{di}$ is negative. By substituting (2.12 a) into this equation, we get (2.12 b).

will be satisfied if i has little or no effect on the decision whether to finance internally or externally and if the ratio of accumulated debt to business net worth has little or no effect on the decision to undertake new investments, possibilities which seem to be suggested by a study by Franco Modigliani and M. H. Miller.[11] In the analysis that follows, the negative relationship between changes in the equilibrium values of i and K will depend upon (2.13).[12]

B. THE GOVERNMENT SECTOR

The government sector is a consolidated monetary system and fiscal authority. It buys bonds and current output from the private sector, it makes transfer payments to households, and it can issue bonds of its own. Its bonds are identical to those issued by the business sector. With the exception of interest receipts from its holdings of private bonds when it is a net creditor on bond account, it has no income.

Assume, for the sake of simplicity, that the government turns over to households, as transfer payments, all of its interest earn-

[11] See Franco Modigliani and M. H. Miller, "The Cost of Capital, Corporation Finance, and the Theory of Investment," *American Economic Review*, XLVIII (June 1958), pp. 261-97.

[12] Is it the case that, with i, p, and L constant, the policy of capital accumulation and borrowing implied by (2.6), (2.7) and (2.8) will lead the business sector's asset position to converge onto a stable equilibrium? (2.9) and (2.10) guarantee at least local stability. (2.6), (2.7) and (2.8) can be approximated in the neighborhood of equilibrium as follows:

$$(a)\quad \dot{K}=I_K{}^\circ(K-K^\circ)+I_B{}^\circ(B-B^\circ)$$
$$(b)\quad \dot{B}=ip(I_K{}^\circ-S_K{}^\circ)(K-K^\circ)+ip(I_B{}^\circ-S_B{}^\circ)(B-B^\circ).$$

The necessary and sufficient conditions for the stability of the linear system are

$$(a)\quad I_K{}^\circ+ip(I_B{}^\circ-S_B{}^\circ)<0$$
$$(b)\quad I_B{}^\circ S_K{}^\circ-I_K{}^\circ S_B{}^\circ>0$$

both of which are implied by (2.9) and (2.10). Alternatively, one could assume the stability of this process as an independent hypothesis and use the implications of this assumption instead of assuming $S_K<0$ in obtaining results of Parts III and VII.

ings, whence all interest on bonds is paid to households, and that these payments are not counted in the sum labeled transfer payments. When the government is a net debtor, assume that it taxes back all interest payments, but that otherwise it does not collect taxes.[13] These simplifying assumptions permit us to ignore the effects of the flow of interest payments between the government and private sectors. Under these assumptions, the budget identity of the government sector can be written

$$\dot{M} \equiv G_c + G_t + G_b \tag{2.14}$$

where M is the nominal stock of money, whence $\dot{M}$ is the rate at which new money is issued, G_c is the money value of purchases of goods, G_t is the money value of transfer payments from government to households, and G_b is the money value of government purchases of bonds, all per unit of time. G_b is negative if the government is issuing bonds.

The consolidation of the monetary system and the rest of the government into a single sector can be given at least two interpretations. First, it can characterize an economy in which there is no private sector in the monetary system, or one in which there is a private sector subject to a system of variable fractional reserve requirements by which the monetary authorities can control the portfolios of the private banks. In the latter case, for present purposes, it does not matter which part of the monetary system buys and sells bonds. Second, it can characterize an economy in which there is a private sector in the monetary system either free of controls or subject to a set of regulations which do not vary, but in which the central bank buys and sells bonds. In this case, our monetary system is the central bank, and the private part of the monetary system should be taken to be a part of the private sector. The essential characteristic of the monetary system assumed in this analysis is that its

[13] These are very much in the nature of simplifying assumptions to remove complicating effects of little importance. Taxes could be thought of as negative transfer payments. Hence, for some purposes, the effects of taxes can be taken to be opposite to those of transfer payments.

holdings of bonds issued by the private sector are the object of direct policy decisions so that the bond holdings of the monetary system can be treated as an exogenous variable.

C. THE HOUSEHOLD SECTOR

The household sector receives wage income, wL, interest on bonds, $\frac{B}{p}$, dividends, $\left(rK-\frac{B}{p}-S\right)$, and transfer payments, $\frac{G_t}{p}$. Letting H represent the real income of the household sector, we have

$$H=wL+\frac{B}{p}+\left(rK-\frac{B}{p}-S\right)+\frac{G_t}{p} \tag{2.15}$$[14]

or, using (2.4),

$$H=Y-S+\frac{G_t}{p} \tag{2.16}$$

Households consume part of their incomes and save part. That part which is saved is divided into increments in household holdings of bonds and money. If households accumulate goods, these accumulations do not affect current consumption or savings decisions. Letting C represent consumption, D_b and D_m, household incremental demands for bonds and money balances respectively, all in real terms, the budget identity for the household sector can be written

$$H\equiv C+D_b+D_m. \tag{2.17}$$

Within this constraint, C, D_b and D_m will be determined as the result of a simultaneous multi-marginal choice depending upon household income, H, the interest rate, i, real cash balances, $\frac{M}{p}$, and real bond holdings. Let the net bond holdings of the gov-

[14] Households receive all of the interest on bonds outstanding because of our simplifying assumption that the government automatically transfers all interest earnings to households.

ernment sector be B_g. Then, since total privately issued bonds outstanding are B, the real market value of household bond holdings can be written $\frac{B_h}{ip}=\frac{B-B_g}{ip}$.

The effects on consumption of increases in consumers' holdings of real bonds and money balances, the "real asset" and "real balance effects" will be assumed to be positive.[15] The effect of the interest rate on consumption has received a good deal of attention.[16] The standard neo-classical hypothesis is that the effect of increases in the interest rate is to reduce consumption.[17] However, this will have no bearing on later conclusions. It is not an important effect. Consumption is also a function of household income. The partial derivative of consumption with respect to income, that is, the marginal propensity to consume, will be positive but less than unity. Again, letting subscripts denote partial differentiation with respect to the indicated argument, the consumption function can be written and the foregoing hypotheses can be summarized as follows:

$$C\left(\frac{B_h}{ip}, \frac{M}{p}, i, H\right) \tag{2.18}$$

$$C_1>0, C_2>0, C_3<0, 0<C_4<1.$$

[15] See *inter alia* Gardner Ackley, "The Wealth-Saving Relationship," *Journal of Political Economy,* LIX (April 1951), pp. 154-61, and William Hamburger, "The Relation of Consumption to Wealth and the Wage Rate," *Econometrica,* XXIII (January 1955), pp. 1-17, for empirical studies of the relationship between wealth and consumption. Patinkin, *op. cit.,* p. 22, cites three studies on the real balance effect itself. See also Thomas Mayer, "The Empirical Significance of the Real Balance Effect," *The Quarterly Journal of Economics,* LXXIII (May 1959), pp. 275-91. The only assumptions that I make are about the signs of these effects. There is no intention to suggest that as a matter of practical policy, downward price flexibility can be counted upon to restore equilibrium when there is a general excess supply of goods and labor.

[16] See, for example, J. M. Keynes, *The General Theory of Employment, Interest and Money* (1936), Chap. 8; L. R. Klein, "The Empirical Foundations of Keynesian Economics," *Post-Keynesian Economics,* K. K. Kurihara, ed. (1955), pp. 277-319, especially p. 292.

[17] See Patinkin, *op. cit.,* pp. 51, 77, 133.

The demand functions for bonds and money, D_b and D_m, are flows. Their dimensionality is the same as that of the demand for consumer goods, that is, acquisitions per unit of time. Their sum, the net household demand for financial assets, is equal to household saving.

Aside from the obvious symmetry with the consumption function, one might ask what is the advantage of formulating the demands in terms of flows instead of stocks. The main reasons are simplicity and compatibility with dynamic analysis. These points deserve some explanation. First, it is important to distinguish between what might be called *temporary equilibrium* and *full equilibrium* for a household or for the household sector. A household can be said to be in temporary equilibrium if its flow of consumption and the allocation of its portfolio are optimal, given its tastes, the prices of goods and securities, its income, *and its total wealth at that time,* but if its wealth is not optimal given the other variables. The household is in full equilibrium when the temporary equilibrium conditions are satisfied *and the size of the portfolio is optimal,* that is, when total wealth is great enough to induce the household to stop accumulating financial assets and to consume all of its income. The same distinction can be applied to the household sector or, for that matter, to any sector.[18]

[18] Incremental demand functions can be defined for each household. The aggregate demand for the sector as a whole is merely the sum of the individual demands. The temporary equilibrium values of the aggregate demands, and therefore of the interest rate and the price level, do depend upon "distribution effects," that is, on the way in which financial assets happen to be distributed between sectors, as Patinkin points out. *Op. cit.*, pp. 200-03. But, on the assumption of the existence, uniqueness and stability of equilibrium, the full equilibrium values of the financial asset holdings are independent of distribution effects. Given time, the results of any distribution effects will disappear (or, strictly speaking, become arbitrarily small). Thus, comparative statics in terms of full equilibrium positions can be done without assuming the absence of distribution effects. This is a point which Patinkin appears to have overlooked. The full equilibrium values depend only on tastes, incomes and prices. For a lucid explanation, see G. C. Archibald and R. G. Lipsey, "Monetary and Value Theory: A

Now, D_b and D_m, the planned increments in real bond and cash balance holdings per unit of time, depend upon, but are not equal to (1) the difference between the temporary equilibrium values of $\frac{B_h}{ip}$ and $\frac{M}{p}$ and their actual values, and (2) the difference between the full equilibrium values of $\frac{B_h}{ip}$ and $\frac{M}{p}$ and their actual values. Except in full equilibrium, however, there is no reason to expect them to be equal. Quite the contrary. For example, if the difference between the actual portfolio and the equilibrium one, either in the temporary or the full equilibrium sense, is at all large, a household may not plan to correct it all in one period. In fact, whether it would or not would depend on the unit of time chosen. However, one would expect D_b and D_m to be increasing functions of these differences and to be equal to zero when they are. D_b and D_m might be said to be determined by these portfolio disequilibria plus hypotheses about the speed with which households will seek to correct the disequilibria.

The statement of demands for and supplies of financial assets in terms of demands for and supplies of stocks can be misleading. Is the "demand for money" the temporary equilibrium stock of money, or is it the full equilibrium stock? It can make a difference. Moreover, for the reason which I have just explained, that is, that households may not plan to correct the portfolio disequilibrium all in one period, neither demand is equal to the current effective demand in the marketplace. D_b and D_m are the effective demands.

The statement of demands in terms of flows is necessary for dynamic analysis because one needs hypotheses about flows in order to study the behavior of the system outside of full equilibrium. In a growing economy, some sectors may never be in

---

Critique of Lange and Patinkin," *The Review of Economic Studies,* XXVI (1) (October 1958), pp. 1-22. The distinction between temporary and full equilibrium is analogous to the distinction between short and long run equilibrium in the theory of the firm.

full equilibrium, but there may be a path of temporary equilibria at which the market is cleared and prices are constant.

To fix ideas, suppose the actual stock of financial assets held by the household sector is $A=\frac{1}{ip}B_h+\frac{M}{p}$. Let the temporary equilibrium cash balances be M^d, a function of A, i, and possibly H if there is a transactions motive at work. Then, we can say that the household sector's real cash balances are equal to their temporary equilibrium value if

$$M^d(A, i, H)-\frac{M}{p}=0. \tag{2.19a}$$

Assuming that neither financial asset is an inferior good, $0<\frac{\partial M^d}{\partial A}<1$. Moreover, $\frac{\partial M^d}{\partial i}<0$. If a transactions motive for holding cash is at work, $\frac{\partial M^d}{\partial H}>0$. Similarly, for bonds, the temporary equilibrium condition is

$$B^d(A, i, H)-\frac{B_h}{ip}=0. \tag{2.19b}$$

But M^d and B^d will not be equal to their full equilibrium values unless A is also optimal, given i and H. Let the full equilibrium values be $M^e(i, H)$ and $B^e(i, H)$, with $\frac{\partial M^e}{\partial i}<0$, $\frac{\partial M^e}{\partial H}>0$, $\frac{\partial B^e}{\partial i}>0$ and $\frac{\partial B^e}{\partial H}>0$. Then we can speak of two kinds of "net demand for cash balances," $M^d-\frac{M}{p}$ resulting from non-optimal allocation of the existing portfolio, and $M^e-\frac{M}{p}$ which will be positive in temporary equilibrium if the sector plans to save and acquire more wealth. D_m is related positively to both, but not necessarily equal to either except in full equilibrium in which case $D_m=0$.

The assumptions that have been made so far are consistent with a broad class of hypotheses about the rationale for household behavior.[19] For example, they accord with the hypothesis that households maximize a quasi-concave (that is, diminishing marginal rates of substitution) utility function of asset holdings, subject to a limited total portfolio value, or, alternatively, with the hypothesis that households maximize the rate of return on their portfolios, discounted for risk, with each discount factor an increasing function of the ratio of the holdings of that particular asset to the value of the total portfolio.

Now, write

$$D_m = \phi\left[M^d(A, i, H) - \frac{M}{p}, M^e(i, H) - \frac{M}{p}\right] \tag{2.20}$$

with the partial derivatives ϕ_1 and ϕ_2 both positive. Then, D_m is a function of A and $\frac{M}{p}$, therefore of $\frac{B_h}{ip}$, and a function of i and of H. Taking $\frac{B_h}{ip}$ as a parameter, the partial derivates of D_m are

$$\frac{\partial D_m}{\partial \frac{M}{p}} = \phi_1\left(\frac{\partial M^d}{\partial A} - 1\right) - \phi_2 < 0,$$

$$\frac{\partial D_m}{\partial \frac{B_h}{ip}} = \phi_1 \frac{\partial M^d}{\partial A} > 0,$$

$$\frac{\partial D_m}{\partial i} = \phi_1 \frac{\partial M^d}{\partial i} + \phi_2 \frac{\partial M^e}{\partial i} < 0,$$

and

$$\frac{\partial D_m}{\partial H} = \phi_1 \frac{\partial M^d}{\partial H} + \phi_2 \frac{\partial M^e}{\partial H} > 0.$$

[19] See, for example, James Tobin, "Liquidity Preference as Behavior Towards Risk," *The Review of Economic Studies*, No. 67 (February 1958), pp. 65-86, and H. Markowitz, "Portfolio Selection," *The Journal of Finance*, VII (March 1952), pp. 77-91.

Thus, we may write

$$(2.21)\qquad D_m\left(\frac{B_h}{ip}, \frac{M}{p}, i, H\right)$$

$$D_{m1}>0,\ D_{m2}<0,\ D_{m3}<0,\ 1>D_{m4}>0.$$

Similar considerations suggest [20]

$$(2.22)\qquad D_b\left(\frac{B_h}{ip}, \frac{M}{p}, i, H\right)$$

$$D_{b1}<0,\ D_{b2}>0,\ D_{b3}>0,\ 1>D_{b4}>0.^{21}$$

[20] Let $D_b=\psi\left[B^d(A, i, H)-\frac{B_h}{ip}, B^e(i, H)-\frac{B_h}{ip}\right], \psi_1>0, \psi_2>0.$

[21] These results are consistent with the household budget identity (2.17). Differentiating this identity partially with respect to real bond holdings, real cash balances, the interest rate (holding real bonds constant) and household income, and equating partial derivatives, we obtain

$$C_1+D_{b1}+D_{m1}=0$$
$$C_2+D_{b2}+D_{m2}=0$$
$$C_3+D_{b3}+D_{m3}=0$$
$$C_4+D_{b4}+D_{m4}=1$$

Multiplying the first equation by $-D_{m2}$ the second by D_{m1}, and adding, we obtain

$$(C_1D_{m2}-C_2D_{m1})+(D_{b1}D_{m2}-D_{b2}D_{m1})=0.$$

Our hypotheses about the demand functions imply that the first expression must be negative, whence

$$D_{b1}D_{m2}-D_{b2}D_{m1}>0.$$

The sense of this inequality is that the positive asset effects on consumption imply that the "own" effects of bond and money holdings on the incremental demand functions are greater, in absolute terms, than the "cross" effects. This is useful in establishing at least the local convergence of the household asset accumulation process.

Let

$$\frac{\dot{B}_h}{ip}=D_b\left(\frac{B_h}{ip}, \frac{M}{p}, i, H\right)$$

$$\frac{\dot{M}}{p}=D_m\left(\frac{B_h}{ip}, \frac{M}{p}, i, H\right)$$

Differentiating C, D_b and D_m partially with respect to K, B, p and i, and making use of (2.10) and (2.16), we have

$$C_K = C_4(F_K - S_K) > 0$$

$$C_B = C_1 \frac{1}{ip} - C_4 S_B$$

$$C_p = C_1\left(-\frac{B-B_g}{ip^2}\right) + C_2\left(-\frac{M}{p^2}\right) - C_4\left(S_p + \frac{G_t}{p^2}\right) \tag{2.23}$$

$$C_i = C_1\left(-\frac{B-B_g}{p_i^2}\right) + C_3 - C_4 S_i < 0$$

$$D_{bK} = D_{b4}(F_K - S_K) > 0$$

$$D_{bB} = D_{b1}\frac{1}{ip} - D_{b4}S_B < 0$$

$$D_{bp} = D_{b1}\left(-\frac{B-B_g}{ip^2}\right) + D_{b2}\left(-\frac{M}{p^2}\right) - D_{b4}\left(S_p + \frac{G_t}{p^2}\right) \tag{2.24}$$

$$D_{bi} = D_{b1}\left(-\frac{B-B_g}{pi^2}\right) + D_{b3} - D_{b4}S_i$$

The necessary and sufficient conditions for local stability are $D_{b1}^\circ + D_{m2}^\circ < 0$ and $D_{b1}^\circ D_{m2}^\circ - D_{b2}^\circ D_{m1}^\circ > 0$, where the superscript indicates that the function is evaluated in the neighborhood of equilibrium.

This result can be thought of as an example of a recent theorem due to F. H. Hahn: "If all goods are gross substitutes, then the Walrasian General Equilibrium is locally stable." The theorem makes use of the budget constraint and the fact that terms analagous to C_1 and C_2 are positive. See "Gross Substitutes and the Dynamic Stability of General Equilibrium," *Econometrica,* XXVI (January 1958), pp. 169-70.

Moreover, if this pair of differential equations is approximated in the neighborhood of equilibrium by a linear expression, the characteristic roots of the approximating pair of equations will be

$$2\lambda = D_{b1}^\circ + D_{m2}^\circ \pm [(D_{b1}^\circ - D_{m2}^\circ)^2 + 4D_{m1}^\circ D_{b2}^\circ]^{\frac{1}{2}}$$

Thus if D_{b2}° and D_{m1}° have the same sign, the roots will be real, whence the convergence of B_h and M to their equilibrium values will be asymptotic and not oscillatory, at least for values sufficiently close to equilibrium.

$$D_{mK}=D_{m4}(F_K-S_K)>0$$

$$D_{mB}=D_{m1}\frac{1}{ip}-D_{m4}S_B$$

$$(2.25)\qquad D_{mp}=D_{m1}\left(-\frac{B-B_g}{ip^2}\right)+D_{m2}\left(-\frac{M}{p^2}\right)-D_{m4}\left(S_p+\frac{G_t}{p^2}\right)$$

$$D_{mi}=D_{m1}\left(-\frac{B-B_g}{pi^2}\right)+D_{m3}-D_{m4}S_i<0.$$

D. MARKET EQUILIBRIUM CONDITIONS

The equilibrium conditions in the markets for goods, bonds and money respectively are

$$(2.26)\qquad C+\dot{K}+\frac{G_c}{p}-Y=0$$

$$(2.27)\qquad D_b+\frac{G_b}{p}-\frac{\dot{B}}{ip}=0$$

$$(2.28)\qquad D_m-\frac{\dot{M}}{p}=0$$

Adding the three budget identities (2.6), (2.14), and (2.17) and the definition (2.16), we obtain Walras' Identity (assuming that the factor markets are always in equilibrium):

$$(2.29)\qquad \left[C+\dot{K}+\frac{G_c}{p}-Y\right]+\left[D_b+\frac{G_b}{p}-\frac{\dot{B}}{ip}\right]+\left[D_m-\frac{\dot{M}}{p}\right]\equiv 0$$

Thus, one of the equilibrium conditions is redundant. When any pair of markets is in equilibrium, the third must be in equilibrium also.

III. The Comparative Statics of The Stationary State

In stationary equilibrium, all aggregate variables are constant. The system reproduces itself period after period without any change in the overall magnitudes. In particular, if all aggregate variables are constant, there can be no net deficits, no net asset accumulation, and no net flow of loanable funds between sectors. Each sector saves nothing and accumulates nothing. $\dot{K}$, $\dot{B}$, $\dot{M}$ and G_b must be equal to zero, and Y and L must be constant. Since $\dot{M}=0$ and $G_b=0$, $G_c+G_t=0$, whence, assuming transfer payments must be non-negative, government expenditure on current output must be equal to zero.[22] The stationary equilibrium values of K, B, p, and i are defined by the equations

$$I\left[K, \frac{B}{p}, F_K(K, L), i, KF_K(K, L)-\frac{B}{p}\right]$$

$$-S\left[K, \frac{B}{p}, F_K(K, L), i, KF_K(K, L)-\frac{B}{p}\right]=0$$

(3.1)
$$C\left[\frac{B-B_g}{ip}, \frac{M}{p}, i, F(K, L)-S\right]-F(K, L)=0$$

$$-D_b\left[\frac{B-B_g}{ip}, \frac{M}{p}, i, F(K, L)-S\right]=0.$$ [23]

[22] Stationariness in this model implies $G_t+G_c=0$. Essentially, this means a balanced budget on income and expenditure account. If the government were to collect taxes, G_c could be positive in a stationary state. However, for the sake of simplicity, we shall assume only non-negative transfer payments. The more general assumption would not change the content of the analysis.

[23] There is a problem in reconciling the existence of a positive demand for cash balances with the existence of bonds offering a positive rate of return in a stationary state. The reasons usually advanced for holding money balances which yield no income are risk avoidance of some kind, and transactions motives. Presumably the persistence of a stationary equilibrium for a suffi-

It is worth making note of the fact that the price level in this model is not arbitrary. Given the exogenous variables B_g, M and L, p is determined by the equations (3.1). To test this proposition, suppose that the system (3.1) is in general equilibrium at $p = p^\circ$ when $B_g = B_g^\circ$ and $M = M^\circ$. Now arbitrarily double p while holding the exogenous variables constant. Will the system remain in equilibrium? It is immediately apparent that the increase in the price level will reduce the real burden of debt on the business sector, causing it to increase investment, reduce the rate of saving and increase the rate of borrowing. The price increase will reduce the real value of the financial assets of households, causing that sector to reduce consumption and increase its rate of saving. In general, the system will not be in equilibrium. Suppose then that B is doubled also. This would leave the business sector in the same position as before, and therefore in equilibrium. However, it would still leave the household sector with smaller real cash balances. If B_g is positive, the change

---

ciently long period of time would eliminate the subjective probabilities of capital loss of even the most timid investor. This point is made e.g. by Leontief in his discussion of Keynesian Liquidity Preference Theory. See "Postulates: Keynes' *General Theory* and the Classicists," *The New Economics*, Seymour E. Harris, ed. (1952), pp. 232-44. Moreover, in an unchanging world, it would be possible for households to improve the synchronization between payments and receipts and reduce, if not eliminate, the transactions demand for cash. Indeed, as Samuelson has argued, ". . . in such a world securities themselves would circulate as money and be acceptable in transactions. . . ." See Paul A. Samuelson, *Foundations of Economic Analysis* (1948), p. 123. All this is to argue that a full theory of demand for real balances would have to be historical and would take into account the history of variations in interest and prices. For present purposes, this possible objection is not a very interesting one. Rather, it is enough to assume a demand for real balances without attempting to explain it. To justify this assumption in a stationary state, one might hypothesize (1) variation in individual rates of income and expenditure within constant aggregate totals; (2) some randomness in the rate of or timing of receipts and expenditures, (Patinkin does this, *op. cit.* e.g. pp. 327-32); (3) a given institutional structure in which transactions costs and the degree of synchronization of payments are fixed. For a lucid discussion of the issue, see James Tobin, "Liquidity Preference As Behavior Towards Risk," *op. cit.*

would leave households with greater real bond holdings; if B_g is equal to zero, the same real bond holdings; if B_g is negative, smaller real bond holdings than before. In the first case, the effect on consumption is ambiguous, but there will be an excess supply of bonds and an excess demand for cash. In the second and third cases, consumption will decline. In the third case, there will be an excess demand for both bonds and cash balances. In any event, the system will not be in equilibrium.

Comparative statical analysis of the equations (3.1) will have little meaning unless the system is stable in the sense that, in the limit, all endogenous variables will converge onto their new equilibrium values when one or more of the exogenous variables has been changed. But the stability of the system depends upon the laws of motion of the endogenous variables. Thus, a meaningful comparative statical analysis requires a prior dynamic analysis. A dynamic analysis of this system will show that it does not *have* to be stable; the assumptions made so far do not imply that it must be. However, the hypothesis that it is stable, when the laws of motion of the price level and the interest rate are specified, provides additional information which will prove valuable in deriving comparative statical propositions.[24]

The rate of change of K has been defined by the investment function (2.7), that of bonds outstanding by (2.6). It remains to specify the laws of motion of p and i. In terms of partial equilibrium analysis, the price of goods is determined on the goods market, that of bonds on the bond market. The price of goods will be assumed to rise when there is excess demand for goods, fall when there is excess supply and to move at a speed proportional to the ratio of excess demand to total supply, that is,

$$\dot{p}=Q_1(C+I-Y) \tag{3.2}$$

where

$$Q_1=\frac{q_1}{Y},$$

[24] This is, of course, Professor Samuelson's *Correspondence Principle.* See Samuelson, *op. cit.,* Part II.

and where q_1 is a positive constant.[25] Similarly for i,

$$\dot{i}=Q_2(I-S-D_b) \tag{3.3}$$

where

$$Q_2=\frac{q_2}{\frac{B}{ip}},$$

and where q_2 is also a positive constant. Combining these hypotheses, we have four simultaneous differential equations in the variables K, B, p and i.

$$\begin{aligned} \dot{K}&=I \\ \frac{\dot{B}}{ip}&=I-S \\ \dot{p}&=Q_1(C+I-Y) \\ \dot{i}&=Q_2(I-S-D_b) \end{aligned} \tag{3.4}$$

If the system (3.4) is stable, in the sense that in the limit over time all paths which the system might follow approach the equilibrium path, then the linear system which approximates (3.4) in the neighborhood of equilibrium must be stable. Differentiating (3.4), and evaluating the partial derivatives in the neighborhood

[25] This assumes that there are no "spillover" effects of excess demand between the goods and bond markets. This assumption has been attacked by Patinkin, *op. cit.* pp. 352-65 and "Limitations of Samuelson's Correspondence Principle," *Metroeconomica,* IV (1952), pp. 37-43. It seems reasonable to argue that in cases of large and persistent excess demands, there would be pronounced "spillover" effects. Thus, one might want to make something of the point in a discussion of inflation, particularly repressed inflation. But the *Correspondence Principle* deals with motions in the neighborhood of equilibrium where disequilibria are small and vanishing. Thus, the validity of Patinkin's point as applied to the *Correspondence Principle* seems dubious at best. For a non-empirical discussion of alternative price reaction equations, see Bent Hansen, *A Study in the Theory of Inflation* (1951), and Alain C. Enthoven, "Monetary Disequlibria and the Dynamics of Inflation," *The Economic Journal,* LXVI (June 1956), pp. 256-70.

$\dot{p}$ is, of course, the first derivative of p with respect to time.

of (stationary) equilibrium to form a linear approximation, we have

$$\dot{K}=I_K^\circ(K-K^\circ)+I_B^\circ(B-B^\circ)+I_p^\circ(p-p^\circ)+I_i^\circ(i-i^\circ)$$

$$\begin{aligned}\dot{B}=i^\circ p^\circ(I_K^\circ-S_K^\circ)(K-K^\circ)+i^\circ p^\circ(I_B^\circ-S_B^\circ)(B-B^\circ)\\ +i^\circ p^\circ(I_p^\circ-S_p^\circ)(p-p^\circ)+i^\circ p^\circ(I_i^\circ-S_i^\circ)(i-i^\circ)\end{aligned}$$

$$\begin{aligned}\dot{p}=Q_1^\circ(C_K^\circ+I_K^\circ-F_K^\circ)(K-K^\circ)\\ +Q_1^\circ(C_B^\circ+I_B^\circ)(B-B^\circ)+Q_1^\circ(C_p^\circ+I_p^\circ)(p-p^\circ)\\ +Q_1^\circ(C_i^\circ+I_i^\circ)(i-i^\circ)\end{aligned} \tag{3.5}$$

$$\begin{aligned}\dot{i}=Q_2^\circ(I_K^\circ-S_K^\circ-D_{bK}^\circ)(K-K^\circ)\\ +Q_2^\circ(I_B^\circ-S_B^\circ-D_{bB}^\circ)(B-B^\circ)\\ Q_2^\circ(I_p^\circ-S_p^\circ-D_{bp}^\circ)(p-p^\circ)\\ +Q_2^\circ(I_i^\circ-S_i^\circ-D_{bi}^\circ)(i-i^\circ).\end{aligned}$$ [26]

A necessary condition for the stability of (3.5) and hence for the stability of (3.4) is that the determinant of the coefficients of the variables $(K-K^\circ)$, $(B-B^\circ)$, $(p-p^\circ)$ and $(i-i^\circ)$ be positive.[27] If we assume that the system is stable, it can be shown, by the ordinary rules of determinants, that this implies that the determinant

$$|\Delta|=\begin{vmatrix} I_K^\circ & I_B^\circ & I_p^\circ & I_i^\circ \\ -S_K^\circ & -S_B^\circ & -S_p^\circ & -S_i^\circ \\ C_K^\circ-F_K^\circ & C_B^\circ & C_p^\circ & C_i^\circ \\ -D_{bK}^\circ & -D_{bB}^\circ & -D_{bp}^\circ & -D_{bi}^\circ \end{vmatrix} \tag{3.6}$$

must be positive.

[26] $Q_1^\circ=\frac{q_1}{Y^\circ}$, $Q_2^\circ=\frac{q_2}{\frac{B^\circ}{i^\circ p^\circ}}$. By assumption, $\dot{G}_b=0$ whence B_g is constant. Thus $B^\circ=B_h^\circ+B_g$ whence, by subtraction, $B-B^\circ=B_h-B_h^\circ$.

[27] See, e.g., Patinkin, *op. cit.* p. 354. Let the matrix of coefficients of $(K-K^\circ)$, $(B-B^\circ)$, $(p-p^\circ)$, $(i-i^\circ)$ be Δ. (3.5) is stable if and only if the real parts of the roots of the characteristic equation $|\Delta-\lambda I|=0$ are negative.

In a stationary state, the government can increase the stock of money by buying goods, making transfer payments or by buying bonds, but the assumption of a return to a new stationary state implies that these flows must be temporary. Thus, the only permanent effect of government deficit finance must be through an increase in the stock of money, or through a change in the government's holdings of bonds, or both. Consider the cases in which the only permanent effect of government expenditure is an increase in the stock of money. This would happen if the government were, once and for all, to buy goods or make transfer payments, financed by issue of new money. Differentiating (3.1) totally with respect to M, we obtain

$$I_K^\circ \frac{dK}{dM} + I_B^\circ \frac{dB}{dM} + I_p^\circ \frac{dp}{dM} + I_i^\circ \frac{di}{dM} = 0$$

$$-S_K^\circ \frac{dK}{dM} - S_B^\circ \frac{dB}{dM} - S_p^\circ \frac{dp}{dM} - S_i^\circ \frac{di}{dM} = 0$$

(3.7)

$$(C_K^\circ - F_K^\circ) \frac{dK}{dM} + C_B^\circ \frac{dB}{dM} + C_p^\circ \frac{dp}{dM} + C_i^\circ \frac{di}{dM} = -C_2^\circ \frac{1}{p}$$

$$-D_{bK}^\circ \frac{dK}{dM} - D_{bB}^\circ \frac{dB}{dM} - D_{bp}^\circ \frac{dp}{dM} - D_{bi}^\circ \frac{di}{dM} = D_{b2}^\circ \frac{1}{p}$$

The determinant of coefficients of the derivatives is (3.6). Solving for the desired derivatives by Cramer's rule, we find [28]

$$(3.8) \qquad \frac{dK}{dM} = \frac{B_g}{ip^3} \frac{(C_2 D_{b1} - C_1 D_{b2})(I_B S_i - I_i S_B)}{|\Delta|} \gtreqless 0 \text{ as } B_g \lesseqgtr 0$$

But the determinant of Δ is equal to the product of the roots. Thus, if the real roots are negative, the sign of Δ must be that of $(-1)^n$ where n is the order of Δ. The complex roots occur in conjugate pairs whose products are positive, whence, if there are complex roots, the sign of Δ must be that of (-1) raised to the power n minus the number of complex roots, i.e. the sign of $(-1)^n$.

[28] For the sake of convenience, the superscripts ° indicating evaluation at equilibrium are omitted in the rest of Part III. For Cramer's Rule for solv-

(3.9) $$\frac{dB}{dM}=\frac{B}{M}-\frac{B_g}{ipM}\,\frac{(C_1\Delta_{32}-D_{b1}\Delta_{42})}{|\Delta|}$$

(3.10) $$\frac{dp}{dM}=\frac{p}{M}-\frac{B_g}{ipM}\,\frac{(C_1\Delta_{33}-D_{b1}\Delta_{43})}{|\Delta|}$$

---

ing simultaneous linear equations by determinants, and for the ordinary rules of determinants, see e.g., R. G. D. Allen, *Mathematical Analysis for Economists,* London, 1938, pp. 482-85.

The steps in obtaining (3.8) from (3.7) are as follows. (1) by Cramer's Rule,

$$|\Delta|\frac{dK}{dM}=\begin{vmatrix} 0 & I_B & I_p & I_i \\ 0 & -S_B & -S_p & -S_i \\ -C_2\frac{1}{p} & C_B & Cp & C_i \\ D_{b2}\frac{1}{p} & -D_{bB} & -D_{bp} & -D_{bi} \end{vmatrix}$$

(2) By (2.9), $I_p=-\frac{B}{p}I_B$. By (2.10), $S_p=-\frac{B}{p}S_B$. Multiply the second column by $\frac{B}{p}$ and add the product to the third column. This leaves the value of the determinant unchanged, but makes the elements of the third column 0, 0, $\frac{B}{p}C_B+C_p$, $-\left(\frac{B}{p}D_{bB}+D_{bp}\right)$. (3) From (2.23) it follows that $\frac{B}{p}C_B+C_p=C_1\frac{B_g}{ip^2}-C_2\frac{M}{p^2}$ Similarly, from (2.24), $\frac{B}{p}D_{bB}+D_{bp}=D_{b1}\frac{B_g}{ip^2}-D_{b2}\frac{M}{p^2}$. (4) Then, by the ordinary rules for expanding determinants, the determinant is equal to $\left[C_2\frac{1}{p}\left(D_{b1}\frac{B_g}{ip^2}-D_{b2}\frac{M}{p^2}\right)-D_{b2}\frac{1}{p}\left(C_1\frac{B_g}{ip^2}-C_2\frac{M}{p^2}\right)\right][I_BS_i-I_iS_B]$ from which (3.8) follows.

The steps in obtaining (3.9) from (3.7) are as follows. (1) By Cramer's Rule,

$$|\Delta|\frac{dB}{dM}=\begin{vmatrix} I_K & 0 & I_p & I_i \\ -S_K & 0 & -S_p & -S_i \\ C_K-F_K & -C_2\frac{1}{p} & C_p & +C_1 \\ -D_{bK} & D_{b2}\frac{1}{p} & -D_{bp} & -D_{bi} \end{vmatrix}$$

$$(3.11) \qquad \frac{di}{dM} = \frac{B_g}{ip^3} \frac{(C_2 D_{b1} - C_1 D_{b2})(I_K S_B - I_B S_K)}{|\Delta|} \gtreqless 0 \text{ as } B_g \gtreqless 0$$

where, for example, Δ_{32} is the cofactor of the second element in the third row of Δ.

The sign of (3.11) is positive if B_g is positive, and negative if B_g is negative. The sign of (3.8) is opposite to that of (3.11). That is, if the government sector is a net creditor in terms of bonds, an increase in M will raise the interest rate and lower the equilibrium level of the capital stock. If the net bond holdings of the government sector are negative, an increase in M will lower the equilibrium value of i and raise that of K.

Perhaps these results can be best understood by comparing them with the standard neo-classical neutral money propositions.[29] Suppose that an increase in the money stock were followed by an increase in B and p in the same proportion with no change in i and K. This would leave the business sector in the same real position as before, and hence in equilibrium. But if B_g is positive, it would leave the household sector with more bond holdings, in real terms, than before. Since it would leave the

---

(2) Multiply the second column by $\frac{M}{B}$, the numerator determinant by $\frac{B}{M}$, leaving its value unchanged. (3) Add $-\frac{p}{B}$ times the third column to the second. (4) The elements in the second column become I_B, $-S_B$, $C_B - C_1\frac{B_g}{ipB}$, $-D_{bB} + D_{b1}\frac{B_g}{ipB}$. (5) Thus, the determinant can be decomposed into the sum of two determinants, one of which is $\Delta\frac{B}{M}$, the other of which is like the original determinant except for the second column whose elements are now $0, 0, -C_1\frac{B_g}{ipM}, +D_{b1}\frac{B_g}{ipM}$. (6) The second determinant can therefore be written $-\frac{B_g}{ipM}(C_1\Delta_{32} - D_{b1}\Delta_{42})$.

The equations (3.10), (3.11), (3.14), (3.15), (3.16), and (3.17) are obtained in similar fashion.

[29] See Patinkin, *op. cit.*

position of the household sector otherwise unchanged, it would result in an excess supply of bonds, whence an increase in the rate of interest would be required to restore equilibrium. Because the private sector as a whole has no money illusion, its net excess demand for real bonds is not affected by a change in M which is accompanied by a change in p in the same proportion. But because the government sector holds its *nominal* bond holdings constant, an increase in p will reduce its *real* holdings $(B_g>0)$, thus creating a real excess supply of bonds. If the government sector is a net debtor in terms of bonds, the results will be the opposite. If the government sector has a zero net position in bonds, changes in M will have no effect on the equilibrium values of i and K.[30]

If the government sector increases the money stock by buying bonds, it must either reduce or leave unchanged the interest rate, the latter in a rather special case. Let the government sector perform an open market operation in which it buys bonds from the private sector in exchange for money. In this case, the value of the change in the money stock must be equal to the value of the change in the government's bond holdings. That is

$$dM=\frac{1}{i}dB_g. \tag{3.12}$$

Differentiating (3.1) totally again with respect to M, but this time employing the relationship (3.12), we obtain a set of equa-

[30] Unfortunately, the hypotheses advanced in Part II and the stability of the system are not sufficient to determine the signs of the second terms on the right hand sides of (3.9) and (3.10). Thus, it is not clear, for example, whether the change in the price level is more than or less than in the same proportion as the change in M. If all the off-diagonal elements of Δ were non-negative, stability would imply $C_1\Delta_{33}-D_{b1}\Delta_{43}<0$, and therefore $\frac{dp}{dM}\frac{M}{p}>1$. However, some of the off-diagonal elements are, by assumption, negative. Alternatively, the same result will follow if the diagonal elements are large enough in absolute value in relation to the other elements.

tions identical to (3.7) on the left hand side, and with the following column on the right hand side:

$$\begin{matrix} 0 \\ 0 \\ -C_2\frac{1}{p}+C_1\frac{1}{p} \\ +D_{b2}\frac{1}{p}-D_{b1}\frac{1}{p}. \end{matrix} \tag{3.13}$$

Solving by Cramer's Rule, we obtain

$$\frac{dK}{dM}=-\frac{\left(M-\frac{1}{i}B_g\right)}{p^3}\frac{(C_2D_{b1}-C_1D_{b2})(I_BS_i-I_iS_B)}{|\Delta|}\geqq 0 \tag{3.14}$$

$$\frac{dB}{dM}=\frac{B}{M}+\frac{\left(M-\frac{1}{i}B_g\right)}{pM}\frac{(C_1\Delta_{32}-D_{b1}\Delta_{42})}{|\Delta|} \tag{3.15}$$

$$\frac{dp}{dM}=\frac{p}{M}+\frac{\left(M-\frac{1}{i}B_g\right)}{pM}\frac{(C_1\Delta_{33}-D_{b1}\Delta_{43})}{|\Delta|} \tag{3.16}$$

$$\frac{di}{dM}=-\frac{\left(M-\frac{1}{i}B_g\right)}{p^3}\frac{(C_2D_{b1}-C_1D_{b2})(I_KS_B-I_BS_K)}{|\Delta|}\leqq 0.\text{[31]} \tag{3.17}$$

Although it is possible that $\left(M-\frac{1}{i}B_g\right)$ could be negative, this

[31] The inequalities in (3.14) and (3.17) are based on the assumption $M-\frac{1}{i}B_g\geqq 0$, discussed below in the text. Notice that (3.14), (3.15), (3.16), and (3.17) correspond to (3.8), (3.9), (3.10), (3.11) with $\frac{1}{i}B_g-M$ substituted for $\frac{1}{i}B_g$.

can be regarded as most unlikely. Given the transactions which the government can perform, the market value of its bond holdings can exceed the money stock only if it has had the benefit of a capital gain which has not been offset by previous deficits. Ordinarily, the money stock will be greater than or equal to the net bond holdings of the consolidated monetary system and government sector. $M - \frac{1}{i}B_g$ can be called *outside money*. It is the net indebtedness of the government sector to the private sector. Our assumption that the government collects no taxes implies that barring capital gains, the amount of outside money cannot be negative.

When there is positive outside money, an open market purchase of bonds, reduces the equilibrium value of the rate of interest and increases the equilibrium value of the capital stock. That this occurs is not at all surprising. When there is positive outside money, B_g is smaller than M. Thus, an equal absolute increase in M and B_g must mean that B_g is increased more than in the same proportion as M. Even if p increases in the same proportion as M, still the real value of the bond holdings of the government sector is increased, whence the interest rate must fall.

On the other hand, if there is no outside money, an equal absolute increase in M and B_g must also be an equal relative increase, whence the effect of the increase, in real terms, can be obviated and equilibrium restored by an increase in the price level in the same proportion.[32]

Finally, if the government should want the effects of its opera-

[32] Of course if it were the case that $\frac{1}{i}B_g > M$, that is, if the amount of outside money were negative, $\frac{di}{dM}$ in (3.17) would be positive. An open market purchase of bonds would raise the equilibrium rate of interest. A heuristic explanation of the paradox is that $\frac{1}{i}B_g > M$ and $dM = \frac{1}{i}dB_g$ imply $\frac{dM}{M} > \frac{dB_g}{B_g}$; that is, the transaction increases M relatively more than B_g, raising the price level more than in the same proportion as the increase in B_g. As a consequence, the net effect of the transaction is to reduce the real value of the government sector's holdings of bonds.

tions to be neutral despite the existence of positive outside money and a net bond position that is not equal to zero—that is, if it should want to change only the nominal price level while leaving all real magnitudes unchanged—it can do so only by changing its (nominal) bond holdings in the same proportion as it changes the money supply. The point, then, is not that the government sector cannot make a set of transactions which when taken together will be neutral in their effects. Rather, it is that the ordinary simple transactions it does make—buying goods and buying and selling bonds—will not leave all real magnitudes unchanged.

IV. Balanced Growth

Comparative statics analysis in a stationary state model is limited in its relevance to the workings of a growing economy by the fact that persistent deficits and surpluses in the different sectors are incompatible with the hypothesis of stationarity, unless the financial assets which are being accumulated have no effect on spending patterns. If, for example, the government were to finance a deficit on current account, period after period, by increasing the money stock, and if cash balances have a positive effect on the expenditures of the private sectors, there would be no limit to the increase in the price level. In a growing economy, on the other hand, sectors can run persistent deficits, paying for them by issuing securities (or money) and still the economy can be in what might be described as a "moving equilibrium." In a model of a growing economy, one can analyze the impact of these flows on the rest of the system. In the stationary state, the government sector is limited to a balanced budget on current account. In a growing economy, a persistent deficit, financed by issue of new money, may be quite compatible with a constant price level. In fact, it may even be a necessary condition for price stability.

The remainder of this study is devoted to the workings of the model in a state of balanced growth. Balanced growth may be defined as a state in which income, factor supplies, assets and expenditure flows are all growing at the same constant relative rate.

If the economy is in equilibrium in a state of balanced growth, the ratios between all of these variables will be constant. Balanced growth is not the only possible pattern of growth. Indeed, it is a very special case of no more, though no less, generality than the stationary state. However, it is interesting because it is a possible path of growth, and a growing economy, as was observed in the previous paragraph, does have properties that a stationary economy does not have. Thus, the results of an analysis of balanced growth may be at least suggestive of conclusions of more general significance.

Assume that the investment, business saving, household demand for bonds and consumption functions are all homogeneous of degree one in the asset and income variables, but not in the price variables. That is, for example, a doubling of $K, \frac{B}{p}$ and $rK-\frac{B}{p}$ with r and i constant will double the rate of investment, and a doubling of $\frac{B_h}{ip}, \frac{M}{p}$ and H, with i constant, will double the rate of consumption, or, more generally,

$$\text{(4.1)} \qquad \begin{aligned} \lambda\dot{K} &= I\left(\lambda K, \lambda\frac{B}{p}, r, i, \lambda rK-\lambda\frac{B}{p}\right) \\ \lambda C &= C\left(\lambda\frac{B_h}{ip}, \lambda\frac{M}{p}, i, \lambda H\right). \end{aligned}$$

Then, if $K^\circ, B^\circ, L^\circ, M^\circ, H^\circ, p^\circ, r^\circ$, and i° are a solution of the equations (3.1), $\lambda K^\circ, \lambda B^\circ, \lambda L^\circ, \lambda M^\circ, \lambda H^\circ, p^\circ, r^\circ$ and i° are a solution also. In other words, if the equilibrium conditions are homogeneous in the asset and income variables, the system is capable of balanced growth.

Now, assume that the labor supply, the money stock, the government's stock of bonds, and government expenditures on goods, bonds, and transfer payments are all growing at the constant relative rate n.[33] That is

[33] This can be actual growth in population or labor supply, or growth in labor supply times a productivity improvement factor.

$$\begin{aligned}
\dot{L}&=nL &\quad \dot{G}_c&=nG_c\\
\dot{M}&=nM &\quad \dot{G}_b&=nG_b \qquad (4.2)\\
\dot{B}_g&=nB_g &\quad \dot{G}_t&=nG_t.
\end{aligned}$$

Will the whole system grow, at least asymptotically, at the same rate? It will be convenient to transform the asset and income variables into ratios to their trend values.[34] Let

$$\begin{aligned}
k&=Ke^{-nt} &\quad g_c&=G_ce^{-nt}\\
b&=Be^{-nt} &\quad g_t&=G_te^{-nt}\\
b_g&=B_ge^{-nt} &\quad g_b&=G_be^{-nt} \qquad (4.3)\\
m&=Me^{-nt} &\quad h&=He^{-nt}\\
y&=Ye^{-nt} &\quad l&=Le^{-nt}
\end{aligned}$$

whence, for example,

$$\dot{K}=(\dot{k}+nk)e^{nt}.$$

Applying this transformation to the dynamic system (3.4), and now permitting $\dot{M}$, G_b, G_c and G_t to take on positive values, we have

$$\begin{aligned}
\dot{k}&=I\left(k, \frac{b}{p}, r, i, rk-\frac{b}{p}\right)-nk\\
\dot{b}&=ip\left[I-S\left(k, \frac{b}{p}, r, i, rk-\frac{b}{p}\right)\right]-nb\\
\dot{p}&=Q_1{}^*\left[C\left(\frac{b_h}{ip}, \frac{m}{p}, i, h\right)+\frac{g_c}{p}+I-F(k, l)\right] \qquad (4.4)\\
\dot{i}&=Q_2{}^*\left[I-S-\frac{g_b}{p}-D_b\left(\frac{b_h}{ip}, \frac{m}{p}, i, h\right)\right].^{35}
\end{aligned}$$

[34] I am grateful to Professor Robert Solow for suggesting this technique to me.

[35] Because of the homogeneity, the term e^{nt} can be factored from both sides

Given the exogenous growth in the labor supply, the money stock, and government expenditure, the whole system will converge onto a relative rate of growth equal to n if the system (4.4) is stable. Of course, the equilibrium position of (4.4) is different from the stationary equilibrium position of (3.4) and the stability of the latter does not necessarily imply the stability of the former.[36]

Expanding (4.4) around the equilibrium point to form a linear approximation, we have [37]

$$\dot{k}=(I_K{}^\circ-n)(k-k^\circ)+I_B{}^\circ(b-b^\circ)+I_p{}^\circ(p-p^\circ)+I_i{}^\circ(i-i^\circ)$$

$$\dot{b}=i^\circ p^\circ(I_K{}^\circ-S_K{}^\circ)(k-k^\circ)+i^\circ p^\circ\left(I_B{}^\circ-S_B{}^\circ-\frac{n}{i^\circ p^\circ}\right)(b-b^\circ)$$

$$+i^\circ p^\circ\left(I_p{}^\circ-S_p{}^\circ+\frac{nb^\circ}{i^\circ p^{\circ 2}}\right)(p-p^\circ)$$

$$+i^\circ p^\circ\left(I_i{}^\circ-S_i{}^\circ+\frac{nb^\circ}{p^\circ i^{\circ 2}}\right)(i-i^\circ)$$

$$\text{(4.5)}\quad \dot{p}=Q_1{}^{*\circ}(C_K{}^\circ+I_K{}^\circ-F_K{}^\circ)(k-k^\circ)+Q_1{}^{*\circ}(C_B{}^\circ+I_B{}^\circ)(b-b^\circ)$$

$$+Q_1{}^{*\circ}\left(C_p{}^\circ+I_p{}^\circ-\frac{g_c}{p^2}\right)(p-p^\circ)+Q_1{}^{*\circ}(C_i{}^\circ+I_i{}^\circ)(i-i^\circ)$$

$$\dot{i}=Q_2{}^{*\circ}(I_K{}^\circ-S_K{}^\circ-D_{bK}{}^\circ)(k-k^\circ)$$

$$+Q_2{}^{*\circ}(I_B{}^\circ-S_B{}^\circ-D_{bB})(b-b^\circ)$$

$$+Q_2{}^{*\circ}\left(I_p{}^\circ-S_p{}^\circ+\frac{g_b}{p^2}-D_{bp}{}^\circ\right)(p-p^\circ)$$

$$+Q_2{}^{*}(I_i{}^\circ-S_i{}^\circ-D_{bi}{}^\circ)(i-i^\circ).$$

---

of the first two equations. $Q_1{}^*=\frac{q_1}{y}$, $Q_2{}^*=\frac{q_2}{\frac{b}{ip}}$.

[36] For example, the equilibrium flow of investment in (3.4) is $\dot{K}=I=0$; in (4.4) it is $\dot{K}=I=nK$. Thus, for example, I_K evaluated at the first equilibrium point does not necessarily equal I_K evaluated at the second.

[37] In equilibrium, i.e., with $\dot{b}=0$, $ip(I-S)=nb$. $Q_1{}^{*\circ}=\frac{q_1}{y^\circ}$, $Q_2{}^{*\circ}=\frac{q_2}{\frac{b^\circ}{i^\circ p^\circ}}$.

The assumption that the system (4.4) is stable implies that the determinant

$$|\Delta^*| = \begin{vmatrix} I_K^\circ - n & I_B^\circ & I_p^\circ & I_i^\circ \\ I_K^\circ - S_K^\circ & I_B^\circ - S_B^\circ - \dfrac{n}{i^\circ p^\circ} & I_p^\circ - S_p^\circ + \dfrac{nb}{i^\circ p^{\circ 2}} & I_i^\circ - S_i^\circ + \dfrac{nb}{p^\circ i^{\circ 2}} \\ C_K^\circ + I_K^\circ - F_K^\circ & C_B^\circ + I_B^\circ & C_p^\circ + I_p^\circ - \dfrac{g_c}{p^{\circ 2}} & C_i^\circ + I_i^\circ \\ I_K^\circ - S_K^\circ - D_{bK}^\circ & I_B^\circ - S_B^\circ - D_{bB}^\circ & I_p^\circ - S_p^\circ - D_{bp}^\circ + \dfrac{g_b}{p^{\circ 2}} & I_i^\circ - S_i^\circ - D_{bi}^\circ \end{vmatrix}$$

is positive.[38]

V. The Stability of Factor Proportions

If the marginal capital-output ratio is fixed, and if the ratio of savings and investment to total output is constant, then there is a unique relative rate of growth of total output which will just keep the capital stock fully employed.[39] This rate, which has been called *the warranted rate* by Sir Roy Harrod, is not necessarily equal to *the natural rate,* the exogenously determined rate

[38] If $n=0$, $g_b=0$, $g_c=0$, and $g_t=0$, then $\Delta^*=\Delta$.

[39] Let total output be Y and let savings be sY. Let the marginal capital-output ratio be z, so that $\dot{K}=z\dot{Y}$. Then, if the new capital, sY, is to be fully employed, $sY=z\dot{Y}$, or $\dfrac{\dot{Y}}{Y}=\dfrac{s}{z}$.

of growth of the labor supply, or the labor supply multiplied by some productivity improvement factor. If the two rates do not coincide, there will be a progressively worsening shortage or excess supply of labor. The reason for this, fundamentally, is that with fixed factor proportions, there is no possibility for substituting the factor in excess supply for some of the factor in short supply. (Of course, equilibrium might still be restored if a declining price for the factor in excess supply were to reduce the amount supplied.)

On the other hand, as Professor Solow has shown, "when production takes place under the usual neo-classical conditions of variable proportions and constant returns to scale, no simple opposition between natural and warranted rates of growth is possible." [40] For the purposes of his discussion, Solow adopted Harrod's assumption that saving is a constant fraction of income and that investment adjusts automatically to equality with saving. Then, if the (relative) rate of growth of K falls below that of L, the rate of growth of Y will be intermediate between the two, exceeding that of K. Since new investment is proportional to income, it will therefore grow at a rate exceeding that of K, pulling the growth rate of K upwards towards that of L. If the rate of growth of K rises above that of L, the growth rate of income and therefore investment will be less than the rate of growth of K, pulling the growth rate of K downwards towards that of L.[41]

[40] See R. M. Solow, *op. cit.*, p. 73.

Very briefly, Solow's model is as follows. Let $\dot{K}=sY=sF(K, L)$, let $\dot{L}=nL$ and $\alpha=\frac{K}{L}$. Then $\dot{\alpha}=sF(\alpha, 1)-n\alpha$. As Solow shows, this equation does not have to have an equilibrium solution. But for many production functions it will have an equilibrium which is stable.

[41] That is, if (1) $Y=F(K, L)$, F homogeneous of degree one, and (2) $\dot{K}=sY$, then $\frac{\dot{L}}{L}<\frac{\dot{K}}{K}$ implies (3) $\frac{\dot{L}}{L}<\frac{\dot{Y}}{Y}<\frac{\dot{K}}{K}$. $\frac{d}{dt}\left(\frac{\dot{K}}{K}\right)=\frac{K\ddot{K}-\dot{K}^2}{K^2}$. But (3) implies $\dot{K}Y>K\dot{Y}$ or, using (2), $\dot{K}^2>K\ddot{K}$. Thus, $\frac{\dot{L}}{L}<\frac{\dot{K}}{K}$ implies $\frac{d}{dt}\left(\frac{\dot{K}}{K}\right)<0$. However, it does not imply that $\frac{\dot{K}}{K}$ must eventually reach $\frac{\dot{L}}{L}$.

The sense of this result can be extended quite readily to include investment which is determined as an increasing function of the marginal product of capital. The marginal product of capital depends upon the ratio of K to L. If this ratio falls below its equilibrium value, the increased marginal product of capital stimulates investment and causes the capital stock to catch up. If the capital-labor ratio rises, the decreased marginal product of capital lowers the investment rate, allowing the labor supply to catch up.

If the investment function (2.7) is homogeneous of degree one in the asset and income variables, it can be written

$$\dot{K}=KI\left(1, \frac{B}{pK}, r, i, r-\frac{B}{pK}\right) \tag{5.1}$$

Taking $\frac{B}{pK}$ and i as parameters, (5.1) can be written

$$\dot{K}=KI^*\left(r, i, \frac{B}{pK}\right). \tag{5.2}$$

$$I_1^*>0, \qquad I_2^*<0, \qquad I_3^*<0.$$

Let the labor supply grow at the constant relative rate n, and let

$$\alpha=\frac{K}{L}, \qquad \text{whence}$$

$$\frac{\dot{\alpha}}{\alpha}=\frac{\dot{K}}{K}-\frac{\dot{L}}{L}. \tag{5.3}$$

Substituting (5.2) into (5.3),

$$\frac{\dot{\alpha}}{\alpha}=I^*-n. \tag{5.4}$$

Now, since the production function is homogeneous of degree one in K and L, the marginal product of capital, F_K, is homogeneous of degree zero in the same variables. In other words, because the production function has the property of constant returns to scale, the marginal products of the factors depend only on the ratio of capital to labor. Thus, we may write

$$r = F_K(K, L) = F_K(\alpha, 1). \tag{5.5}$$

Substituting into (5.4), we have

$$\frac{\dot{\alpha}}{\alpha} = I^*\left[F_K(\alpha, 1), i, \frac{B}{pK}\right] - n \tag{5.6}$$

and

$$\frac{\partial I^*}{\partial \alpha} = I_1{}^* F_{KK} < 0, \tag{5.7}$$

that is, I^* is a decreasing function of α. The relative rate of change of α can be divided into two branches, I^* and n. When $I^* = n$, α is constant; when $I^* > n$, α is increasing; when $I^* < n$, α is decreasing. This is illustrated in Figure I. Therefore, the equilibrium capital-labor ratio, α^*, that is, the one at which $I^* = n$, is stable.[42]

The effects of $\frac{B}{pK}$ and i on investment are negative. Therefore, higher values of these two variables must correspond to lower values of the investment function. This is illustrated in Figure II. As $\frac{B}{pK}$ and i increase, I^* shifts to the left, and with it, the equilibrium capital-labor ratio. In the figure, $I_1{}^*, \cdots, I_4{}^*$ correspond to successively higher values of $\frac{B}{pK}$ and i.

[42] Diminishing marginal returns to capital is not a necessary condition for the stability of factor proportions in Solow's model, but it is a necessary condition in mine, although diminishing marginal returns alone does not guarantee the existence of an equilibrium value of α. In Figure *I*, I^* *could* approach some constant greater than n asymptotically, in which case α would always be increasing. However, quite simple and plausible assumptions such as $I^*\left(0, i, \frac{B}{pK}\right) = 0$, $\lim\limits_{\alpha \to \infty} F_K(K, L) = 0$, and $n > 0$ would guarantee the existence of an equilibrium. The shape of the I^* curve is drawn as it is in order to suggest that $\frac{\partial I^*}{\partial \alpha} < 0$ is the only property that has been assumed for it.

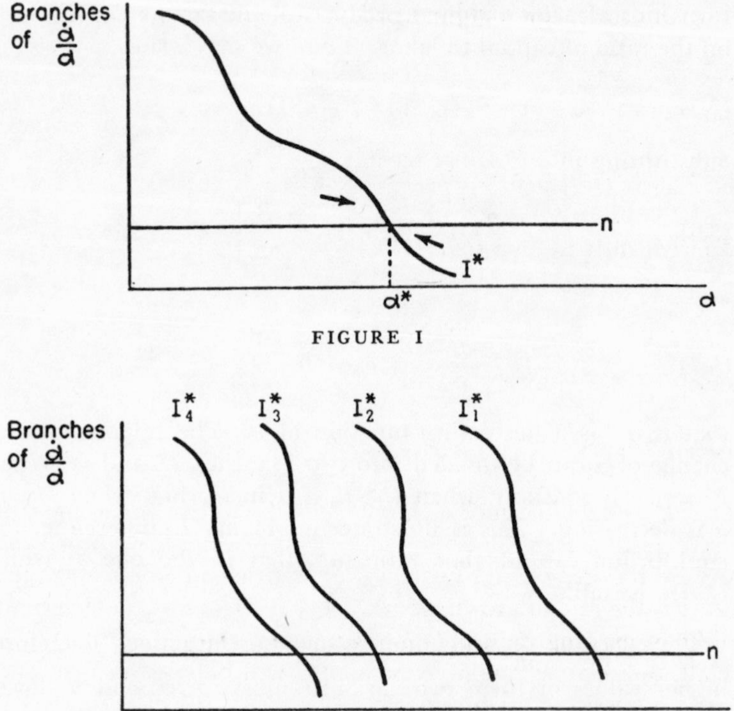

FIGURE II

Thus, the capital-output ratio and the marginal products of both factors depend upon i which, in turn, can be influenced by monetary policy.

VI. The Growth of Debt

Abstracting momentarily from the model which has been presented so far, suppose that the rate of net new borrowing, $\dot{D}(t)$, is positively related to aggregate income, negatively related to the total stock of debt outstanding, $D(t)$, and linearly related to both.

$$\dot{D}(t) = q_1 Y(t) - q_2 D(t) \qquad (6.1)$$

$$q_1 > 0, \qquad q_2 \geqq 0.$$

Let income grow exponentially at the rate n. Then

$$Y(t)=Y(0)e^{nt}, \tag{6.2}$$

and

$$D(t)=\left[D(0)-\frac{q_1}{n+q_2}Y(0)\right]e^{-q_2 t}+\frac{q_1}{n+q_2}Y(0)e^{nt}, \tag{6.3}$$

from which it follows that

$$\lim_{t\to\infty}\frac{D}{Y}=\frac{q_1}{n+q_2} \tag{6.4}$$

and

$$\lim_{t\to\infty}\frac{\dot{D}}{D}=n. \tag{6.5}$$

That is, as debt and income grow, the ratio of debt to income will converge to a stable limiting value. This limiting value will be greater the greater is the effect of income on borrowing, the lower is the rate of growth of income and the less is the deterrent effect of existing debt on new borrowing. Moreover, if $D(0)$ is small, the relative rate of growth of D will be large at first, and it will approach n asymptotically from above. That is,

$$\frac{\dot{D}}{D}=\frac{q_1 Y(0)e^{(n+q_2)t}}{\frac{q_1}{n+q_2}Y(0)[e^{(n+q_2)t}-1]+D_0}-q_2. \tag{6.6}$$

At $t=0$,

$$\frac{\dot{D}(0)}{D(0)}=\frac{q_1 Y(0)}{D(0)}-q_2 \tag{6.7}$$

whence, if $D(0)$ is small, $\frac{\dot{D}(0)}{D(0)}$ is large.[43]

[43] This point about the "normal" behavior of the growth of debt has been made in several places. See, e.g., Evsey D. Domar, "The 'Burden of the Debt' and the National Income," *American Economic Review,* XXXIV (December 1944), reprinted in *Readings in Fiscal Policy,* American Economic Association (1955), pp. 479-501; John G. Gurley and E. S. Shaw, "The Growth of

Similar conclusions can be demonstrated, under simplifying assumptions, for the model presented in Part II. In particular, the ratio of bonds outstanding to the capital stock, and to income, can be shown to be stable on the assumption that the capital stock and the labor supply grow at the constant relative rate n. Again the price level and the interest rate are assumed to be constant. The assumption that the capital stock grows at the constant relative rate n independently of B is, of course, inconsistent with the form of the investment function assumed in Part II. However, the assumption does facilitate a partial analysis of the growth of debt, and the results of the analysis do yield insight into the nature of the early stages of the debt-growth process. Later, the assumption will be relaxed in order to study the interaction of K and B in the growth process.

Let

$$K=K(0)e^{nt} \quad \text{and} \qquad (6.8)$$
$$L=L(0)e^{nt},$$

where $K(0)$ and $L(0)$ are the values of K and L in some arbitrary initial period. Because of the homogeneity of the business saving function in the asset and income variables, we may write

$$S=(S_1+rS_5)K+(S_2-S_5)\frac{B}{p}. \qquad (6.9)$$

Substituting (6.8) and (6.9) into (2.6), we have

$$\dot{B}=ip(n-S_1-rS_5)K(0)e^{nt}-i(S_2-S_5)B, \qquad (6.10)$$

which is the analogue of (6.1).

Debt and Money in the United States, 1800-1950: A Suggested Interpretation," *Review of Economics and Statistics*, XXXIX (August 1957), pp. 250-62; Alain C. Enthoven, "The Growth of Instalment Credit and the Future of Prosperity," *American Economic Review*, XLVII (December 1957), pp. 913-29. The models used in these articles are similar to this one with $q_2=0$.

Assign S_1, S_2 and S_5 their equilibrium values, that is, their values when K, L and B are all growing at the same relative rate. Let

$$(6.11)\qquad \begin{aligned} a_1 &= ip(n - S_1^\circ - rS_5^\circ)^{44} \\ a_2 &= i(S_2^\circ - S_5^\circ). \end{aligned}$$

Then (6.10) becomes a first-order non-homogeneous linear differential equation with the solution

$$(6.12)\qquad B(t) = \left[B(0) - \frac{a_1}{n+a_2} K(0) \right] e^{-a_2 t} + \frac{a_1}{n+a_2} K(0)\, e^{nt},$$

which is analogous to (6.3) with a_1 and a_2 replacing q_1 and q_2 respectively. The term a_2 has been assumed to be positive in (2.10); a_1 must be positive if debt is to grow. If a_1 is negative, saving will grow faster than investment and debt will decrease indefinitely, a possibility which cannot be excluded *a priori*. Thus, as t grows large, the ratio of B to K converges to $\frac{a_1}{n+a_2}$. Unlike (6.4), however, the effect of n on the limiting debt to capital ratio in this case is ambiguous. The reason for this is that at a higher n, there is more investment and hence more borrowing, which may offset the fact that the denominator of the ratio is also growing faster.

From (6.12) we obtain

$$(6.13)\qquad \frac{\dot{B}(t)}{B(t)} = \frac{a_1 K(0)\, e^{(n+a_2)t}}{\frac{a_1}{n+a_2} K(0) [e^{(n+a_2)t} - 1] + B(0)} - a_2.$$

At $t=0$,

$$(6.14)\qquad \frac{\dot{B}(0)}{B(0)} = \frac{a_1 K(0)}{B(0)} - a_2.$$

[44] The use of a_1 as a shorthand expression for $ip(n - S_1^\circ - rS_5^\circ)$ should not be taken to suggest that a_1 is a constant independent of n.

As t grows large

$$\lim_{t\to\infty}\frac{\dot{B}(t)}{B(t)}=n. \tag{6.15}$$

Thus, when the initial stock of debt is small, the relative rate of increase is large at first, always greater than n, but asymptotically approaching n with the passage of time.

The stability of the ratio of B to K, under these assumptions, is not dependent on a linear approximation. The homogeneity of S permits us to write (2.6) as follows:

$$\dot{B}=ipnK-ipKS\left(1, \frac{B}{pK}, r, i, r-\frac{B}{pK}\right). \tag{6.16}$$

Let

$$\beta=\frac{B}{K}, \tag{6.17}$$

whence

$$\dot{\beta}=\frac{\dot{B}}{K}-\frac{B}{K}\frac{\dot{K}}{K}. \tag{6.18}$$

Substituting (6.17) into (6.16), we have

$$\frac{\dot{B}}{K}=ipn-ipS\left(1, \frac{1}{p}\beta, r, i, r-\frac{1}{p}\beta\right), \tag{6.19}$$

and

$$\dot{\beta}=ipn-\left[ipS\left(1, \frac{1}{p}\beta, r, i, r-\frac{1}{p}\beta\right)+n\beta\right]. \tag{6.20}$$

By (2.10)

$$\frac{\partial S}{\partial\beta}>0. \tag{6.21}$$

$\dot{\beta}$ is equal to the difference between two branches. When β is below its equilibrium value, ipn exceeds $ipS+n\beta$ and β rises; when β is above equilibrium, forces are set in motion which drive it back down. This is illustrated in Figure III. The second branch is an increasing function of β because of (6.21). Clearly the equilibrium is stable. Thus, if K and L, and therefore Y, are growing at the same relative rate, the ratio of bonds outstanding to each of these variables will be stable.

If we wish to consider the simultaneous variation of K and B around their steady growth path, we must again be content with

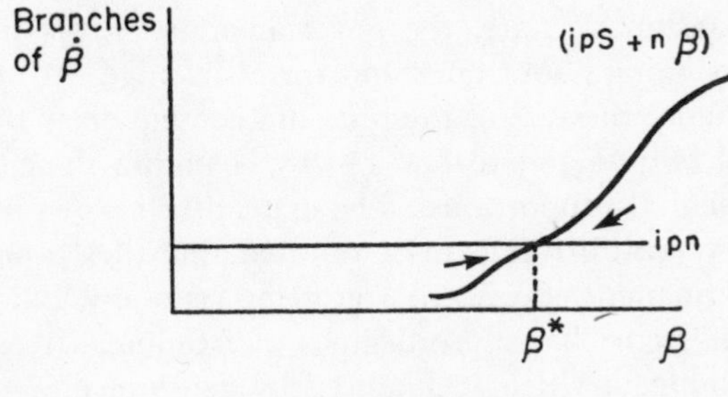

FIGURE III

local results. If i and p are held constant at their equilibrium values, the equations (4.5) become

$$\begin{aligned} \dot{k} &= (I_K{}^\circ - n)(k-k^\circ) + I_B{}^\circ(b-b^\circ) \\ \dot{b} &= i^\circ p^\circ (I_K{}^\circ - S_K{}^\circ)(k-k^\circ) + i^\circ p^\circ\left(I_B{}^\circ - S_B{}^\circ - \frac{n}{i^\circ p^\circ}\right)(b-b^\circ). \end{aligned} \tag{6.22}$$

The necessary and sufficient conditions for the convergence of b and k from any initial values to their equilibrium values are

$$\begin{aligned} &(I_K{}^\circ - n) + i^\circ p^\circ\left(I_B{}^\circ - S_B{}^\circ - \frac{n}{i^\circ p^\circ}\right) < 0 \\ &I_B{}^\circ S_K{}^\circ - I_K{}^\circ S_B{}^\circ - \frac{nI_K{}^\circ}{i^\circ p^\circ} - nI_B{}^\circ + nS_B{}^\circ + \frac{n^2}{i^\circ p^\circ} > 0, \end{aligned} \tag{6.23}$$

fulfillment of both of which is implied by (2.9) and (2.10). Thus, if B and K are sufficiently close to their equilibrium growth paths, they will converge onto those paths. In this case, the limiting relative rate of growth of both variables is n. Clearly, if one or both variables are below their equilibrium paths, their *average* relative growth rates will exceed n for a time, but the convergence may be either asymptotic or oscillatory.

VII. Comparative Dynamics

In the stationary state, the government sector is limited in effect, to bringing about once and for all changes in M and B_g. It can influence the rate of interest, and consequently the capital stock, total output and real wages, by changing these two variables in unequal proportions. The expenditure flows must stop, if stationary equilibrium is to be restored, and they can therefore have no permanent effects. In a growing economy, however, the government sector has more degrees of freedom. It can run a persistent budgetary deficit, financed by issues of new money or bonds, in order to buy a part of the current output of goods or bonds, or in order to make transfer payments. Increases in the money stock must be accompanied by one or a combination of these three classes of expenditure flow. The effects brought about by changes in the pattern of expenditure flows in the growing economy generally (though not always) reinforce the effects of the corresponding changes on the asset side. Thus, for example, if the government sector issues new money to finance the purchase of goods, with B_g constant, the equilibrium value of i will increase if B_g is positive (Equation 3.11). The pure effect of increasing G_c in the growing economy is also to increase i. In this section, the influence of variations in the rate and pattern of government expenditures on the growth path of the economy is examined. Each flow is varied, relative to all the other expenditure flows in the economy, and the resulting changes in k and i are calculated.[45]

[45] By similar means, one can find the effects of changes in the exogenous variables on p and b also. In general, these changes will not be in the same

The equilibrium values of k, b, p and i when the economy is in a state of steady balanced growth are defined by the following equations:

$$I\left[k, \frac{b}{p}, F_K(k, l), i, kF_K(k, l) - \frac{b}{p}\right] - nk = 0$$

$$I - S\left[k, \frac{b}{p}, F_K(k, l), i, kF_K(k, l) - \frac{b}{p}\right] - \frac{nb}{ip} = 0$$

(7.1)
$$C\left[\frac{b - b_g}{ip}, \frac{m}{p}, i, F(k, l) - S + \frac{g_t}{p}\right] + \frac{g_c}{p} + I - F(k, l) = 0$$

$$I - S - \frac{g_b}{p} - D_b\left[\frac{b - b_g}{ip}, \frac{m}{p}, i, F(k, l) - S + \frac{g_t}{p}\right] = 0.$$

The budget constraint of the government sector, (2.14), can be written

(7.2)
$$\dot{m} + nm = g_b + g_c + g_t.$$

In balanced growth equilibrium, $\dot{m} = 0$, whence

(7.3)
$$nm = g_b + g_c + g_t.$$

Also, when the economy is in a state of equilibrium balanced growth, though not necessarily otherwise,

(7.4)
$$g_b = \frac{n}{i} b_g.$$

From (7.3) and (7.4) follows

(7.5)
$$g_c + g_t = n\left(m - \frac{1}{i} b_g\right),$$

that is, along the equilibrium growth path, the stock of outside money must grow at the same exponential rate as M and B_g.

---

proportion as the changes in m, but our hypotheses do not determine unambiguously the direction of the variation from proportionality.

Now let the government sector increase g_c, its rate of purchase of new goods deflated by the average growth factor for the economy as a whole, while holding g_b and g_t constant. This means a permanent increase in G_c relative to the rest of the expenditure flows in the economy, and not merely a temporary injection. The purchases are financed by an increase in the rate of issue of new money. When the system returns to its moving equilibrium, m will have increased according to the relationship

$$dg_c = n\,dm. \tag{7.6}$$

The effects of this change on k and i can be found by differentiating (7.1) totally with respect to g_c or m, using (7.6) to relate changes in those variables. Differentiating totally with respect to m, we have [46]

$$\begin{aligned}
&(I_K - n)\frac{dk}{dm} + I_B\frac{db}{dm} + I_p\frac{dp}{dm} + I_i\frac{di}{dm} = 0\\
&(I_K - S_K)\frac{dk}{dm} + \left(I_B - S_B - \frac{n}{ip}\right)\frac{db}{dm} + \left(I_p - S_p + \frac{nb}{ip^2}\right)\frac{dp}{dm}\\
&\qquad + \left(I_i - S_i + \frac{nb}{pi^2}\right)\frac{di}{dm} = 0\\
&(C_K + I_K - F_K)\frac{dk}{dm} + (C_B + I_B)\frac{db}{dm} + \left(C_p + I_p - \frac{g_c}{p^2}\right)\frac{dp}{dm}\\
&\qquad + (C_i + I_i)\frac{di}{dm} = -\frac{1}{p}(C_2 + n)\\
&(I_K - S_K - D_{bK})\frac{dk}{dm} + (I_B - S_B - D_{bB})\frac{db}{dm}\\
&\qquad + \left(I_p - S_p + \frac{g_b}{p^2} - D_{bp}\right)\frac{dp}{dm} + (I_i - S_i - D_{bi})\frac{di}{dm} = \frac{1}{p}D_{b2}.
\end{aligned} \tag{7.7}$$

[46] All partial derivatives in this section should be taken to be evaluated at the point of equilibrium. For the sake of convenience, the superscript ⁰ is omitted.

It will be convenient to abbreviate two expressions which appear in all of the following results. Let

$$Z_1=\frac{1}{p^2}\left[I_iS_B-I_BS_i+I_B\frac{nb}{pi^2}+I_i\frac{n}{ip}\right]<0, \qquad \text{and}$$

$$Z_2=\frac{1}{p^2}\left[I_BS_K-I_KS_B+nS_B+\frac{n^2}{ip}-nI_B\right]>0.$$

Then (2.9), (2.10) and (2.13) imply $Z_1<0$ and $Z_2>0$.

Solving (7.7), we have [47]

$$\text{(7.8)} \qquad \frac{dk}{dm}=\frac{Z_1\left[\frac{b_g}{ip}(C_1D_{b2}-C_2D_{b1}-nD_{b1})+\frac{g_b}{p}(C_2+D_{b2}+n)+\frac{g_t}{p}(C_2D_{b4}-C_4D_{b2}+D_{b2}+nD_{b4})\right]}{|\Delta^*|}$$

[47] For the reader who wishes to reconstruct the solutions (7.8), (7.9), (7.11), (7.12), (7.14), (7.15), (7.17) and (7.18), the following suggestions may be helpful. We wish to solve for two elements in the vector $d=\left(\frac{dk}{dm}, \frac{db}{dm}, \frac{dp}{dm}, \frac{di}{dm}\right)$, defined by the equations (7.7) which can be written, in matrix notation, $\Delta^*d=v$, where $v=(0, 0, v_1, v_2)$. In (7.7), $v_1=-\frac{1}{p}(C_2+n)$, $v_2=\frac{1}{p}D_{b2}$. In later differentiations, v_1 and v_2 will assume different values. The equations can be solved by matrix inversion. That is, $d=\Delta^{*-1}v$. Because we are interested in only two elements in d and two in v, we require only four elements in the inverse. Let $Z_4=\left(-g_b+D_{b1}\frac{1}{i}b_g-D_{b2}m-D_{b4}g_t\right)$ and let $Z_5=\left(-g_c+C_1\frac{1}{i}b_g-C_2m-C_4g_t\right)$. Then, let a_{ij} be the element in the ith row and j^{th} column of Δ^{*-1}. We then have

$$a_{13}=\frac{Z_1Z_4}{|\Delta^*|}, \quad a_{14}=\frac{Z_1Z_5}{|\Delta^*|}, \quad a_{43}=\frac{Z_2Z_4}{|\Delta^*|}, \quad a_{44}=\frac{Z_2Z_5}{|\Delta^*|},$$

and $\frac{dk}{dm}=v_1a_{13}+v_2a_{14}$ and $\frac{di}{dm}=v_1a_{43}+v_2a_{44}$. The simplification of the results as presented in the text also makes use of the relationships (7.4) and (7.5).

$$(7.9)\quad \frac{di}{dm}=\frac{Z_2\left[\frac{b_g}{ip}(C_1D_{b2}-C_2D_{b1}-nD_{b1})+\frac{g_b}{p}(C_2+D_{b2}+n)+\frac{g_t}{p}(C_2D_{b4}-C_4D_{b2}+D_{b2}+nD_{b4})\right]}{|\Delta^*|}.$$

The consequences of an increase in g_c and m are similar but not identical to the consequences of an increase in M in the stationary case (Equations 3.8 and 3.11). If b_g and g_b are positive, that is, if the government sector is a creditor on bond account, the expression in brackets in the numerator of (7.8) and (7.9) is positive whence $\frac{dk}{dm}$ is negative and $\frac{di}{dm}$ is positive.[48] The effect of the transaction on the asset side, which is described by (3.8) and (3.11) is reinforced by the effects operating via the expenditure flows g_c and g_t. If b_g and g_b are negative, however, that is, if the government sector is a debtor on bond account, $\frac{dk}{dm}$ may still be negative, and $\frac{di}{dm}$ positive, if g_t is large enough in relation to b_g. The effect at work here is that the increase in m will raise the price level and reduce the real value of the flow of transfer payments. This, in turn, will reduce somewhat the demand for bonds, working in the direction of increasing i. If there are no transfer payments, however, the sign of $\frac{di}{dm}$ will be the same as the sign of b_g. That is, as in (3.11), increases in m and g_c will increase i if the government is a creditor, lower it if the government is a debtor.

[48] The coefficient of $\frac{g_t}{p}$ can be written $C_2D_{b4}+(1-C_4)D_{b2}+nD_{b4}$, all of whose terms are positive.

The statement of these derivatives in terms of m as the independent variable should not be permitted to mislead one into thinking that it is essentially the change in m which produces the results, any more than the use of g_c as the independent variable, were it used, should be taken to mean that it is the change in government expenditure alone which produces the results. The results are, in fact, produced by the transaction as a whole. The choice of independent variable is arbitrary; either can be used.[49] This point deserves emphasis because so much writing on monetary theory analyzes the effects of changes in M alone, neglecting the expenditure which brought about the change, while much income theory is based on the expenditure side and neglects the manner in which the transaction was financed. In fact, both sides are relevant.

To illustrate the significance of the method of financing, suppose the government were to increase g_c and pay for it by reducing g_b, keeping m and g_t constant. The effects of this transaction on k and i can be found by differentiating (7.1) totally with respect to g_c using the relationship

$$dg_c = -dg_b.^{50} \tag{7.10}$$

With the help of (7.3) and (7.4), the results can be written

$$\frac{dk}{dg_c} = \frac{Z_1\left[\frac{m}{p}\left(D_{b2}+\frac{1}{n}C_1D_{b2}-\frac{1}{n}C_2D_{b1}+C_2+n-D_{b1}\right)+\frac{g_t}{p}\left\{D_{b4}\left(1+\frac{1}{n}C_1\right)+(C_4-1)\left(1-\frac{1}{n}D_{b1}\right)\right\}\right]}{|\Delta^*|} \tag{7.11}$$

[49] By (7.6) we have $\frac{dm}{dg_c}=\frac{1}{n}$ whence, for example, $\frac{di}{dg_c}=\frac{di}{dm}\cdot\frac{1}{n}$.

[50] The equations so obtained are like (7.7) on the left hand side, and have the column of elements 0, 0, $-\frac{1}{p}\left(\frac{1}{n}C_1+1\right)$, $+\frac{1}{p}\left(\frac{1}{n}D_{b1}-1\right)$ on the right hand side.

$$\text{(7.12)} \quad \frac{di}{dg_c} = \frac{Z_2\left[\frac{m}{p}\left(D_{b2}+\frac{1}{n}C_1D_{b2}-\frac{1}{n}C_2D_{b1}+C_2+n-D_{b1}\right) + \frac{g_t}{p}\left\{D_{b4}\left(1+\frac{1}{n}C_1\right)+\left(C_4-1\right)\left(1-\frac{1}{n}D_{b1}\right)\right\}\right]}{|\Delta^*|}.$$

When an increase in g_c was financed by an increase in m, if there were no transfer payments, the sign of $\frac{di}{dg_c}$ was unambiguously the same as the sign of b_g (Equation 7.9). This is not the case, however, if the increase in g_c is financed by the sale of bonds. In the latter case, if $g_t=0, \frac{di}{dg_c}$ must be positive. Thus, if the government is a debtor or bond account, the effect of an increase in g_c on the rate of interest will be negative if it is financed by an increase in the rate of issue of new money, positive if financed by bond sales (all assuming $g_t=0$).

Now let the government sector increase g_t and m while holding g_c and g_b constant. Differentiating totally with respect to m, and letting

$$\text{(7.13)} \quad dg_t = ndm,$$ [51]

one obtains

$$\text{(7.14)} \quad \frac{dk}{dm} = \frac{Z_1\left[\frac{b_g}{ip}\left\{C_1D_{b2}-C_2D_{b1}+nC_1D_{b4}+nC_2(1-D_{b4}) +nC_4(n-D_{b1}+D_{b2})\right\}+\frac{g_c}{p}(C_4D_{b2}-C_2D_{b4}-D_{b2}-nD_{b4})\right]}{|\Delta^*|}$$

[51] The equations are like (7.7) on the left hand side, and have the column of elements $0, 0, -\frac{1}{p}(C_2+nC_4), +\frac{1}{p}(D_{b2}+nD_{b4})$ on the right.

$$\text{(7.15)}\quad \frac{di}{dm}=\frac{Z_2\left[\frac{b_g}{ip}\{C_1D_{b2}-C_2D_{b1}+nC_1D_{b4}+nC_2(1-D_{b4})+nC_4(n-D_{b1}+D_{b2})\}+\frac{g_c}{p}(C_4D_{b2}-C_2D_{b4}-D_{b2}-nD_{b4})\right]}{|\Delta^*|}.$$

The coefficient of b_g in the expression in brackets is positive; the coefficient of g_c is negative. Increasing the money supply, via transfer payments, raises the price level and lowers the real value of g_c. This works in the direction of lowering the rate of interest. As before, the sign of $\frac{di}{dm}$ is related positively to the sign of b_g.

Finally, let the government sector increase the rate at which it purchases bonds, financing the purchases by increasing the rate at which it issues new money. The effects of this change can be found by differentiating (7.1) totally with respect to m, and applying the relationships

$$\text{(7.16)}\quad dg_b=ndm$$

and (7.4).[52] Solving, one obtains

$$\text{(7.17)}\quad \frac{dk}{dm}=\frac{Z_1Z_3}{|\Delta^*|}\quad \text{and}$$

$$\text{(7.18)}\quad \frac{di}{dm}=\frac{Z_2Z_3}{|\Delta^*|},$$

where

$$\text{(7.19)}\quad Z_3=\left(\frac{m}{p}-\frac{b_g}{ip}\right)(C_2D_{b1}-C_1D_{b2})-\frac{g_t}{p}\{C_4(n-D_{b1}+D_{b2})+C_1D_{b4}+C_2(1-D_{b4})\}-\frac{g_c}{p}\{n-D_{b1}+D_{b2}+C_2\}.$$

[52] The resulting equations are like (7.7) on the left hand side, and have the column of elements 0, 0, $\frac{1}{p}(C_1-C_2)$, $\frac{1}{p}(n-D_{b1}+D_{b2})$ on the right.

Z_3 is negative unless there is no outside money, in which case it is equal to zero. Thus, if the government sector increases the rate at which it buys bonds (or reduces the rate at which it issues them), financing the change by an offsetting change in the rate of issue of new money, the interest rate is unambiguously reduced and the equilibrium level of the capital stock increased, that is, $\frac{di}{dm}<0$, $\frac{dk}{dm}>0$.

VIII. *Conclusions*

This analysis has raised at least as many questions as it has answered. For example, what are the characteristics of the equilibrium growth path if the demand and production functions are not homogeneous? Or if the exogenous variables do not grow exponentially, or at the same rate? It is difficult even to conjecture answers to these questions. Is the impact of neutral technological change inflationary or deflationary? Evaluation of the relevant determinant proves to be complicated.

However, the analysis has shown that, given the neo-classical assumptions, there is no essential instability in the growth process. There is no necessary opposition of warranted rates and natural rates of growth. There is no inevitable debt saturation. This is not to say that cycles, depressions, and inflations will not occur. The empirical validity of the neo-classical hypotheses, both in the short run and the long, is another question. But instability is not intrinsic in the process of economic growth itself. On the other hand, I have not been able to prove that the neo-classical hypotheses imply stability in the stationary case or stable proportions in the balanced growth case. But it does not seem unreasonable to conjecture that there is a close relationship between the two. Samuelson, and Arrow, Block and Hurwicz have already shown that diminishing marginal rates of substitution and the stability of equilibrium are closely related.[53] Solow and Samuel-

[53] See Samuelson, *Foundations of Economic Analysis, op. cit.*, pp. 301-02; Kenneth J. Arrow and Leonid Hurwicz, "On the Stability of the Competi-

son have shown that any system of differential equations of the form

$$\dot{Y}_i = F^i[Y_1(t), \cdots, Y_n(t)] \qquad (i=1, \cdots, n) \tag{7.1}$$

in which the F^i are homogeneous of degree one and have all positive partial derivates will have a balanced growth equilibrium whose proportions are stable in the large.[54] Perhaps by extension of these results it will be possible to show that constant returns to scale and diminishing marginal returns do imply stable prices and factor, output and asset proportions in a wide range of cases.

Finally, it has been possible to show the (or restate what should be the obvious) non-neutrality of public expenditure. Like private expenditure, public expenditure does have an impact on prices and the allocation of resources, and the direction and extent of the impact depends on the method of financing it. If, for example, the central bank or the monetary system increases the rate at which it buys securities, relative to all other expenditures in the economy, the equilibrium value of the rate of interest will be lowered. The neo-classical critic might dismiss this point as attributable to "money illusion" in the monetary system or to the existence of government bonds—positive or negative—and therefore not at all surprising. But the important point is that the monetary system acts in monetary terms, not in "real" terms. By its nature, it has "money illusion," but a money illusion that cannot be dismissed as a form of irrationality. Moreover, it is not enough to assume away the existence of bonds issued by the government in order to get netural money. The neutrality of money, as a general principle, requires that the monetary authorities be out of the business of dealing in debt altogether, or that the government have no control over the portfolio of the monetary system.

---

tive Equilibrium, I," *Econometrica,* XXVI (October 1958), pp. 522-52; also Arrow, Hurwicz and H. D. Block, "On the Stability of the Competitive Equilibrium, II," *Econometrica,* XXVII (January 1959), pp. 82-109.

[54] Robert M. Solow and Paul A. Samuelson, "Balanced Growth Under Constant Returns to Scale," *Econometrica,* XXI (July 1953), pp. 412-24.

Glossary and Index

Glossary

Balanced growth—Growth of all real and nominal stocks and flows at the same rate.

Banking Bureau—An embryonic governmental banking system that purchases current output, primary securities, or other assets, and creates money on orders from a Policy Bureau.

Debt burden—Ratio of a sector's outstanding real debt to its capital goods.

Deficit rotation—The transfer of deficits on income and product account from one sector to another over time.

Direct finance—The sale of primary securities by ultimate borrowers directly to ultimate lenders.

Distribution effects—Effects of price changes on real demand and real supply, resulting from the way income, spending, financial assets, and debts are distributed among spending units.

Explicit deposit rate—Interest payments on money balances expressed as a percentage of those balances.

Financial intermediaries—Financial institutions whose principal function is the purchase of primary securities and the creation of claims on themselves.

Gross-money doctrine—An approach to monetary theory that takes account of both inside and outside money.

Implicit deposit rate—The marginal utility of money, based on the advantages of holding money instead of alternative assets.

Indirect finance—The sale of primary securities by ultimate borrowers to financial intermediaries.

Indirect securities—Obligations of financial intermediaries, including currency, demand deposits, savings deposits and shares, policy reserves, and similar claims.

Inside money—Money based on private domestic primary securities.

Mixed asset-debt position—The position of a spending unit that has both holdings of financial assets and outstanding debt.

Money illusion—Adaptation of economic behavior to nominal rather than to real quantities.

Net debt position—The difference between the debt of a spending unit and its financial assets.

Net-money doctrine—An approach to monetary theory that consolidates inside money against its counterpart in private domestic primary debt, leaving only outside money.

Neutrality of money—The inability of changes in the nominal stock of money to affect the rate of interest, real output and wealth, and other real variables.

Nominal bonds—Bonds at face value, not deflated by a price index of current output.

Nominal money—Money that is not deflated by a price index of current output.

Nonmonetary financial intermediaries—Financial institutions whose principal function is the purchase of primary securities and the creation of nonmonetary claims; these institutions include savings and loan associations, credit unions, insurance companies, savings banks, and others.

Nonmonetary indirect financial assets—Claims on nonmonetary financial intermediaries, such as savings and loan shares, savings deposits, policy reserves.

Outside money—Money that is backed by foreign or government securities or gold; or fiat money issued by the government.

Policy Bureau—The monetary authority; an embryonic central bank that issues instructions to the Banking Bureau.

Primary securities—Obligations of nonfinancial spending units, including government securities, corporate bonds and stocks, mortgages, and various short-term and intermediate-term debt.

Pure asset-debt position—The position of a spending unit that has only financial assets or only outstanding debt, and not both.

Real bonds—Bonds whose face value is deflated by a price index of current output.

Real money—Money deflated by a price index of current output.

Rental rate—Rate of return on capital; equal to the sum of firms' net profits and interest payments as a percentage of their capital stock.

Reserve-balance rate—Rate of interest paid by Central Bank to commercial banks on their deposit balances.

Static price expectations—Expectations that the current price level will be the future one.

Stationary equilibrium—An equilibrium in which financial and real quantities remain unchanged.

Index